LIZ KAVA

COUNTRY

The Author

For nearly twenty years, Corkwoman Mary Lynch ha
known to many people as Liz Kavanagh. *Country Livir*
first volume of her collected writings from *The Irish F*
Journal.

To Eoin
'the quiet poor hoor'

LIZ KAVANAGH
COUNTRY LIVING

WOLFHOUND PRESS
& in the US and Canada
The Irish American Book Company

First published 1997 by
WOLFHOUND PRESS Ltd
68 Mountjoy Square
Dublin 1
Tel: (353-1) 8740354
Fax: (353-1) 8720207

Published in the US and Canada by
The Irish American Book Company
6309 Monarch Park Place
Niwot, Colorado 80503
USA
Tel: (303) 530-4400
Fax: (303) 530-4488

© 1997 Mary Lynch

British Library Cataloguing in Publication Data
A catalogue record for this book is available from the British Library.

ISBN 0 86327 609 1

10 9 8 7 6 5 4 3 2 1

Typesetting: Wolfhound Press Ltd
Cover photograph: The Slide File, Dublin
Cover design: Slick Fish Design, Dublin
Printed in the Republic of Ireland by Colour Books, Dublin

Contents

PREFACE

'Who is this Liz Kavanagh anyway?' is a question frequently asked by readers, especially by those who suspect her column is all made up in some office at the *Irish Farmers' Journal*, and is even, perhaps, the work of a male journalist! Well, those doubting souls are totally wrong, on both scores. Liz Kavanagh is real and has written for all the past twenty years from the firsthand experience of her *alter ego*, Mary Lynch, who is indeed a farming wife.

'This Week – the diary of a farmer's wife' was the full title given to the new weekly column which Liz Kavanagh began to write for the 'Country Living' section of the *Farmers' Journal* way back in 1977. The title given to the column has changed with the succeeding editors, as has Liz herself changed with the years. Yet, I personally have a great affection for the original title because the column was inspired each week by some happening in the lives of Liz, her long suffering husband Eoin, their five sons and the parish at large. Therefore, *this week* is a phrase used in practically every article. Indeed, the very first column, came with the following introduction:

> Our new column, THIS WEEK, introduces Liz
> Kavanagh, a farmer's wife, who is going to share
> with us some of the pleasures and problems of her
> life.

I, Mary Lynch, always speak of Liz Kavanagh in the third person because it is not I, but this other person, Liz, who takes over when I sit down to write. The name Liz Kavanagh was not even of my own choosing, but came with the job. Liz is a very determined person, so determined in fact that she quickly emerged in her own right. I very soon became aware that I could have it all set in my mind what to write about, each week, but once I got down to it, Liz took over, and the finished work is never, ever, what I first set out to write. My proposed subject matter is quickly scrapped. The column, not only in subject matter, but also in language, each week finishes up decidedly hers alone.

Therefore, in this book, I have neither updated nor elaborated on the original pieces. I cannot now write as Liz felt then. Indeed, on reading over the pieces, it is as if I am reading them for the first time. The same themes, of farm, family, ageing, illnesses, depression, good times and bad, however, are common to all years. Each year, also, the two highlights of spring are the cows first going out to grass and the picking of the first bunch of daffodils. Each autumn Liz bemoans the coming of winter, and the problems of getting the cattle in off the land in time.

However, in between the ordinary farming activities, the boys grow up, leave school, go to work, travel, fall in and out of love, crash cars, break their parents' hearts at times, but are always there until the time they all get married. So, as the size of the family grows, so do Liz's topics of universal interest. Grandchildren then begin to figure large in the life of Liz.

With five sons and five daughters-in-law, it is inevitable that all is not always sunshine. In fact some of the family would cheerfully kill Liz if she does write about them, while others complain that they do not seem to count, being rarely mentioned. If they but knew it, what Liz really would love to do is to write the real book, the unabridged version. But that had better come later, or best of all, posthumously.

The first two years' efforts were carefully pasted into scrap-books, with pride, by my eldest son. However, that soon became a chore nobody, least of all myself, wanted to undertake, and the weekly columns of the next eighteen years had to literally be hunted down in the attic, where most things that might possibly be of use some day are stored away in this house.

This collection is divided, more or less, into the twelve months of the year, to echo if not coincide with the farming year. It begins with the coming of the New Year to the Kavanagh household, and the realisation by Liz that they, as a family, possibly have celebrated their very last Christmas together.

Then Liz reflects on her life. The months which follow show just how true her premonitions were, with changes in the family, and the farm, gradually altering Liz, over this period of twenty years, from a woman very active in both farming and child-rearing to a grandmother of seven, and a person who has given in, with a certain grace, to the inevitable push which has left her on the sidelines of the actual farming enterprise. This book also hints at the difficulties in farm family succession and life for a woman with sons and their wives, but no daughters. Liz frequently looks back into her personal experiences of life to illuminate her present situation.

Liz went to university some five years ago, because, as she said, 'it seemed like a good idea at the time'. Perseverance led to a first class BA degree, and now an attempted MA. Leaving the farm work for academia has been a turning point in her life, as has been her 'coming out', in 1994, to her readers.

Until 1994 I put the weekly offering into an envelope and posted it up to Dublin. And once a month a cheque came back in the post, my squander money, and that was the only contact I had with the outside world under a series of editors despite the fact that Gay Byrne, one morning in the late eighties, read out a letter from a fan saying that her greatest ambition was to see Liz Kavanagh on the *Late Late Show*, and would Gay please fix it for her. Gay asked 'Who is this Liz Kavanagh anyway?' But neither I nor the *Farmers' Journal* answered that question.

Then Mairead McGuinness changed all that with the unveiling of Liz at the 1994 Ploughing Match. The results were spectacular, with Liz being literally mobbed by the public for the few hours she was on the stand. I had no idea that Liz had so captured the public imagination. One woman said that reading my column gave her the delicious feeling of insight that one normally only gets from reading somebody else's private letters. But many men also said that Liz was the first thing they read in *The Journal*, since her farming troubles so often helped to ease their own pain in a similar misfortune.

At that Ploughing Match the idea of a collected edition of Liz Kavanagh was born. Liz repeated her success to an even greater degree in 1995, being on display for three days. The pressure was thus intensified for a more widespread publication.

Once again, at this year's Ploughing Match, several people asked me when I was going to publish a book of my collected writings, saying that they would be more than interested in such a publication for themselves, and as presents for all their friends. One particular man said that every farmer in Ireland would buy a copy for both his wife and his mother, for Christmas or birthdays, and as an excuse to read it himself.

This book is dedicated to Eoin, the mainspring of my life, the source of my inspiration. The particular form of the dedication came about because, one day at a Grassland Association meeting, while we sat in rows waiting for the first speaker to commence, two men in front of us began to discuss, of all things, 'that one Liz Kavanagh who writes in the *Farmers' Journal*.' My ears were, of course, well and truly cocked as I discreetly leant forward. The two men concluded that Liz must be real, quoting incidents that only a person in the job could know. But then one turned to the other, and in all seriousness remarked: 'Do you know who I feel really sorry for always? I feel right sorry for Eoin – that quiet poor hoor!'

JANUARY

Enter the New Year

'How did you get over the Christmas?' That's the greeting I've heard on all sides these last few days. The answer is always, 'Oh grand, but 'twas quiet somehow!'

I wonder what did they expect? – an orgy! Christmas is, and always has been, to the best of my memory, quiet. Still, I was as sentimental as the next, when dusk came so early on Christmas Eve and all the preparations were finally finished. We gathered together, the seven of us, to light the candle. The tradition here is that the youngest capable member of the household lights the Christmas candle and then says a prayer for the whole family.

Now our youngest also happens to have been born on a Christmas Eve, so it is very much his day. The same lad is a bit of a showman anyway, and his prayer varies every year, depending on the humour he's in. This year we had the usual quick gabble-gabble-gabble through a few formal prayers, and then he prayed for us all to be together again this day next year.

That really set me back on my haunches. I had never really considered the possibility that we might not all be together again this time next year. But seemingly, my youngest son had. And he was right. Because, with my eldest son sitting his Leaving Cert in June, next Christmas will not be the usual, home from school holidays, for him. As yet Michael has said nothing about his future plans. So, does my youngest know something we don't? The parents, I find, are often the last to know, although, in my heart of hearts, I am sure we will have him home for many's the Christmas to come. I'm not ready yet for things to change.

The boys really enjoyed their Christmas dinner. And for once things went smoothly enough. They could see that there was plenty for all, so each, for once, was not jealously watching his rights. So often I have seen them taking more than they wanted, for fear one of the others might get even a little bit extra.

For the same reason I can never, not even at Christmas, put a box of chocolates, or a tin of fancy biscuits, in front of them and tell them to have at them. They would get sick from gobbling them down with unseemly haste, just to make sure that none of the others got even the one extra. A box of chocolates can only be passed around here in a strict rota, with even the 'first choice' being rotated by age. Is this state of affairs confined to young males? Little girls I fondly imagine to be all 'sweetness and light'. My boys remind me too often of young cockerels circling each other, tail feathers spread, looking for a fight, and usually getting it too.

So, when such goodies normally come into this house, as presents, I confiscate them on the spot. These, with the exception at Christmas of one big box of chocolates and a tin of their favourite biscuits, go into my store, a locked drawer in my bedroom, to be passed on when I, in turn, go visiting. The sons, for all the good it does them, deeply object, saying that the presents are really meant for them.

However, much suspicious hilarity ensued when a certain box of biscuits came here with good friends this Christmas, and I proposed opening that one. When the boys were so vehement that they'd prefer to open any other tin, my suspicions were really aroused, and I refrained, in front of the visitors anyway. It usually pays to be suspicious with my lot. Eventually, the full story emerged. This time last year, when getting ready to go out to a party, I got the eldest to festively wrap a tin of biscuits from my store. Which he did, even to the extent of Christmas-sellotape-sealing the lid in great style. But there was a purpose to his helpfulness. That tin of biscuits was well attacked, while I was in the bath, with all their favourites being replaced by the plainer sorts I keep in the kitchen. So the Christmas sellotape was to conceal their raid. And here was the self-same box back to us, unopened, exactly twelve months later. Clearly, I am not the only one to have a store!

But Christmas is over and my real news is to do with the New Year. On New Year's day, Eoin and Seamus came in after milking the cows, and they were in great good form. 'It's here already,' they said in unison, just standing there without taking off their boots. We were all attention immediately, wondering just what was there.

'It's here already,' repeated Eoin. 'The first of the calves, and it's grand – maybe a bit on the small side, but there's no fear of it!' And he told how our second son Seamus, our farmer-to-be, had found the calf sucking away at his mother up in the corner of the shed, where he himself had never bothered to look, anxious and all as he was to get to his breakfast. We all trooped out to inspect the new arrival. And there he was, still wet and shiny, hard at work, sucking with gusto, himself and his mother now safely in a pen.

The cow lowed with pride while licking all she could reach of her offspring. The calf's tail wagged furiously and the biestings frothed and dripped from his pap-filled mouth. Then I knew that the Christmas season was well and truly over and the new season, and a new life, had begun.

Isn't there something so exciting about the start of things, especially when all is well? Last year, with its troubles and pleasures, is forgotten, and the New Year, full of hope and promise, stretches away ahead of us, like our lives. And there it was all personified for us, in one slightly premature, spindle-legged, milk-flecked baby calf. Happy New Year everybody. (1977)

The early, the middle years & now

For years, when I was surrounded by small children, had too much work on my hands, and very little money, I looked forward to the middle years. I saw them as long blissful days in the sun, with grown children needing no care, attention or money, meals eaten in a relaxed mood, with pleasant family conversations, and, above all, time to spare; time to follow my own interests; time to do my own thing; maybe even time to improve myself.

That was the dream. Now, here I am beginning to live the reality. However, the only thing that worked out for me is the fact that I reached those middle years. In every other way the dream was false. Yes, I am now undoubtedly middle-aged but busier than ever, and with even less time for myself. And I still worry and fret about my children, my sons, without now the benefit of even the odd hug or the loving bunch of wild flowers, clenched in a hot, sticky fist, and picked for me on their way home from national school.

An article I read this week in a glossy magazine at the dentist's, while waiting for the sons' dental work to be completed, helped me to clarify my situation. This article described the early years as the 'achieving years', when you achieve adulthood, a home, husband, children and possessions. Then come the 'joining years' when you join societies, have outside activities and a lively social life.

It sounded so familiar that I put down the magazine there and then to take stock, without reading on. 'Yes,' I thought. 'That is what is wrong with me. I have joined so many groups, and taken such an active part in everything, and asked so many people to the house, that really, I have used up all the time there is.'

I began to think about all the active members in our groups, the ICA, the flower club, the country market... and realised we have all, each and every one of us, left the first fair flush of youth behind. We are the doers, the ones who get things moving. And what would happen to the country without us?

So, when I thought about it like that, I decided there was a lot to be said for the way I spend my time after all. And anyway, according to the article, the years to come are the retiring years when we are content to give up everything, little by little. So, some day I maybe will get some time to myself after all.

Yesterday was my monthly stint at the country market, which wasn't too bad a market considering the time of the year. It was also pay-day and the extra from the Christmas markets was nice to see in the cheque. Whatever did we do for our squander money before this market started? And what do women do in places which haven't got one going yet? Traditionally, the eggs paid for the messages and, in many cases, it was practically a barter system with the village shop or travelling van.

Now, however, with all the Common Market rules about packaging and grading, not to speak of quality control, no supermarket manager wants to see the farmer's wife coming in the door with her baskets of eggs hanging from each arm.

Even the village shops are now mini-supermarkets, bound by the same rules and regulations, so, from where is that extra pin-money to come? I know of no farmer's wife getting a regular housekeeping allowance from which she might save a little for herself. And, take it from one who knows, there is nothing like a little squander money of your very own, money which can be spent with not even the slightest prick from our ever-active consciences.

Our country market has solved the problem of a little money of our very own for a lot of women in my area. It's been trading just over a year and going from strength to strength. It started, more or less, as an offshoot of the ICA, but was soon taken over by a middle-aged outside committee. And this band of women has more than a sprinkling of what were once known as 'the gentry'.

How is it that rural English or Continental women are always those who make the best jam and cakes, keep marvellous ornamental and kitchen gardens and manage to organise things so much better than we do? Is it a legacy of being accustomed to such things for generations, when most of our forebears had more than enough to do to try to keep sufficient food on the table to have time for the niceties of life?

Anyway, at our country market, this past year, I have bought and tried more vegetables than I ever did before in my life. I started with seakale in the spring: this had a superb sort of asparagus taste with a broccoli texture. Even my husband Eoin, and my sons, liked it. And they are as conservative in their food tastes as most Irishmen. 'Crambe maritima' is the proper name for seakale. I discovered this when I had to search through several cookbooks to discover what to do with the stuff once the curiosity had made me buy it.

Then out came the gardening books to find out how to grow it. It is supposed to be grown from root cuttings in the autumn. But I stuck a few ends of the blanched stalks into a choice corner of my garden, and I think they have taken. So I may well have managed to both have my cake and eat it.

Anyway, even if they haven't rooted, I can always order some plants in the plant section of the market for the autumn. This, to me, apart from the money I make, is the best part of the country markets, since so many people bring pieces of their herbaceous plants to sell here. Nurserymen in my corner of Ireland never seem to stock herbaceous plants. Consequently, the only way one could add to one's stock was to beg, or even steal, from an established garden. I'll always remember the words of a rather grand old lady who advised me to always cultivate gardeners, as assiduously as I did my garden, if I wanted to be a good gardener. I, and my garden, owe a lot to her.

Isn't it great to see Irish people becoming so garden conscious? It is a hobby guaranteed to last through all the stages of one's life. It can be quite profitable, too, through a country market outlet. It never ceases to amaze me that the bunches of flowers, which I have always given away so freely, are in fact worth hard cash. Fruit too is a great seller, especially raspberries and loganberries.

Twenty years ago, indeed it was the first autumn after we had got married, I planted an orchard with all kinds of fruit, the usual apples, gooseberries, raspberries etc. The few small bushes and straggly lines looked so pitiful that I put in some more the following year.

I could not visualise the changes the years would bring. Just as my family has grown from one tender infant to five teenage tornadoes, so has the fruit spread, grown and thickened. Indeed, it has practically taken over, just like them. So for many years I found I had lots of friends calling when it came to the fruit season.

But the country market has taught me a lot. I too have skills, which can make me my very own squander money. And, as the man said, they ain't seen nothing yet. (1977)

Back to normal after the boys' big discovery

Well, it's back to a quiet life again for the Kavanaghs, and that, despite the fact that the calving season is now in full swing. By this, no doubt, you have gathered that the boys, with the exception of Eoin Óg, have all gone back to school after the holidays. Padraig, who is in his first year at boarding school, was extremely loth to leave home.

It is funny how, in their first year at boarding school, each one of the four of them so far has really hated going back after the Christmas holidays. In September it is a great adventure for them going away from home for the first time.

This euphoria lasts through the Hallowe'en break. But after Christmas, it is all as flat as uncorked lemonade. The novelty of school has completely worn off and home never seemed so good as when the time of leaving approached. Each of the four has shown their upset in differing ways. Number two, Seamus, I well remember! For days before the back-to-school date we could not even look at him or he was stumping off up to his room, banging the door shut in his temper.

Number three, Sean, showed his upset by fighting with all and sundry, even the dogs. Each time, when I remonstrated with him, he accused me of caring nothing for himself, only the others, and then he too departed up the stairs. Wasn't it well they had a room each to go to?

Poor old number four, Padraig, the latest recruit, must have had a fair old knot of misery in his stomach. His loneliness took the form of going completely off his food. That really showed that something was very wrong. Nothing would tempt him and I was afraid to press him since floods of tears might follow and I'd never be forgiven his humiliation.

Indeed, tears were not too far away from more than him. I was not much better myself as I watched the lonesome look of him. Still, on the night in question, I took them back by myself; Eoin had a heifer in the throes of calving. Padraig walked manfully through the school door with the rest. It was I who then had the knot in my stomach, as I left to face the quiet lonesome journey home, and I was very sorry I hadn't brought the youngest with me, for distraction. I was remembering only too well, from my own days at boarding school, being sick with misery, missing home while lying on the hard school bed on that first night back after Christmas.

His letters, I know, will be very sorrowful for the next few weeks, as he pours out some of his misery on paper. The first time this happened with Michael, our eldest. I agonised with him and my fresh tears mingled with his dried ones on his weekly letters home. He, however, got over it and his letters were quite cheerful again, long before Patrick's Day.

Never again did we hear complaints on the score of loneliness from him. In fact, the same lad, when he felt that he was being overworked on the farm during the holidays, has often told us, and quite churlishly too, how glad he was to be going back to school – for his holidays.

These were the times, did he but know it, that we were completely happy with our decision to send all our sons to boarding school. Living so far from any bus route I would never have been off the road with them if we hadn't taken that decision. And, more importantly, they would never have been left get on with their school work whenever there was work to be done on the farm. Michael will never make a farmer anyway, I fear.

Now Seamus, who loves anything to do with the farm, and whose help we sorely missed, was just as lonesome his first time back after the Christmas holidays. When his first sorrowful epistle arrived it was a case of no way was he going to stay in that awful place; he was so unhappy; he had nothing to do; everyone was horrible to him; it was cold; it never stopped raining; etc. and etc.

Then, in my pain and uncertainty, I remembered Michael's letters and got them all out again; I keep every letter I ever get from my sons. This was very useful in that I could then chart the course this son's loneliness and his letters would take. And so I shed less salt tears over this son's plight. In fact, because he is games-mad, and the rain obviously stopped, his very next letter was all about who scored what goal, when, where, and how. Unlike his older brother, little other information, indeed, did we ever get from him ever again, in any of his letters, about how he was really feeling.

Last year Sean survived too and so, no doubt, will my present problem. Still, when his first letter home this term arrives, I suppose I will be agonising over him too, in spite of knowing that this is something he just has to live through, all by himself.

But mothers always, in spite of knowing better, suffer along with their children. I wonder does there come a stage, when they are all grown up, that we no longer suffer the pangs of their pains? While I look forward to that, I doubt somehow that I will ever see that day. But only time will tell. In the meantime, having four of them safely back in school does ease my mind considerably. You see, something really significant happened in our house this holidays. My older boys discovered girls.

Yes, I know I should have anticipated this perfectly natural development, especially since Michael has been shaving now for some time. But somehow, I didn't. After all, for years they had all literally taken to the hills when daughters of visiting friends were seen coming up the avenue. I gave up on them, blaming our all-male family, and our segregated school system, for the fact that my sons were growing up gauche and inarticulate in the presence of females. But when I asked my mother for advice on the subject, she just laughed and said: 'Give them time'.

It was in church, of all places, that I realised things had changed. For several weeks, both before and after Christmas, my two eldest boys seemed to have become very devout. There they knelt, both before and after communion, seemingly rapt in prayer, heads buried in their hands. I wondered was I witnessing the first signs of a priestly vocation, and I already began to feel a little of that intense pride that every Irish mother is supposed to feel at her son's ordination and first Mass.

Then I looked a little more closely at my devout duo and found that the eyes, sunken in prayerful hands, were really peeking through open fingers. No contemplation of deep spiritual matters there: they were observing the girls going up and down the aisle. They spotted form on the way up to the altar rails and had a good look at the glorious front views of the young girls on their way back. So much for my pious imaginings. Well, they are all out of harm's way now until the Easter holidays, at the very least! (1978)

Men, of course, do not gossip

Men, of course, do not gossip. Leave it to the men, that wonderful capacity to be able to disseminate all the news without actually gossiping. I would be lost at this writing job without that ability of Eoin's to bring back to me the latest story going the rounds, as well as what actually happens to himself personally.

Our local repair shop is a great meeting place for these non-gossiping men, as good as the creamery ever was in its heyday, before it was amalgamated, or the forge was before that, when horses needed shoeing or wheel rims needed mending. Eoin came back from our local repair place today, and for no reason at all, except association of place, we started talking about a retired priest who once lived in the parish.

Father O was a great character – just so long as you didn't get on the wrong side of him. He said a grand quick Mass, even if it was at eight o'clock in the morning. But woe betide you if you arrived late, especially as he was as liable to swing into action at ten to eight as he was at eight on the dot. I have seen him, myself, stop everything to welcome the laggards and enquire if their alarm clocks had let them down again? He has even offered them a lend of one of his own, if they'd just come up to the house to him for it!

One Sunday morning, quite a few years ago, Father O was well into the Mass when Eoin and I arrived, just a minute before eight. But it was our great good luck that he had his back turned to us. That will tell you how long ago all this was. So, thankful for small mercies, we slunk into the back pew as quiet as mice. But, *mo lear agus mo leain*, when he turned around again he stopped up short and at the top of his stentorian voice bellowed:

'You down there! You were not here when I started. Is it the way you thought I would not see you back there? Come up here, this minute, to where you always sit!'

Eoin and I shrank smaller and smaller into our strange seat at the very back of the church. But it was no use for us. Still louder came the roar.

'Yes, I mean you, the Kavanaghs. Come up here this minute. And next Saturday night turn off that television set, and get to bed early enough!'

And up we had to make our blushing way to our customary seat in the church. You can be sure we were always ten minutes early ever after that episode. Moreover, we were by no means the only ones to get this kind of treatment.

Another Sunday morning, Father O came out on the altar seemingly all ready to go. However, on looking all around him, he sat himself down at the side of the sanctuary and said, in his customary bellow, that, as Mrs Murphy wasn't here yet, we would all wait for her. And, sure enough, we did, while he pontificated from the altar on the *Late Late* of the night before.

When poor Mrs Murphy came in, a minute or two later, and it still wasn't eight o'clock, he clapped his hands together several times, loudly, said he was delighted to see her, and now, that she was here, he would go on with the Mass. She was mortified and the Mass was nearly over before the blush on her neck subsided.

Then there was the time when Eoin went into him to have a Mass said. 'Who are you?' he barked. 'Eoin Kavanagh, Father,' said Eoin. 'Right, Mr Kavanagh...' Father O continued. 'Eoin – Father...' Eoin interjected: he has no great liking for being called Mr Kavanagh by anybody, least of all a priest. Yet he didn't get very far, because Father O stopped him short with:

'I don't know you! Therefore you will remain Mr Kavanagh to me if I choose, or until I do get to know you...'

So, from these snippets, you can gather that Father O's doings and sayings were much discussed in the parish during his sojourn here. Indeed, he had quite a following determined to get as much amusement as possible out of their Mass-going duty. The poor altar boys were the ones who were most in terror, ever since the morning he castigated them publicly for not knowing the name of the grandfather of Jesus. The rest of us in the congregation were scared that he would extend his catechism down the body of the church. Joachim is not a name to spring readily to mind after all, and I still have no idea of what the other grandfather of Jesus, Joseph's Dad, was called.

Father O lived with his brother, a totally different kind of man, and a sister who looked after them both. They were right from the other side of the country but settled in well here. He was always keen to take part in everything that was going on in the parish. So when he said he would take the Stations nobody was really surprised. And a lot of neighbours, who would not normally go to Station Masses, went that morning for a ha'p'orth of look. They were all made very welcome. The Mass was duly said and the dues collected. Then, while everybody sat around awaiting the call to breakfast, the smell of rashers and eggs frying quite tantalising all noses, Father O suddenly stood up and said.

'Doubtless you all want to see my house? Well! Come along then...'

And up they all got, officiating parish priest and all, and followed him from room to room. Then, shepherding all down the hall he ushered them out to see his garden. And out they all trooped, past him, as he politely held the hall door open. However, the minute the last of them stepped outside that door, he did a quick turn about and slammed the door shut on the lot of them.

There was plenty to talk about the Stations in the village pub that night as the men recounted how they smelt the rashers frying, the sister having gone out to the kitchen before ever the collection of the dues began. Then the real debate began as to whether the rashers and eggs were for them or just for her brothers.

Anyway, the sister died. And seeing the death notice in the paper the whole parish, of course, wanted to go to the removal, knowing that the funeral would be too far away to attend comfortably. But beyond noting the fact that she had died in hospital, there was no time specified for her removal from the mortuary there.

However, the remains were expected about seven that night in the church, or so the chapel woman informed all who inquired. Therefore, we all went to the hospital about six, so as to be in good time, to make sure to be seen to be there: there is no good at all in going to a funeral, God knows, if you are not seen to be there. But when we personally got in to the hospital mortuary, there was no trace of the two brothers, or of the sister either. She was gone, coffin and all.

Once this became clear, we all – and a good half of the parish was there by now – high tailed it out towards home again, hoping to catch up with the cortege on the way. Devil the sight we got of it, however. And, when we got out to the church we met Father O and a few of the local hard men making their way back out of the church, and we discovered it was all over. The men looked kind of sheepish and abashed, but they were saying nothing. Well, they said nothing at least until they got safely back into the pub.

It was there Father O had found them when he brought his sister to the church without benefit of undertakers or hearses. He had simply backed his own van up to the hospital mortuary, and rounded up a few of the hospital porters to put the coffin into it. Which they did.

So he was all set, easily enough, for the twenty-mile journey here. When he got to the church, however, there was nobody around: all had gone into town to escort him out in style. In that case what did Father O do but go into the local pub and command the few hardy boys there, who were going to make a short cut of it, to come out with him, that he had a little bit of a job for them.

'Right, Father,' said they, thinking that his old van wouldn't start for him or some such thing. So you can imagine their surprise to find that the little job was bringing his sister's coffin out of the old van, and up into the church. And, what's more, they were told to be there again at half past six the next morning, to load her up again, so that he'd make his family burial place at the appointed time. He and his brother were going driving up there, with her in the back of the van, for her funeral Mass at eleven o'clock.

Anyway, to finish my story, a day or two after all this, while the repairing of a piece of a broken machine was going on down at our mechanic's place, Father O drove up with his lawn-mower for John to fix. Passing our jeep, he, without a word, stopped, opened the back door and stretched himself out full length along the back of it.

The lads around the welder nudged each other and said out of the sides of their mouths: 'Will you look at his Reverence now? Is he going for a sleep or what?'

It was an 'or what' all right. Having had a good stretch, he came to the door and asked which of the men owned that jeep there: every four-wheel drive vehicle in our part of the country is a jeep, regardless.

Eoin admitted ownership, wondering what on earth was to come, Father O not being a man much given to idle conversation. And, while Eoin was drawing breath to sympathise with him on the death of his sister, Father O came right out with the request that when he himself should die Eoin would take his coffin to the family plot for him. Then he continued.

'I'll see you'll be all right – you won't be at a loss – anything would be better than those blasted undertakers. There's neither rhyme nor reason to what those boyos wanted, even when I tried to beat them down.

'You must have heard, of course, that I took the sister in my own van on Tuesday? But I can't take myself to my grave, much as I'd like to, and the brother doesn't have the stomach for it!'

He then proceeded to tell Eoin, and the lads listening, the whole story, just as I've told it to you. So, for once, it wasn't a yarn made up by some of the local bright boys.

''Twas a long old drive for you, Father,' said Eoin sympathetically, with as straight a face as he could muster, while the rest of the lads he could hear smothering their laughter as they suddenly became absorbed in the mechanical problems which had brought them there in the first place.

'Ah sure, no,' replied the priest. 'Didn't we stop for breakfast where we always stop, on the way up to Dublin, and I had a fine feed of rashers and sausages, black puddings and eggs for myself. After the early start I had a right good appetite on me. But the brother was only able for tea and toast: he has a weak stomach, you know.'

Then the woman of the house asked him where was his sister that day: they usually all travelled together. So, Father O told her she was out in the van. And the woman nearly took a fit at that. She said that he was to go out at once and bring her in. 'The poor creature,' she added in pity, 'she must need her breakfast too...'

'But,' Father O continued, 'I said to her that there was no point in my doing that, that my sister wouldn't ate nothing.'

'And why wouldn't she ate nothing? Isn't she on the road as long as yourselves?' said the good woman, now really upset. Therewith Father O told her straight out:

'She won't ate nothing, Missus, 'cos she's dead.'

There was a mass exodus of the lads out the door and across the fields at this point. Eoin, however, was captive, so he had to keep a straight face, even at this, and he finished up giving his word that he would do the needful for his reverence when that day came.

'Right,' said Father O then, with no further ado. 'I can sell this van so. I was only keeping it on because I thought it would come in useful for the coffins for us all. You'll do the brother too I'm sure? Of course you will...'

And then Father O finally released Eoin, and looking into the darkness of the garage bellowed,

'Come out here, John, and tell me what you think of my van. What do you think she's worth? I put new tyres on her only the day my sister died...' (1985)

Taking a backward look

Well, even if you don't normally make New Year resolutions, how about some new decade resolutions for this, the beginning of the 1980s? Not that it will make the slightest bit of difference to any of us. My guess is that we will still all be the same, in the 1980s, as we were in the 1970s, only a little more so. We'll just get more set in our ways, and of course older. I don't mean to be pessimistic, but I have long ago learned that it is an utter waste of time to yearn after the impossible. We are as we are and it is a mighty hard job to make modifications of any major sort.

Now basically I am the least domesticated of women and all the good resolutions in the world won't make me so. I should plan menus for weeks in advance and clean the house daily. Then I wouldn't have all that mad dash around when visitors threaten. However when the sun shines and the garden beckons, out I go, all good resolutions forgotten.

Maybe the 80s will bring me a domesticated daughter-in-law? Wouldn't it be marvellous if I were lucky enough to get one who'd delight in running the house, one of those super girls who washes the kitchen floor every day! I'd have no bother at all in handing my house over to her, as long as she stayed out of my garden.

''Tis you will be getting your specs out, then, to look her over,' said Eoin with a laugh, when I mentioned the possibility of daughters-in-law for us before the decade was out. He thinks that day is forever away.

As to that, I will just have to wait and see. They tell me anyway that it is hard to let a son go, but haven't you first got to let them go in order to keep them, say I, the hurler on the ditch. Thankfully, all those problems are still, I think too, far away in the distance.

But where did the 70s go? It seems only a year or so since 1970, and yet think of all that has happened to us, and the country, in the meantime. There has never been such a decade of change for farmers and farming. Leaving aside the Common Market and all that, in fact it is only in the past decade that farmers have become socially acceptable. Before that nobody wanted to know us. We weren't fit company, socially, for bankers or civil servants – not to mind doctors or solicitors. I never once in the 1950s or 60s got invited to a charity coffee morning not to mind a dinner party. But it is amazing the change, and the parties we got invited to over the past few years. There is nothing like money, or at least the name of money, for others to become socially aware of one's existence, or am I just being entirely too cynical?

While we were at the bottom of the social ladder nobody gave the farmer a thought, except by way of a joke, some of those jokes very nasty indeed, or indeed as a warning. There was even a nun in my convent school who used to say to us, when we failed to reach her exacting standards in Irish:

'Watch it girls, for without Irish to get you into a good job in the civil service, you'll get nowhere today and you will finish up married to some poor farmer and struggling for the rest of your lives!'

Well, some of us did finish up married to farmers even if our Irish was good enough for us to go to Dublin and be civil servants or teachers. But since we joined the Common Market, it seems that a lot of those girls, whether they still have their jobs, or are ensconced in typical suburban houses, now act as if they would change places happily with us, once the pitied ones, but now designated as 'rich farmers' wives'.

Of course the grass is always greener on the other side of the fence and I too have often thought that life in a suburban house must be very peaceful indeed, with no calves, callers, or men to feed. Imagine the luxury of feeding just myself and my children in the middle of the day while my good man lunched in town. And a pocket handkerchief of a garden could be whizzed around practically before breakfast. Still, I'd probably be bored stiff and find some mischief to get into. Or even more likely Parkinson's Law would operate and 'the work would expand to fill the time available.'

Work is always available here, but time runs so short that my dream for the new decade is to find some way of making my time expand to cover all the necessary work. Right here and now, because of having to write this column in time for the post, I shall have to feed the baby calves after supper. I dare not give hungry calves precedence over hungry men and boys.

So, my new decade resolution really must be to do things when I should do them, and not when I have to. Inasmuch as, the old proverb went, *procrastination is the thief of time*, that is the only practical way I can even begin to hope to expand the time available to me in the decade ahead. I'm not yet ready to give anything up, on any front. Time enough for that when I have to. (1980)

FEBRUARY

Frustration fighting to get out

It is a stinking, wet, cold day outside, a real dark, dreary day, and everybody here is right cross and grumpy in themselves. The menfolk in this house are always, I notice, much crankier anyway on a wet day, especially when winter lingers on into spring.

I know, I got the head bitten off me at dinner, by the sons, because I asked some question or other about the cows. Next, the stew wasn't to their liking. I counted silently to ten standing at the cooker. But because I then took my eye off it, for a moment, to put more potatoes on the table, the milk for the custard boiled over on me, making its usual stinking mess.

Then, you'd swear that I had committed a capital offence, at the very least, from the remarks of them, and the eyes thrown up to heaven, especially by that pair of sons who had been snapping at each other ever since they came in and had fought bitterly over the bar of soap at the sink. Now they were all one, when I, the *old dear*, was the object of their derision.

Eoin, infuriatingly, just sat there, eating solidly through his meal, apparently oblivious to all this carry-on. I had a mad overwhelming urge to sweep everything off the table, in one glorious crash to the ground, throw the custard at those sons of mine and stick Eoin's face right in his dinner plate – as it was interesting him so much!

I did no such thing, of course. I just stuck the kettle on the Aga for their cup of tea after the dinner. But how I would dearly love, just for once, to go really berserk like that, and get it all out of my system. Do any women, I wonder, ever really let fly with the teacups and plates, just as you see in the films?

Now, I have never thrown anything at anybody in my entire life. But I can well understand the urge to do so. It must be the most glorious feeling, to be able to give vent to your frustrations like that, just letting fly with the nearest piece of crockery, at the wall, even if not at the real source of irritation. Anyway, the men always duck, successfully, in the films.

So why don't I just go and do it? I suspect it is because I know full well, in my heart of hearts, that it would do me no good at all and it is me who'd be left picking up the pieces, in every sense of the word, all by myself, at the heel of the hunt. I doubt very much if it would all finish up in a beautiful reconciliation scene, à la Hollywood, with me being swept up in Eoin's manly arms as he kissed my tears away. He'd just clear out to the yard as fast as he could, and the sons with him no doubt, with ne'er a flea in their ear.

So what do other people do, instead, when they feel like a marvellous smash-up? Or should I just ask, what do other women do? Men, those farming anyway, seem to have no problems at all in giving vent to their frustrations. I gather this is not the only farmyard you'd want to be careful passing by, if and when a repair job is not going too well. Supposing your sensibilities survive the language polluting the air, you may not physically survive the odd tool or spare part let fly in pure and utter temper.

And, if a poor old cow is foolish enough to kick, when the humour is vicious, retribution can be swift, vocal and, indeed, often quite brutal. But woe betide anybody who points out to them that that sort of thing does no good at all, only makes the poor animal worse, and upsets the rest of the herd as well, in a ripple effect. You'd be safer not to try such remonstration, especially when they have a stick in their hands and the tempers are really up!

Now the urge to go walloping a poor cow, I would suggest, is the self-same reaction to stress as the urge to dump a jug full of custard on top of a head. But I bet you anything you like that there are a lot more cows walloped, unfairly, every day in Ireland, than jugs of custard dumped on deserving heads!

So, what do women do instead, to ease their frustrations? One woman I know, when that kind of humour is on her, tackles a load of washing. She literally strips beds, curtains, wardrobes, the lot, and sorts them all out on the floor to go into the machine. And, usually, by the time the first lot is pegged out, and the second lot swirling away in the washing machine, she is feeling a whole lot better.

The family now know to beware, she says, if they come in and find great heaps of washing awaiting attention. Not that it is all washed, ever, she admitted, somewhat ruefully. Even in that first mad urge to wash everything in the house, she still puts the perfectly clean things separately. So, when she feels better, and the thought of all the ironing intrudes, the clean things can go straight back where they came from, and not via the washing machine. I do hope that urge is not striking her today the way the rain is lashing down out of the heavens!

Now, another friend of mine solves her problems by just leaving everything there, when things get too much for her. She goes and gets her hair done, a full facial, the lot. Then she goes shopping. And she is grand by the time she gets back, late in the evening. Her family cope fine in the meantime, she assured me. 'I owe it to myself anyway' is the expression I have regularly heard her use, in many contexts, which always makes me smile each time I hear it. Easy known she isn't married to a farmer!

Another woman I know has a much more economical cure. She just goes for a good long walk when she finds things really getting on top of her. 'Then,' she said with a grin, 'I can't take it out on the family, when I clear off out myself. And,' she continued, patting her enviably flat stomach, 'my way is very good for the figure as well as the temper.'

Now, that is funny, in a way, since this woman always gave me the impression, at the country market, of being the most even-tempered woman imaginable. But I did remember her just leaving the hall, unexpectedly, a few mornings, right in the thick of things. At the time I just thought that she was short-taken. Now I wonder, each time she leaves, just why she is going for that walk?

I have no reason to wonder what another market member does when she can't stand her husband another minute. I know quite well since one famous evening, when, collecting her for a meeting, I found her, all dressed up, but stripping the wallpaper in their hall. 'Serve him right,' was all she said as she stopped and picked up her coat, which was all ready hanging on the banister, so she had not forgotten I was coming.

'Now he'll have to redo that wall tonight...' she continued with pure venom, and she pointed out the spare rolls of wallpaper, resting against the door into the kitchen, all ready and waiting for him. Another time, she told me that she had jerked all the wires out of half a dozen plugs, the ones he himself uses the most, the lamps on his side of the fire and the bed. And, if he was too late home, she was quite capable of pouring a bucket of water on the fire, to give him a cool reception, while she went off to bed with a book, she confided as we drove to our meeting. I told her there and then she was asking for trouble, advice which, in turn, got a pretty cool reception as well. I did not ask what her husband had done to annoy her this time...

In connection with all that, do you know that farmers have a much lower than average rate of heart attacks, or so a doctor friend of ours told us recently. He said this is because farmers can 'f... their animals and machinery from a height, and doctors and others always have to smile at even their most stupid and demanding patients or clients'.

Those words are his, not mine. He was deadly in earnest. So perhaps letting off steam is a good thing after all. And having this weekly column ensures that I don't ever have to smash the crockery over anybody's head! (1986)

Flat as a pancake

Pancake night is almost with us again, but it might as well be nothing. Oh, I'll make pancakes all right, and, doubtless, they will be eaten too, but without any fuss, excitement or even comment.

Pancakes are no great novelty to my family, you see. The sons often make themselves pancakes when they feel like a snack at night – or when they are getting their own supper, or, more likely still, when one of them decides that he doesn't like what I have provided.

Not for them, though, all that laborious beating of flour, eggs and milk, for ages and ages, and then letting it stand for a few hours to give the flour time to swell. They read my mixer instruction-cum-recipe-book more thoroughly than I had done, and found their own method of making pancake batter.

They just fling two eggs, a pint of milk, eight ounces of flour and a teaspoon of salt into the liquidiser, cover it and switch it on for half a minute. And hey presto! their pancakes are ready for cooking. So within five minutes of taking the notion to make pancakes they are actually eating the first one straight from the pan.

How different it was in my childhood. Immediately after the one o'clock dinner was cleared away the great big bowl was brought out to hold what were pounds of flour, the sweet tin full of milk, and egg after egg after egg. All these then had to be beaten, and beaten, and beaten with the wooden spoon.

If we were by any chance home from school on Shrove Tuesday we were not very keen to help wield that spoon, not like the rare occasions when cakes were being made. Then, there was never a shortage of willing helpers. And if you have ever tasted pancake batter, you will understand why. It is very different from the succulent mouthfuls of cake mix which could be purloined in safety while one was helping with cake-making. So there was never a queue to help with the pancake batter, or to bags the bowl or the spoon.

It was a different story, however, when, about five o'clock, the big iron frying pan was brought out from under the dresser and put on the open fire, and the first pancake poured on to sizzle and brown and tantalise those of us who were down the queue. The eldest got the first pancake cooked, and so on down the line, until the youngest got her go. And then the process started all over again.

How my mother managed, crouched as she was on a low stool over the furze fire, I'll never know. But that was during the war years when the big old range just stood there, black, cold and coal-less, fated never to return to glory when the times of austerity ended. Coal prices did not return to pre-war levels and it was replaced by a green anthracite-burning monster, also long since obsolete.

There was no electricity then either, or for many a long year later: all the cooking in my early childhood was done either on an open fire, or on a primus stove. Do you remember how that spat and sputtered and constantly needed pricking? The great big open fire was a lot more reliable with the furze heap in the yard to put jizz in the wet war-time turf. This made the *griosach*, the half burned fuel, really red hot and plentiful, to be put, by the shovelful, on top of the bastible oven when all was ready.

I remember the bastible, on the crane, being swung over the fire to make it good and hot, while my mother made the brown bread. Then, she would carefully take off the lid and scatter a little flour on the base to see if it was sufficiently hot. She knew, by how quickly the flour browned, exactly how hot the bastible was.

We children, however, thought her method of testing extremely dull. In one of the houses we used to call in on our way home from school, the woman of the house there had a much more interesting method. She used to spit into the bastible and, if her spit rolled and did not spatter, the bastible was ready. No way, though, would our mother do the same, or even allow us to test it for her, by this most interesting method. And, did she but know it, I, at one stage in my career, held the championship against all comers, both male and female, for the long-spitting competition in the school yard.

Still and all, I got in quite a bit of practice at bastible-spitting at that neighbour's house, and happily relished the bread cooked there too, when offered a slice on my long and weary way home from national school. With hindsight, I think the baking of the bread was kept for me to see on my way home: they must have been the lonely old couple with ne'er a chick or a child of their own. Mrs Murphy also made her pancakes in the bastible oven, tested in exactly the same way as her brown bread. So I had an advantage over my older brother in pancake consumption, even though he was the first in the line at home. He never went into that house with me. I was the one who rambled happily.

However, the time was not far away when, on coming home from my convent boarding school, full of notions, I was to refuse a piece from the same kind woman. And, when it was forced on me, I carefully left after me the bottom crust where it had touched the bastible.

Isn't it too bad that nice friendly children have to grow into hypercritical teenagers? Sure, the spit had been well sterilised by the heat of the bastible before it ever rolled to the opposite side and disappeared entirely, and the brown bread, or pancake, was put in.

But open fires, bastibles and all that went with them are now very much things of the past. So too are the sweet tins which, filled twice a day, stood on the dresser, holding handy the milk for drinking or cooking. The shopkeepers got those tins, I think, holding their bull's-eyes and acid drops. Then, when empty, they were given to favoured customers, or sold for a few pence to the less favoured ones.

Ah, well, I'll enjoy my pancakes and my memories on Tuesday night – whatever about the rest of my crowd. And if they act shocked when I tell of the bastible-cooking episodes of long ago, I think I'll remind them of the times when they were really young. All five of them used to then sit in a row at the kitchen table. If there was something they particularly liked for supper, like sausages, there was regular war in the camp if they did not each protect their own plates with their elbows. Because if one turned away, distracted for any reason, a fork would spear a sausage like lightning and it would be gone. So they developed the bright idea of visibly spitting on their plates as soon as they were put in front of them. That stopped the marauding forks. But how they hate right now to be reminded of that. I wonder, will the day ever come when they too see the humorous side of things? Right now I doubt it greatly. But then, look how long it took me. (1979)

The Stations in the house

Well, thank God, it is not my turn this time. Otherwise I would be in the horrors by now. I hadn't realised Lent was on us quite so soon, until the Station list was read out last Sunday at Mass. The first Monday in Lent signals the beginning of the Stations in this parish. And our area is the first on the Station list and always has been. The Stations have never been a moveable feast here, except, of course, for the parish priest and curate. They, for the next four or five weeks, will both pray and eat their way around both ends of the parish, as all the neighbours meet up in their Station areas. And great is the exchange of gossip and news in the different Station houses.

The first question asked, when one goes home afterwards, is 'And what did the P.P. have to say for himself this morning?' The Stations have traditionally been the time when communication between priest and parishioners, as well as the exchange of the dues, takes place, even if such communication is inclined to be kind of one-sided. But we at least get an inkling then of what is in the great man's mind, or what is expected of us, by way of contributions, or moral improvements, for the year coming. Later that night, his pronouncements are discussed and evaluated in all the homes and pubs of the parish, as word gets speedily around.

Now, it seems to me that we are experiencing something of a social shift, in that, for most people, the sociable aspect of the occasion is beginning to totally outweigh the religious and historical meanings of the Station morning. The rituals are changing. For one thing, we no longer have to collect the Station box the night before, from whoever had the Station that day. The priest now carries that around himself, in his car, from Station to Station. That separate collection was a reminder, in itself, of the times when it would not have been safe for the priest to have been caught with the accoutrements of Mass in his possession, the reason for the Station Masses, in country houses, in the first place.

I also no longer notice all the men staying outside in the yard, out of respect, come hail or shine, until the priests arrived. It would have been a very bad mark indeed for the man of the house not to have been there, at the door, waiting to receive their reverences, no matter what. The woman of the house was given more leeway, having to supervise the kitchen. She thus had the few minutes extra to whip off the cross-over apron and tidy her hair, before making her appearance. The man of the house almost inevitably seemed to have bits of paper stuck to his cheeks and chin, staunching the blood where his hand had been none too steady with his cut-throat razor, and the fuss of the morning. It was no joke getting all the cows and calves done, and the final sweep-up to the yard completed, before eight-thirty in the morning, which was the time stipulated by the priest here at the time.

It was the woman's job to take both priests to sit in two separate places, in order that the confessions might begin. The man of the house welcomed in all comers while organising the queues in the hall for confession, as best he could. The timid women and children were less able to slip him by, so they were directed to the P.P. The men usually favoured the curate, the younger man, for the open, face to face confrontation, with their sins. We all, men, women and children, decidedly missed the obscurity of the confessional box on the Station morning.

As a child, I remember being absolutely terrified facing in to kneel at the priest's black-clad knee, even if his sideways stance kept his feared face averted from my downcast eyes.

Now, these days there is no rush at all for confession, with only the curate hearing any morning. I wonder is the lasting power of the confessional all that much stronger these times? Before, people would never dare receive Communion unless they had been at confession mere hours earlier. Yet, for the life of me, I cannot see that people were more sinful when I was young, whatever about there being a lot more sins then for them to commit. But then again, in spite of the fasting from midnight rule, absolutely everybody did receive on the Station morning, or great was the comment later on any defaulters. Now, I don't think anybody takes the slightest notice of those whose hands are not raised when the priest asks how many for communion.

The food too is another thing that has changed a lot over the years. Gone is the day of the porridge and the boiled eggs, with plenty of brown and white soda bread. Toast, from baker's bread, was for the priests alone, or the men chosen to sit beside them. *Sean Laidir*, as the strong brown bread was called, did for the rest of us. Don't forget that this was in the days well before the electric toaster, and the women helpers making the toast, with their carving forks, got well roasted at the open fire.

When I first married it was beginning to be rashers and eggs for the autumn Station, with the porridge dropped at both, in favour of the more stylish grapefruit, never served, of course, without its red cherry in the centre. For the last five or six years the fashion has changed once more. Now it is great platefuls of chicken or turkey and ham, with all the trimmings, down to the obligatory lettuce leaf and mound of potato salad. Slices of apple tarts and chunks of flans must always be put on the side plate too, before the meat course is fully finished. And the drops from the bottle then follow, needless to mention.

It all adds up to a really superb meal; but not at ten o'clock in the morning. My poor old stomach is no way fit for it at that hour, and yearns for comforting porridge or just plain bread and marmalade. So I do have a certain pity for the priests, facing into this food, morning after morning, for the coming month. But I can see there is much less to go wrong with that meal than with boiled eggs not fully cooked, or rashers and eggs for those kinds of numbers.

There is an unwritten law, anyway, that anything that can go wrong does go wrong on a Station morning. Great are the tales told of men sticking to freshly painted dressers, and bringing the lot down when they moved away from their support after the Mass. The smell of fresh paint was always overpowering in any Station house, mixed with that of the new linoleum on the floor.

The first of our many Station disasters was on my very first Station here. I tried too hard to have everything perfect. Therefore, I went out to buy a brand new kettle especially for the occasion. The old kettle, which I had inherited on marriage, was bent, battered and somewhat on the blackened side. Perfect saucepans I had enough of, as wedding presents, to boil the eggs and make the porridge. And, to my great comfort, the eggs were neither too runny nor too hard when I opened one in the kitchen before sending the lot up to the room.

So, relaxing, I made the tea, and went up myself to pour it out. The first cup, of course, was for the parish priest and it came out black. Now, I was generous with the tea leaves all right, so as not to be thought mean. But this was B-L-A-C-K. Just like liquid soot it came out the spout.

I was covered in confusion. Eoin looked at me, from his seat next to the P.P., but I had no idea what was wrong, or what to do. So I hastily departed, taking the filled cup, and the teapot, with me. Dumping the lot, I made a whole fresh pot of tea from the now re-boiled kettle on the Aga. Alas and alack, it made no difference. It still came out black. At this stage all the women in the kitchen knew the young bride was in trouble. They had also had the same tea, but from a different teapot. However, one kind neighbour had the answer for me.

It was my new kettle. I, in my youth and inexperience, never knew that always one had to season a new aluminium kettle by first boiling spuds in it, at least once. The old kettle I had dumped only that morning, with the last of the rubbish from the Station clean-up. The breakfast inside was nearly over. Boiling fresh water in a saucepan was the obvious answer. But that would take such a long time from cold.

'Never mind, Liz,' said the same neighbour. 'I'll fix it for you.' And she made the tea, right there and then, from the boiling water off the saucepan full of eggs. 'Sure the men won't know the difference!' said she. And neither did they, as both parish priest and curate had three cups apiece with their toast and marmalade before they left. (1978)

The difference between faith & superstition

'There's not a bit of religion left in *you* anyway!' said Eoin to me in absolute disgust and with strong emphasis. 'So is it any wonder *your* sons are as bad as yourself? If you did more praying and less laughing – the lot of you – perhaps we'd all be better off...' This unexpected outburst made me watch my step a little bit more carefully then, as I finished my story at supper. It is always a really bad sign when our sons become teetotally *'your sons'*.

You see, I had been doing the shopping that day, and somehow or other I had mislaid my car keys. High up or low down, I couldn't find them as I retraced my steps from bank to shop to post office to car. I was only glad that, as usual, I hadn't bothered to lock the car as I was then able to make my search unencumbered by boxes and bags.

On my second round, searching, I met Maggie, an old neighbour, who saw my problem very simply. 'You just run over to the chapel there, love,' she said, 'and promise St Anthony a few pounds, and he'll find them fast for you.'

My ignorance must have been writ large on my face because she went on, like someone instructing a school-child on

self-evident facts – 'but be sure you only promise the money
now, like! That way he'll get a return visit from you when you
find your keys and go back to pay him....'

I was telling all this to my family over supper. And the saga
of St Anthony led on to my telling of this other woman I know,
who, to this very day, when an animal is sick, gets into her car
and goes down to the local church to light a candle for its
recovery... and the boys found all this simply uproarious, the
very thought of anybody rushing to light a candle instead of
dashing for the vet or trying to get to grips themselves with the
problem, whatever it was at the time.

I was only repeating what I had heard this woman say, that
she does precisely that, especially on those occasions when it is
a difficult calving and there is no man around. And it has
never once failed her, she had added. Always, by the time she
is back from the church, the calf is out safely and being licked
by the proud mother.

'You'll know what to do the next time now, Mom!' the sons
teased, and I answered that I didn't go in for bribery and
corruption at any level, not to mind the highest... And so the
crack was mighty as the banter flew back and forth over the
supper table. But I should have noticed Eoin going ominously
quiet. Then I would not have been taken so much by surprise
when he brusquely intervened and told us that it wasn't right,
that we should not be making a mockery of anybody's
marvellous faith. And then he went on to lay the blame fairly
and squarely at my door before firmly changing the
conversation. Well, at least he hadn't stalked off in total
disgust. So I did have the rest of my supper in peace and
hadn't to leave it to go and sooth down ruffled feathers.

Anyway, we weren't really mocking anybody's faith, or at
least we did not intend to be. To me, promising St Anthony, or
anybody else either, money if they do something for you is
pure superstition, just as much as putting the Infant of Prague
statue out under the hedge to ensure the next day will be fine.
I was long married when I first heard that one. And to be quite
honest I did try it, once. I can't for the life of me remember the
occasion now. But I do remember it didn't work.

However, I was told afterwards that it doesn't work if you do it for yourself. It has to be somebody else puts it out for you, before nightfall. It works best, and so is most used, the night before a wedding. It has also to face in the direction the fine weather is required. And, above all, the best Infant of Prague statues have the heads broken off, totally accidentally.

'There is no use in the wide world in it happening accidentally on purpose, like!' I was once told when I complained of my own personal failure with the Infant, even though I had fulfilled another very serious prerequisite. I had not gone out to buy the statue: it had been given to me as a present, and a wedding present at that.

Now one form of what I suppose you could call either superstition or faith was the custom we had in our convent school. There, if we lost anything, we set about the task of saying three Creeds while looking for the lost object. And then we added an additional three Creeds, in thanksgiving, immediately, regardless or not of whether we had found the lost object in the meantime.

And of course this often worked, for the very simple and practical reason that it takes a fair bit of time to say six Creeds and that much searching has to have a good chance of success. Now, it was one good nun who pointed out this indubitable fact to us, young, impressionable girls, while other nuns in the community were busy encouraging it. She, however, said that while saying those prayers was, in itself, very good, we should be careful not to mix it up with superstition.

I shall be eternally grateful to her for making me think beyond the obvious, in this, as in English literature, the subject she taught us.

But then again, my home influence was very strong as well. I never remember any such religious practices at home when I was a child. We said the Rosary each night without fail, and went to Mass each Sunday and Holiday of Obligation. But I have no recollection, whatsoever, of any special visits to holy wells, novenas, First Fridays, Second Tuesdays, or anything like that in my childhood. I have never in my life lit a candle, for instance, because there was no such thing then as petition

candles in our local church and I doubt if I ever, as a child, set
foot in any other church. There would have been no reason to,
when I was growing up in rural Ireland, with no cars on the
road. So I was also unaware of having three free wishes each
time I visited a strange church.

Eoin grew up in a city, as did my friend with the money for
St Anthony, and the woman who lights all those candles,
successfully. Therefore, churches and everything else were
more easily available to them. Actually, come to think of it, the
superstitions of my country childhood were more of a pagan
origin.

On Bonfire night, like everybody else, we lit a bonfire and
took a burned stick into the potato field, after all the cows had
been driven over the dying fire. Everybody in the house was
also supposed to jump the bonfire, which took both skill and
courage. The first year that I was married, I was interested to
see that the bonfire was lit here too, and amused that I got
great urging to be the very first to jump it. In fact, if I recall
things properly, nobody else was allowed to jump until I first
did so, and Eoin, holding my hand, helped as he ran along just
outside the flames. It was years later that I discovered that this,
in fact, was an old fertility rite for all women, but especially for
those newly wed. It did not arise that Eoin would have to jump
the bonfire too, since fertility, or the lack of it, was the
exclusive business of women in those days.

I jumped that bonfire for years and accepted it, quite
happily, as an amusing relic of old beliefs, just like the customs
of Hallowe'en. Getting the stick or the money in my slice of the
barmbrack was just a source of banter. However, what do you
make of the custom of blessing yourself each time you first see
the new moon?

Shortly after his outburst at supper, Eoin saw the new moon
when he went to the sink with his plate, and he blessed himself
automatically, as he always does whenever he sees the new
moon for the first time in the sky. Our youngest, I suppose
because of the earlier conversation, asked him why, and
neither of us were able to explain it. I don't do it myself, but I
well remember the consternation there used to be in the

kitchen at home, if the new moon was first noticed through glass. One particular man, who worked for us for years, used to go outside immediately, and bow several times to the said moon, turning the money in his pockets as he did so.

Could Eoin's making the sign of the cross be a vestige of some more ancient belief? Indeed, Eoin Óg, after recovering from the thought of us all having to go out and bow to the moon, and mischievously adding that he himself had no money in his pocket to turn, but he'd go if he had, asked Eoin if he blessed himself if he first saw the new moon out of doors? Eoin, again, was unable to answer. In fact, I would say that he wasn't even aware that he had blessed himself there that night in the kitchen, so automatic was the action.

It then struck me quite forcefully that our generation are the transitional generation, the last link between the myriad of the superstitious practices of the past generations, and the total disbelief, of any sort, in the present crowd. As for customs of the past, they'll have the mistletoe at Christmas, because it suits them, and the same goes for Valentine's Day, Easter eggs and the Christmas presents. But otherwise nothing. There are no mysteries, no unexplained happenings and mystical doings in their lives.

Of course, circumstances have changed so much that the occasions of many of the superstitions are gone too. Take, for instance, two men washing their hands before dinner in the one bowl of water put out for that purpose. One of them would always quickly spit into it, to prevent a quarrel arising between them later in the day. Now, of course, the washing of the hands is done under a running tap, despite my roars that they are wasting all the hot water. Spitting now disgusts us anyway. But once it went on all the time, to avert bad luck, as when meeting a red-headed woman or a four-legged beast on the way fishing, or on the palm of the hand to seal any bargain.

Now, to finish the story I started, I did not go over to petition, or bribe, St Anthony in the church across the road. I sat into the car instead for a moment, to gather my courage to go and phone home for help, and the spare set of keys. And there I found my own car-keys after slipping down between the two seats. I did offer up thanks then – for not having to call home for help, as I finished my sixth Creed! (1987)

Tea dinners

I put down a joint of roast beef in my electric oven today, and then we had a power cut before I had even the potatoes washed. 'Sure a tea dinner will be fine,' said Eoin, when I told him of my predicament. I had to laugh because, when he had it said, suddenly memories came back to me of times past when tea dinners were so unusual as to be remarkable. But the rest looked blankly at me when I mentioned that we'd all have to have a tea dinner today. Every meal in this place seems to be a moveable feast nowadays.

Long ago dinner was at one o'clock, regardless, except for the days we'd be going somewhere and then that's when we'd have a tea dinner. A tea dinner would be a plate of cold meat and tea and bread and butter, or even a boiled egg, tea and bread and butter: it would be a dinner purely by virtue of it being at dinner time.

And it was a poor woman of the house indeed who served up tea dinners too often. In the years when neighbours helped neighbours, the *meitheals*, and a work man would often be sent off early in the morning with his pike on his shoulder, the comment that they only had a tea dinner there the day before, would be pointedly made, later, as a clear warning that they were not to be sent to that particular house again. Farm labourers were very badly paid, so 'diet' and a good feed once a day was all important to them.

Not all farm labourers got their 'diet', however. I had some friends out here during the week and something arose about conditions of life on farms at the turn of the century. To settle an argument I looked for, and found, Eoin's grandmother's account book for farm workers, which she started in 1891.

Now this grandmother of Eoin's was a powerful woman by all accounts. A second wife, she herself was widowed when her husband died of pneumonia at forty-six years of age. She was left with one step-child and five children – well, four actually, since Eoin's father was a posthumous baby. And the story goes that it was my own grandfather who shaved him when he was dead, this being a sign of great friendship indeed, a signal honour.

But this friendship did not last, because my grandmother soon objected to the time that my grandfather spent helping the poor widow woman, to the detriment of his own work. Not that the same widow woman needed that much help if her account books are anything to go on. She was some operator as they would say today. Indeed, she was proof positive that the only women allowed to be good business women, in the Ireland of those days, were widows and reverend mothers. Once there was a man about the house, his was the control. But has much really changed in rural Ireland, in the years since, except perhaps for the reverend mothers? To this day, when the son grows up, even the most efficent widow woman will begin to find callers to the door asking her once more, 'Is himself around by any chance?'

This widow woman, my grandmother-in-law, milked a bawn of forty cows on this farm in the early part of this century, when such a thing was unheard of. And, as her family grew, she took on the contract for the repairs of roads locally, and ran a horse drawn bus and delivery service twice daily to the local train station some five miles away. In her account book I have the flyers for this service.

I also have some of the work contracts drawn up at gale days, for the men working on the farm here. These are full legal documents and make fascinating reading, once one has deciphered the fading copperplate writing. One went as follows:

Memorandum of agreement between Margt. J Kavanagh of Granig and James Sullivan, also of Granig, also his brother-in-law, Patrick O'Keeffe.

They are to work for me as general farm labourers from the 25 of March 1901 until the 25 of March 1902, James Sullivan as ploughman and at all sorts of farm work. I am to pay the said James Sullivan at the rate of 7s..6d per week, at the rate of 1s..3d per day, for every day he works for me, without diet, Patrick Sullivan at 7s per week, 1s..2d for every day he works for me, without diet. I am to give him the grass of two sheep each, also a quarter of manured ground, planted, to each of them, also 1/2 ton of coal to each of them. They are to do their work for me cheerfully and willing to attend on Sundays and holidays to the feeding of cattle and horses. Also, their two women are to work, when required, on the farm, or otherwise, binding and about turnips and mangolds at the same rate, to be paid 1s. per day for binding and 8d for other work. For the milking of cows also is required Hanora Keeffe.

Signed by
Witness Margaret J Kavanagh
Thomas Murphy James X [his mark]
Patrick X [his mark]

What poor Hanora was to get for the milking of cows was not spelled out, or who she was in relation to 'their two women'. But why on earth did James take control of his brother-in-law, Patrick and his family, and get a penny a day more pay? All Eoin remembers are near neighbours, called Sullivans, who were that fond of tea that his uncle used to say of them that if they had tea for their dinner, they'd still have tea after their dinner!

However, what Eoin remembers most was the 'bee' wine in that house, which he used to be given to drink there as a child. It was the most wonderful drink, he says, made in a glass sweet jar with the 'bees', which weren't bees at all but some form of African bean seeds or pods, constantly moving up and down it. What on earth were they? I would dearly love to know. And, no wonder Eoin felt good after his 'bee wine': it must have been quite an intoxicating mixture, since sugar was constantly added to the 'bees' to keep them active, when and if they stopped their perpetual movement.

I would say that his grandmother was no joke either at ensuring perpetual movement, during their working hours, from her workforce. A big studio portrait of her had pride of place over the dining room sideboard when I first came here. From the look of her I would say that she didn't have too many tea dinners in this place! I dearly wish I had found more of her history than this one account book. But I did get her only grandson, and her farm of land! (1988)

MARCH

Eoin does hate Sundays

'You just wait and see,' Eoin muttered to me as the day went on. 'I'll kick the bucket myself on some fine Sunday!' 'I'm glad you're going to wait for a fine one anyway,' was my reply, which was fair enough in that last Sunday was a particularly wet Sunday, with a wind straight from the Siberian plains that would skin a brass monkey. Eoin was doing his nut, because, despite all his care, we had to have a caesarean done on a cow last Sunday morning. We barely survived the ordeal ourselves, but neither the mother nor the calf did. 'She'd have been all right if it was any other day but a Sunday,' was Eoin's bitter reaction.

Poor Eoin. He does so hate Sundays! Everything that can possibly go wrong for him does so on a Sunday. We had been to early Mass, otherwise we might never have made Mass that Sunday. Which was just as well when I consider a certain man in this parish who had a cow calve while he was at Mass and not there in attendance. The calf was dead when he got home. So from that day until the day he died, almost forty years later, that man never again set foot in the house of God. The same man was equally unforgiving to some of his neighbours.

While I doubt that Eoin would ever take it that far, against God or man, he does sometimes shake his fist up to heaven and shout at the top of his voice 'God! God above! If there be a God above! Why are you doing this to me?' Nevertheless he really does have a thing about Sundays. It can be rather like a litany with him once he starts naming out all the annoyances and calamities of Sundays past. And he remembers each one vividly as if each was a personal affront to him on the part of God.

Cattle, grazing peacefully all week, take it into their heads to break out and go on a rampage on a Sunday. The like of the milking machine and water pump also choose Sundays to break down, when no mechanic is ever available. Remember the big freeze-up last month? Well, it also was early on a Sunday morning that we woke up frozen in our electric-blanket-warmed bed. The electricity was obviously off. There was no water in the cold tap when we tried to fill the kettle to stick on the Aga. All over the farm, every water pipe was frozen solid. The misery of that Sunday, with the cows neither milked nor watered, is something I do not care to remember. And we never made Mass at all.

Then there was that dreadful Sunday when the hay-barn went on fire, while we were at Mass, the first Sunday in December, and all our winter fodder went up in smoke. The two youngest sons, who were not at Mass with us, were missing. And for some hours it was missing, presumed dead, until they were found hiding behind the bulk tank in the dairy. That easily was the worst in our litany of dreadful Sundays, and it still gives me the horrors even to think of it, many years later.

I wonder do others find Sundays as catastrophic as the Kavanaghs do? Or is it all a form of superstition with us at this stage? Regardless of what we may think, we all do have our pet superstitions. Eoin has his Sundays. Personally, I think that Sundays are no worse than any other day in this place. Eoin just notices Sundays more because he can't get help to fix his problems until the Monday, and so has to live with them for that much longer.

When he is at his most despairing I invariably ask him one question, to point up this fact, before he goes over the top entirely and declares, once more, that he'd be better off dead! I ask if money will cure our problem. I know it drives Eoin mad when I do. But I reckon if the answer is in the affirmative, then basically we have no problem, since it will be curable, sooner or later, depending on the cash-flow or the bank manager.

Alternatively, Eoin's trouble with Sundays may be more to do with the day that is in it. He was brought up to strongly believe Sundays to be days of rest from all servile work, which is a relatively easy thing if, like Eoin, one is not brought up on a farm. I am farm bred, and while I once got into trouble in school for admitting to doing knitting on a Sunday, I was quite accustomed to work continuing on more or less as usual on Sundays. Cows still had to be milked, pigs fed, eggs collected. Come to think of it, it was really only field work that was never touched on a Sunday. The neighbours could see one at that. And my mother enjoyed her knitting, be it Sunday or Monday, sitting by the fire or outside in the sunshine.

So I have no complexes whatsoever about doing both what is necessary and what I enjoy on Sundays. Eoin, I suspect, feels just that little bit guilty, subconsciously, when he is compelled by circumstances to do a lot of extra work on a Sunday. This may well be the real reason behind his 'always on a Sunday' syndrome.

Now I pride myself on being a very practical woman with no time at all for the usual superstitions. I willingly walk under ladders. By the way, do you know that the thing about walking under ladders started because the triangle formed by a ladder against a wall, in medieval times, was reputed to be a sign of the Trinity, three persons in one God? Hence, to show proper respect, one walked around it.

Still, I do have one odd belief, call it a superstition if you like, which it well may be. In a peculiar way I am glad, grateful even, for all the small things that so regularly go wrong on us here, even the ones on a Sunday. Then, even in the pain, I feel we are safe from major disasters. I have often noticed that people who have all things in their lives running really well for them, the ones on whom the gods always smile, are the very ones to whom fate finally deals a cruel blow, the kind of misfortune which money does not cure.

It is so much easier to put up with many little pin-pricks from life, which is all that basically happens to us on Sundays anyway, how ever much Eoin may curse and swear and shake his fist at the heavens, than dealing with really serious problems. Eoin, when he isn't getting mad at me for it, laughs at my saying that it could be very much worse. You see, whenever we have a few weeks' plain sailing, Eoin says I am then on the look-out for trouble, 'inviting it in, in fact' are his very words.

This may connect back to my own mother. Strange how we never get away from our upbringing, no matter how hard we may try. She has her very own form of superstition. She hates us to praise anything at all of ours, be it farm or family. We can't say a child or cow or calf is doing real well, without her jumping down our throats. Saying something is doing well, she says, is the surest way possible to make something go wrong. When that does happen then, as indeed it often seems to, it is no use our saying that it would have happened anyway, regardless. It is no use pointing out that it was only the fact that we remarked on something that makes her remember it at all. She strongly holds onto her view that it is the praising of anything that brings on the trouble, and that is all there is to it.

This must be a remnant of our pagan days and customs, with a ring of 'let's not make the gods jealous of our good fortune' to it. Could that also be partly the reason why so many farmers indulge in their perpetual 'poor mouth syndrome'? Inasmuch as, if we were to substitute 'urban population' for 'the gods', perhaps that is the right attitude for us all to take! (1978)

The principle of the thing

I'm afraid I've been caught again. There is no doubt about it that people are peculiar and that I'll never learn from experience. I've been caught before so I should have known better. But still I walked into it, with my eyes open, and all because I thought she was a friend! It really isn't the few pounds that bothers me. It's the principle of the thing. Or could it be that, when it is somebody I know, a friend, I am too nice, or even too cowardly, to do anything about it?

The cause of my annoyance this time is a seed order. At the country market last autumn I was asked by a fellow gardener if we would combine our seed and bulb order from a specialist catalogue she had from an English concern, and so save ourselves money and bother. We both wanted to grow a lot of perennials from seed and one packet would give each of us many many more plants than either one of us would need.

It seemed so sensible to split the packages between us. There and then we made up our order, and, foolishly enough, I offered to write the cheque to cover the cost. As always with gardeners, our enthusiasm for plants ran away with us. What was to be a few packages of seeds turned into a sum that gave us both cause to pause. But what matter, we said. It would be only half each, so that was all right. And it was also very much cheaper growing them from seed than paying God knows what per plant to have somebody else grow them. Privately anyway, I determined to recoup my cost by sales from the market, knowing I am a better grower than she.

So it was done, so many split half each, and some that only one or the other wanted. We did not stop until the order form was complete and the total cost for each of us was calculated. During a lull in the postal strikes, both here and in England, the seeds and bulbs duly arrived at my house. I spent a whole

Thursday night scrupulously putting my portions into separate containers, writing out the names and instructions for same as I went. Next day, at the market, I handed over her share, in the original packages, to my 'friend'. 'Aren't you very good indeed, Liz?' said she to me in her plummy accent – but not a thing more as she took them from me and immediately turned to a nearby crony, telling her of all the marvellous things she was about to grow this year. I even heard her promising to give her a few plants of a very special and new form of Anthemis I had specially chosen because I had read of it in a gardening magazine.

I was hurt at my immediate exclusion from the conversation. They carried on as if I wasn't there at all and dark uncomfortable thoughts of my being considered as a mere peasant papist, after all, intruded. I was also flabbergasted that there was no mention of money. But I genuinely thought that she would be back to me with her share of the cost, during the morning. Because really I had been expecting my money, for weeks, since her share of the total had been determined the very first day we made out our joint list.

Devil the sight of money did I see that morning though, or at any other market morning since. The question is what should I do now? Should I ask her straight out for what she owes me, and risk upsetting and offending her, for of course she must just have forgotten she hadn't paid me. Or will I, as I have done on a few other occasions, grin and bear it, while swearing never again to get involved in anything that involves paying out money for others? Cash on the nail will be my motto from now on.

'That's right, Mom,' echoes a son, who just sneaked a look at what I'm writing this week when I left the room. They have only just discovered their mother writes this column and are slightly uptight about the whole thing, lest their friends find out, or I write something about them. 'Remember the raspberries we picked for your friend, Mrs Nyhan, and how you wouldn't let us ring her up to ask her for the money for them?'

And I wouldn't either, even though it cost me dear, as I there and then reminded him. To stop them making a disgrace of me I had to pay those Shylock sons of mine the full price for forty pounds of raspberries, an order for both her mother-in-law and herself, that my friend so conveniently forgot all about. It was rough, buying my own raspberries from my sons. And more fool I, since I had even delivered the wretched things myself, on my way to town, to spare Nora the bother of coming out to collect them.

Her mother-in-law was the only one in the house when I arrived. She rhapsodised over the raspberries, and then said Nora would pay for them next time she saw me. And actually the next time Nora saw me was at a dinner party at her house. And guess what we had for dessert? But that was hardly the time, nor the place, in front of her husband and my fellow guests, to remind her that my sons had never been paid for those raspberries we were eating.

Now a little discreet questioning around and about has revealed the fact that I am not the only one with a similar problem. Many people, when I broached the subject, jumped in with, 'Do you know what, Liz, something very similar happened to us as well.' I say us, advisedly, because one woman told of her husband who organised a group of neighbouring farmers in a drainage scheme. They agreed that he was to meet all sundries, advertising etc, and the shortfall, if any, in the grants. Then, when the job was completed, they would settle up with him, share and share alike. The land is long reclaimed. But the settlement day never came. Now, years later, the memory still rankles with that pair, even though, as they freely admit, the money concerned now seems small to them. But it was quite a lot at the time and, once again, it is the principle of the thing as much as the actual money.

Another woman told me how she was to provide the car to take a group on an outing and her passengers were to provide the petrol. But never once, either coming or going, was it suggested that they stop at a petrol pump, and she lacked the courage to do it herself, lest it cause embarrassment. Thus, she nearly ran the car dry before she got home, rather than pull into a petrol station. There was war next day when her husband ran out of petrol on his way to the village. 'Stupidly enough,' she explained, 'I started out the day with a fairly full tank, a mistake I never made again.'

Is all this a form of mean stinginess with people or do they genuinely forget? Does the brain subconsciously block out all memories that one does not want to remember? Will those reading this recognise themselves? And how do you think it will go if I give the subconscious mind of my seed-sharing friend a good jog some market day soon, by sweetly and casually asking her how *my* seeds are coming along – and tell her that *my* half of the packages, *which I* bought, are slow enough about germinating, which in actual fact they are. Sure it will be worth a try anyway. But it will probably be like water off a duck's back – or off a duck's subconscious. (1979)

The basic dilemma of farm life

I know my son is right, but I for one could never do it. And I doubt if Eoin could either. Killing calves goes against what we have always felt and done – keeping them alive regardless of our time, trouble or effort has always been our way. Money did not really come into it at all, as my farming son was quick to point out, when I was so aghast at what he wanted to do, which was to kill the lovely little heifer calf just that minute born.

'What are you killing *yourself* for, anyway, Mom?' he said, laying on the sarcasm. 'Why don't you just throw your money straight into the slurry pit and go and play with your plants in the garden? And you'd be better off pouring all that milk powder into the slurry pit as well while you are at it. It might do some good, eventually, on the land, because it is doing no good at all in those bitches of calves and that's for sure!'

Although I hated the thought of it, the boy was right. I could not fault his logic. He had been all day at the mart with calves. The price he got for the bull calves was bad. But disastrous was too good a word for what he got for our lovely heifer calves. They only made between £18 and £35 each, and most of them were a good six weeks old at that. Which Seamus was not slow about pointing out to me.

'You may as well go in home now, Mom, like a good woman, and let me do it. Those calves today were at least 42 days old, and drinking over a pound's worth of milk a day. So they all cost you well over £40 each, not counting your time at all, nor any of the injections you gave the sick ones... nor the cost of the straw to bed them... nor the calf nuts they ate...' Then, as he went on and on, he became all determined and continued with 'I don't care what you say, Mom. From now on I am knocking any heifer calf born on the head, the minute it hits the ground.' Then, to make matters worse, he pointed out the batch of heifer calves we had not considered strong enough that day to take to the mart and said that those were going to cost us good money as well. So they were going off to the very next mart, regardless!

I had to listen to him, even though it went completely against the grain. And yet, and yet – I have been conditioned, in all my years farming, to go to any lengths humanly possible to keep a calf alive. Even the calves with something wrong with them I have laboured over, coaxing them to drink their milk and so have some chance of survival. Whenever I succeeded I have felt quite ridiculously proud of myself, and attached to the calf in question. But now I have to face the fact that I may have been quite wrong all those years. Or is it that I am not flexible enough to change with the changing circumstances? That is the one great thing about young people, like this strapping seventeen-year-old son of mine trying to make me see sense. They look at things with fresh eyes, and maybe see more that we, with the scales of tradition distorting our vision.

Perhaps, after all, Eoin and I are inclined to fall into the very real trap of looking on farming as a way of life and not a business. Animals are a means to an end in themselves, and nothing more. So, while it normally pays to be kind to our animals, perhaps these are not normal times and our farming son is right.

Still and all, I don't know – killing these helpless creatures just because they will not pay their way! But then again we are farming to make money, not just to rear animals. All this account-keeping we now have to become involved with is going to do one thing for sure, and that is to make us question everything we do. Fresh eyes – account-keeping eyes – are being brought to bear on many facets of farming, in these days of diminishing returns. People like me will find it very hard to change. But as in the case of the calves, what are we to do? We already have more than the land will carry for the year, as our farming son has proved with his calculation of stocking units and acres.

However, I keep pointing out to him that we lived through this sort of thing before. Do you remember 1974, the year of the great fodder shortage, when there were no bids at all for beautiful calves at all the Marts? Many stories were then told of men, when faced with returning home with trailer-loads of unsold calves, going into the pub to help ease the pain, and then coming back out to find extra unwanted calves dumped in with theirs. Other farmers were unable to do the dread deed themselves and chose one easy way out. I also know that we have mart dockets somewhere, where a bunch of calves actually cost us money to sell them, since the entry fees and the commission charged were more than the value of the calves themselves. The mart then billed us for the difference.

Still and all, those who held their heads and reared their calves were well paid in 1976 when the price of beef dramatically improved. And what about the days of the Economic War? I bet many then found it impossible to kill their calves for a handful of silver, even though on production of the hide they were paid ten shillings.

Times were a lot harder then, I'm told, tough and all as times are now. But as I always say, we never died a winter yet, and here we are, with the grass now growing well, the daffodils out in great yellow clouds, and spring is well and truly here. I won't even begin to think of next winter, and the fodder to keep those calves I am determined to save, because who knows what will have happened to any us, calves and all included, by then? (1980)

One confession is the making of another

Eoin and I, in the car driving along, started talking, of all things, about stealing, and what we personally had got up to when young. Well, that wasn't surprising actually, because we were listening to a mother on the radio to Gay Byrne, in an awful tizzy, because her child was stealing money from her. She really was in an dreadful state over this. The guest psychologist told her that she shouldn't be too worried: most children at some time or other steal things. Which is true enough, God knows.

Eoin and I then started to reminisce about that son of ours who used to steal from us, when he was a very small lad at national school. Eoin had, and still has indeed, the habit of emptying the small loose change out of his pockets into a redundant ashtray by his wardrobe. And there it stays, a temptation to any young child, until I gather it all up. I am not totally innocent either, as I was always inclined to just drop my handbag on the nearest chair, on coming home from any outing.

But all that had to change when the teacher called me one day after school, to say that she did not think it right that my son should have so much pocket money. He was buying sweets, every day, for the whole class, which she did not think right, she said. She may have had her suspicions about where he was getting the money, but I left her in no possible doubt that it wasn't with our knowledge that those sweets were being purchased, even if it had to be with our money. We both decided that the lad must have been trying to buy popularity.

Naturally Eoin and I were upset at this turn of events, and while we determined not be too hard on him, we set out to ensure that it didn't happen any more. However, despite changing our habits, and talking kindly to our son, and even searching his pockets and school-bag before he left each morning, within a week the teacher hailed me again to say that matters had not improved. So rather than keeping every penny in the house under lock and key, an impractical solution, we resolved to do a complete body search the very next morning. And sure enough, we discovered a half-crown safely tucked into the toe of one of his socks.

We knew then that he really had problems in school, when he was going to such extremes, so we showered him with extra attention and kept on inviting children from his class home with him to play. In a way we bought him the popularity that he himself was endeavouring to buy with sweets. But we also kept a strict eye on him, and our money, since appeals to his conscience did not seem to have the slightest effect. He had no conception of conscience, of right and wrong, we reluctantly decided.

There was no word about conscience, or the rights and wrongs of stealing, that morning either on the Gay Byrne show. And suddenly I found myself telling Eoin about my thefts, at that age or even younger. Personally I went to town on it, in every sense of the word. It was about the time of my First Holy Communion; I was in Woolworths on my own. Times were so different then, children at quite a young age were free to wander as they pleased, more or less.

My parents would leave us off at Woolworths' door and go off about their business while we spent a very happy time looking at all the wonders on those long, flat, glass-divided counters. There was so very much to dream over because the shilling we had each for the week didn't go very far, even with putting several weeks together and having no Peggy's Leg at all, any day, on the way home from school. Those yellow sugar sticks were a great long suck for the three-mile walk we had home. Sweets were just too scarce on our menu for profligate crunching.

So, while our parents were busy on whatever kept farmers busy those times in the city, we were free to wander, unobserved, in Woolworths' wonderland. Now, that day at the jewellery counter, I fell for this bracelet of beads, looking like flower heads, with a double row of elastic running through them so it stretched to go over my hand and then fitted back so snug on the wrist. I tried it on, and how I craved it! I cannot remember ever wanting anything quite so badly ever since. But I had no money.

Then I saw my father coming in the door. The jewellery counter at that time was just inside the left-hand door, the sweet counter was next to it, and then the stairs. Dad never liked to be kept waiting when he came back for us. So we were supposed to be ready near the door to go on the spot, which I did, the bracelet still on my wrist.

And it wasn't the case that I forgot to take it off, either. It was quite deliberate. It stayed under my coat sleeve all the way home in the pony and trap. And then, once home, I scooted up to my bedroom to drool over it in private. How I swanked all week in school with my bracelet. And my conscience didn't bother me in the slightest because a week or two after this I was taken to town again and this time I went into Woolworths, deliberately, for a matching bracelet for the other wrist.

Then, to my utter confusion and consternation, my conscience was developed for me, very shortly after, by a catechism lesson in school on the seventh commandment. This was bad enough, to have it confirmed that I had committed a sin, twice, and would have to tell it in my First Confession. But the really hard part was yet to come, when the teacher went on to explain that, for this particular sin, going to confession was not enough. Any child who had stolen anything could not make their First Communion with just going to confession. No, the only way to be forgiven was to make restitution first. And to go to Communion after a bad confession would mean the most terrible of unforgivable sins – going to Communion in the state of mortal sin.

I wonder how many others of the First Communion class got that sudden sharp shock of self-recognition as a dreadful sinner? All the way home I was in torment. What was I to do? Where was I to get three whole shillings? I was old enough to calculate that two bracelets at one and six each made three shillings, an impossible amount in the time available before my First Communion. Or else I would have to take back my two beautiful bracelets.

Instead, I stole the necessary amount from my mother's purse. Well, I did better than that, actually. I took a red ten-shilling note and went into the shop on the way to school to have it changed. But the shopkeeper said no, I think because I was buying nothing, or even because she did not have that much change. Ten shillings was an almighty amount of money then, of course. That left me in a proper cleft stick, because the shopkeeper told me that the pub next door would change it, but there my courage failed me. All day at school that ten-shilling note bothered me lest I lose it, or be seen with it. And if I took it home, the chance of detection would be even greater.

So I eventually told my brother the whole sorry saga and asked him to go into the pub for me. Which he did, but only on condition that he could keep half of my ill-gotten gains! He justified this by saying that girls were never allowed into pubs, and anyway I'd still have money over and above what I needed. We both crunched on Peggy's legs on our way home that evening.

How I justified taking the money from my mother's purse showed how little I really understood. For the teacher had said that restitution did not have to be made for stealing a spoonful of sugar from our mothers, that taking things at home, while still a sin, was different. Why anybody could possibly want to take a spoonful of sugar on its own was a mystery to me. But we had also been taught that God dealt very much in mysteries.

Then, that very week, I came around my father to be taken to town on the Thursday when he was going in with the butter and the eggs. There was no lingering around Woolworths this time. I went to the jewellery counter and left the three shillings on the counter and then ran out the door as fast as ever I could. Restitution was made. In fact, during that dash to the door was when I discovered guilt, and the way it makes us feel. I felt much worse in the act of restitution that in the actual thefts. But I was ready for my First Confession on the Saturday.

Now it was Eoin's turn for confession, when he had finished laughing at mine. He had kept watch for another boy on the way home from school while that boy stole a jam roll from the local shop. And the pair of them ate it there and then on their way home from school. But Eoin was sick as a dog after the over-indulgence. So the next day, when it was his turn to do the stealing, he refused point blank, saying that he didn't ever want to see a jam roll again. And to this day he won't look at a shop-bought jam roll. But a home made one lasts no battle if he's around.

But his perfidy did not end at that. Like me, even if for more straightforward reasons, he also helped himself from a convenient handbag. He stole half a crown from his grandmother's purse one day, and spent the lot on sweets and red lemonade. But then, like me, he too got a crisis of conscience, but not until the supply of sweets was gone. Then he went and told his grandmother the awful thing he had done. And what did she do but open up her purse and give him another half-crown for being so honest. But he couldn't remember what he did with that half-crown, what he spent it on. The guilt of the ill-gotten coin imprinted its spending on his memory. He was able to describe in detail the exact kind of sweets he got with the first half-crown. He also remembered very clearly his lessons on certain of the commandments in his school.

So small children do develop consciences, but only if they are taught what consciences are all about. All the telling in the world by parents that stealing is wrong is not half as effective as the teacher doing the same thing in school. I wonder is it still being done by teachers in all this new curriculum stuff, because on that radio programme the concept of a child developing a conscience was never once raised? The problem was totally a problem of the adults and not the children. Has the pendulum swung a little too far, I wonder, in these child-centred times? (1982)

Johnny, the missing pants & the frying-pan

'You'd better watch out that I don't do a Johnny on you,' said Eoin to me when the phone call came from the doctor's secretary that the hospital is now all organised. Eoin has to have elective surgery done for his cataract, and is very much in two minds about going for it at all. He is only looking for an excuse to put the whole thing off still further. He is really quite uptight about this, his first ever full anaesthetic.

But I hope to God he doesn't do a Johnny on us all the same, to give him courage. I'd never be able for that. Now Johnny, who was old, unmarried and a character, was a class of a relation of Eoin's. Johnny was a continual torment to his sisters, also unmarried, with whom he lived: he just would not have manners put on him and they got quite particular in themselves as they grew older. Johnny always made us laugh. But as Eoin pointed out, it would be a different story entirely if one was dealing with him every day of the week.

I well remember how we laughed the day he came up the hill to ask Eoin for the loan of a pair of pyjamas. 'Themselves below' – which was how he always referred to his sisters, as a collective term – 'tell me I must get a pair of them things before I go into the hospital,' he explained. He was having some trouble with his waterworks, he said to Eoin, in a loud whisper behind his hand, lest I hear what was taking him to hospital.

Now Johnny was one of those who put a clean shirt on his back every Sunday morning, and that then had to do him, night and day, until the following Sunday morning, when he had his weekly shave and change of clothes. Don't forget that any money spent on fripperies was so much less for the nightly pints, and his sisters managed his finances anyway for him. There was no need at all for him to have pyjamas once he was out of hospital again, he went on to explain to a flabbergasted Eoin. But he knew that Eoin, since he had honeymooned in foreign parts, had probably got some pyjamas for the occasion. And he said that of course now that Eoin was home again, those pyjamas were of no further use to him, so could himself have a pair of the things!

Johnny got his pair of pyjamas, no bother, and went off back down the hill again, delighted at his cleverness. Next day he was safely deposited, by Eoin, in the hospital, after making a suitable stop at a pub on the way. Of course Johnny had to buy the driver a drink. That meant two pints for Johnny since, naturally, Eoin then had to return the compliment.

Eoin came home, finally, full of amusement at your man and his carry on with the poor nun who was given the task of extracting information from him for her records. When she asked how old he was she got the answer, accompanied by a ferocious wink as he stuck his face up to hers:

'Old enough to have sense, but young enough to have fun – if you're game, Sister!"

She must have been nearly bowled over by the smell of porter, if not the wit, because Johnny had been in the pub ever since Mass time after all, before Eoin ever picked him up. The drink was the source of his courage, since he had been notoriously slow, I heard, about coming forward when he should have, during his one and only courtship when he was younger. But that never stopped him having an eye for the young ones, especially if he hadn't a hope in the world of success.

Eoin left after this sally, while the going was good, having given our phone number to the good sister in case of any emergency. That night, we were just thinking of going to bed at our usual early hour, when the phone rang and it was the hospital, inquiring if we had any idea if Johnny had gone home: he was nowhere to be found in the hospital, or in the hospital grounds. They had carried out a complete search. We, of course, had no notion where Johnny might be. So there was nothing for it but to go and face 'those below'.

When we eventually got an answer to our knocking – I had gone down with Eoin, lest they be frightened hearing only a man's voice – they had seen nothing of their brother since he had left with Eoin earlier that day. But somewhat bitterly, sticking her head out her bedroom window, one of them suggested that Eoin phone back the hospital to tell them to go and search all the local pubs before they disturbed any more people in their beds!

Eoin felt he couldn't very well do that. So he set off himself, into the city, to try all the pubs. And sure enough he found Johnny in the one nearest to the hospital, happy out with a new bunch of drinking buddies, whom he said had promised to see him safely back into the hospital once the pub closed. It was well nigh that time then anyway, so Eoin hadn't too long to wait before he got him safely, if a little unsteadily, back to the hospital gates.

Having rung the bell, he didn't wait long enough to see what kind of a reception Johnny got there, only handed him over to the night porter who seemed to think it was all a huge joke. 'Wait till Sister Mary Margaret gets hold of you and you'll get who-began-it!' was all he kept saying to Johnny with the rueful air of one who knew only too well the sharp edge of Sister Mary Margaret's tongue. Well, Johnny may have got the sharp edge of her tongue all right but he didn't get the sharp edge of the surgeon's knife next morning, as intended. His operation had to be put off until he was well sobered up and fasted.

It was a day or two later that Eoin and I got in to see him. It was a surprisingly subdued Johnny we met when we found him in his bed in the ward. 'Did Sister Mary Margaret give you a bad doing-off?' we asked, after inquiring how he was feeling after his operation. 'Faith, no,' he replied, 'I'm too well used to the sharp edge of women's tongues by now to take any notice of her. But she did something far worse, which no other woman has ever done before to me – she took the pants fair and clean off me!'

And sure enough, as he made to demonstrate, he had no pyjama-legs on, only the top, and his good suit trousers, which he had on coming in, were also gone out of the press. 'Now try to get to the pub like that!' Sister Mary Margaret had said to poor old Johnny, when the fell deed was done, that first night, once he was safely back in the hospital bed from the local pub.

Johnny was confined to bed anyway with the various tubes, or so he explained. But he added: 'Fat lot of chance I have of moving anything anyway. Do you know what those jades did to me the morning after my operation ? To add insult to injury, this young nun came in, handed me a frying pan, and told me to sit on it to do my business. Now Eoin, is that any way to treat a decent God-fearing man?'

Eoin's offering of a naggin of whiskey was going down well now with Johnny, so I was not really surprised when he next turned to him to say: 'Tell you what, Eoinín, if you have e'er another pair of those pyjamas at home, left over like from your honeymoon, bring them in here to me. Then, when I get on my feet, and get back the legs of the first pair, I'll do the rounds with them. Any poor devil without his pants will gladly pay dear for a pair of yours, and maybe I can get a wear out of them in the meantime myself!'

We departed on that note, as we then saw some more neighbours heading in Johnny's direction. Eoin had a bit of business next day in town, so he bought a pair of brand new pyjamas for your man. With one thing and another, visiting hours were over when he got to the hospital. So he was not surprised to be stopped in his tracks going in the door to Johnny's ward by an old nun. She, the formidable Sister Mary Margaret we had heard so much about, was dying laughing, however, as she said: 'Do you know what that Johnny is after saying to me now? I came in to confiscate any drink he might have, since he kept the whole place awake last night with the sing-song he had organised. So I told him that I had my eye on him, in as severe a tone as I could muster up. And do you know the answer he made me? "Well, Sister, it may not be too late for me, but it is definitely too late for you to have your eye on me!" So, for pity's sake, Mr Kavanagh, don't give him any more drink.'

Eoin gave him the pyjamas instead, and took back home the naggin of whiskey for another day. Later we heard how, on the day he left hospital, Johnny had indeed gone from ward to ward trying to sell both pairs of pyjamas, to the mortification of the sister and a closer relation who had gone in to bring him home. Now, whether he ever sold the pyjamas or not I don't know. All I do know is that Eoin was never offered them back, or the money for them either. And, when all that family had gone to their eternal reward, the farm went to that closer relation. (1985)

APRIL

A flurry of polish & dusters – Why?

'Only for Christmas and Easter the Irish would rot!' the old people around here used to say when I was young. They were remembering the days when these holidays meant a lot of whitewashing and disturbance. Only the Stations caused more cleaning and refurbishing when their turn came around. Even all the blankets had to be washed for Christmas! Just think of the job of drying them again at that time of the year!

However, it is many the time since, in my married life, that I have found myself saying 'only for Christmas and Easter the Irish would rot – and only for visitors the Kavanaghs would rot.' I never see the dust on the furniture until I see it through somebody else's eyes. Or, even worse, if I notice somebody running their fingers over the surface, and then glancing at them with pursed lips. And it isn't just the women who do things like that!

Have you ever watched the men at a farm-walk examining the clusters in the milking parlour? Even at open days down in the research station at Moorepark, I have seen this. First, they run their fingers under the flab to see what emerges. Then, some of them then take an obvious deep sniff to see if the teat cups are really, really clean. To me, watching on, they are checking up on the housekeeping, just as much as the old biddy checking up on the dust on my mantelpiece.

Eoin says it is a completely different thing. But I can't, for the life of me, see why. The men may laugh and complain at us for sprucing up for the Stations and visitors. But when the Macra lads were having a farm walk here, I saw Eoin cleaning out corners that had not seen daylight for years. Trailer-loads of rubbish, from empty paint tins to rusty old bedsteads, went to the dump in the quarry. Some of the walls in the yards even got a slap of whitewash for the occasion.

Before that farm walk of ours, the dykes of the road, and each and every field, also got a quick once over for plastic fertiliser bags left go with the wind, by us or by our neighbours. For fear of the fears, even the fields where nobody was likely to go were given a quick once over. Now, if every farm had a farm walk every year what a lot of rubbish would be cleared out of the countryside. The same applies to the Stations in the house. Still, I, for one, would never survive the Stations that often. Once in five years sounds a much better idea.

I am only flogged anyway at the moment, sweeping and dusting and frantically polishing all the old brasses, and the furniture both old and new. This is all because Eoin's eldest sister from England is coming tomorrow to stay for a few days, so there is no doubt about it but his other sisters will also be calling to see her. Now, I am not ordinarily in the least fussy about people staying. My theory on the whole is that they can take us as we are, and it is better to clean up after guests are gone than before they come. It is a much more lasting job that way.

Still, all my vaunted common sense deserts me when I hear that any of Eoin's sisters are coming here. Immediately then I am off in a flurry of polish and dusters. The spiders that have spun undisturbed for months, if not years, get turned out of house and home. The boys are threatened and warned to behave themselves, and then nagged at to help, until they, and I, are near screaming point.

The net result of all this is that they invariably are not at their best when their paternal aunts are here. Whether this is from sheer piggery on their part, or pure nervousness from all my scoldings, I am never quite sure. But then I am not at my best either, I must admit, even if it is not now quite the blind panic of the early years. Why do I carry on like this, time after time, exhausting myself with all that unaccustomed cleaning? By tomorrow evening I know I won't be worth tuppence and my hand will have developed that nervous shake as I pour out the tea into my very best china cups for the visitors.

The oddest thing is that I remember quite well the self-same rattle of the teapot on the cup when my own mother poured out the tea for her sisters-in-law on my father's side. And I never could understand what on earth was the matter with her. But there is no doubt that we never understand our parents until we find ourselves in the same position ourselves, and by then it is usually too late. She also had the added problem of two of her sisters-in-law being nuns, and all that entailed, especially all those years ago when nuns and priests were of the world apart.

So it looks as though it will be a long, long time before I can expect understanding from my brood. To them, at the moment, I seem to be both unreasonable in attitude and ancient in body and intellect, fit for nothing but the scrap heap in fact, where they would willingly dump me before the aunts come. Now their aunts, Eoin's sisters, my sisters-in-law, are all fine women. They also all have their own families, homes and interests, so I am quite sure they couldn't care less whether I dusted under the beds or not. While I may feel that in fact they would be happier to find signs of neglect here, that is all in my mind, I am quite sure. I may feel they are looking to see if their mother's home and possessions are now as cared for as they were in her day, and if I am looking after their only brother properly. However, because I am living in their old home after all, they have an interest in the place and all the changes made over the years. And not a word of criticism of those changes has ever passed their lips, although they must, in their hearts of hearts, feel a certain nostalgia for things as they used to be, long ago, when they were all young together. An undertone of disapproval of the changes is probably totally in my own mind. Their game of 'do you remember?' is no reflection on the new woman now in possession.

However, their coming to visit brings back to my memory all my old feelings of inferiority and, dare I say it, intense jealousy, of those days when I, a young bride, came into their old home. They, then, were so much older, so sure of themselves, and knew so much, when I knew so little about anything. Perhaps that is why I now try to bolster up my self-confidence by proving that I can do things pretty well now, even if it nearly kills me and mine in the process.

Now my other sisters-in-law, my brothers' wives, don't affect me in the least. They can pop in and out as often as they like and I don't take a blind bit of notice of any of them. I drop in on them too quite happily, without feeling I have to give them prior notice or anything like that.

Nevertheless, when I do drop in on the sister-in-law married to my brother in my old family home, when visiting my mother, I always get tea brought to me in the best china sitting on an embroidered cloth. So could it be that I too, her husband's sister, am also one of that other kind of sister-in-law? (1978)

Running with the herd

I had Eoin Óg, my youngest, in town with me the other day, to get him a pair of sandals for the summer, only to find he's now getting just as bad as all the rest of them. Buying even a pair of jeans for the older ones can turn into a major shopping expedition in no time flat. To me a pair of jeans is a pair of jeans. My only demand is that there be plenty of leg length there, for turning up.

But for those fashion-conscious sons of mine, the cut – the style – the set of the pockets – even the precise shade of blue – all has to be perfect before a pair is finally purchased. Then I am expected to turn them up to the exact length they want. If they are a fraction too short I am asked is it the way I want to make boot boys out of them. But then, if too long, when they change out of those thick soled shoes they now favour, the ends rub off the ground and get all frayed. And I want to be able to let them down again, some time in the future.

Not that they stay too long, for long. I am beginning to think that teenaged boys must be just like plants, getting their main spurt of growth at this time of the year. I can count the months since winter by the paler blue, let down rings, at the ends of all their jeans. On their monthly free days at home from school, as well as the endless cooking, I spend a lot of my time washing, ironing and leg sewing. And doesn't it take quite a while sewing their flared jeans all around by hand? My old sewing machine just can't cope with the thickness.

Once, in a going-back-to-school rush, I stapled all around a pair, and quite attractive they looked too with the silver glint of the staples. They were soon back to me for sewing, however, because of the comments of some of the other boys – not that I was told what they had said. But the herd instinct was just too strong. No way did my lad want to be in the least different from any of the rest of his peers.

And so it was with my youngest in town this week. Only girls wore that kind of sandal now. Another sort were old-fashioned, not 'with-it', I was told. And so it went, until he got what he wanted, which wasn't sandals at all but another pair of sweaty canvas shoes. This was the herd instinct again. I wanted him to know the delicious coolness of sandals alone after a winter in heavy shoes and socks. But he wanted to be the same as the rest of the boys at his national school.

It was my memories of comfort and rightness I was trying to enforce on him. He, however, wanted things done exactly the same as everybody else, and I had to admit, as I gave in, that I really was no different to him in my day.

I too went to a very small, mixed, national school. The boys there would not let me play football with them if I was wearing boots or shoes. The fact that I was a girl did not bother them in the slightest. Other girls played football with them as well, since we were needed to make up the numbers in our small school. What did bother them was that my boots hurt when my kicks connected, accidentally or otherwise, with opposing shins.

This was in the days when most children went to school barefoot. So I developed the stratagem of leaving home, all quiet and demure, with my plaits tied with red ribbon bows, and wearing neatly laced-up boots. However, half way to school there was a certain hollow tree. There I stopped every morning. Off came the hated ribbons, leaving my plaits to work their own way free. Then the boots and socks joined them in the tree. And off I ran, free as a bird, to meet the others on the main road, with my hair and my feet flying.

I was one of the fellows then, you see, the same as the rest, accepted freely into all their sport and activities. Modern children can never even begin to appreciate the fun we had in going barefoot in summer. They have never experienced the delight of thick black muck squelching up through their toes. On those hot days we used to deliberately seek out those cool, shady, muddy spots, just to get that satisfying squelch.

This must be a primitive urge in all youngsters. I laugh to see even the little ones on the street, how they jump into every puddle they can find, even though, poor things, they have to do it in their best shoes. How things have changed in my lifetime, and I'm not half finished yet. I went without shoes to be accepted. But nowadays everybody has shoes. There is no longer a clear cut line between the 'haves' and the 'have-nots'.

My happy 'have-not' days came to an abrupt end, alas. I cannot now be sure just how long I went blissfully barefoot to school, because you know how it is in childhood. A month can seem years, or years can telescope down into weeks. Anyway, the end came one fateful afternoon in summer. I remember well coming to my tree, and flopping down on the warm grass to make the change back from hoyden to well-brought-up little girl. I reached in for my footwear. But my fingers met nothing. Frantically I searched, pulling out handfuls of rotten timber in my panic. But there were no boots, socks, or even ribbons to be found in there.

A search all around yielded nothing. They were in neither ditch nor dyke. Finally, as it grew late, I had to head for home. You can imagine how I felt, creeping into the kitchen barefoot and grubby, although I had re-plaited my hair just outside the back door. A quick look around assured me that the roof wasn't going to fall in on me just yet: the room was empty. Neither my father nor my mother were there. And my brothers and sisters who might still have been at their dinner, even though they must have been home for ages while I willfully delayed each step, were missing. But instead, on the table, where my dinner would normally be, were my missing socks, my boots and my two bright red ribbons. And so ended my barefoot days at school.

Much later I discovered that the schoolmaster had complained about me to my father. He had strong things to say about how unsuitable it was for me, from my good farming background, to be going to school with no shoes on and in a generally untidy state. My poor father, knowing that I left for school each morning very suitably attired indeed, had followed me that day and saw all. Quiet man that he was, he never said a cross word there and then, just let me go. Then he left my shoes, socks and ribbons in place of my dinner, to do the talking for him.

It worked, for I never again went barefoot to school. And I didn't ask where my dinner was either that fateful day. (1979)

Parking is a problem – I must confess

'...And I was done in confession too!' That seemed to be the final straw for Eoin, as he told us about his day in town.

Poor Eoin. He does so hate the city, and only goes there when driven by absolute necessity for something he can't get locally. This time, being the Thursday before Easter, he had a double purpose to his journey. He needed a new part for the plough, and he hadn't done his Easter duty. Being of the generation to whom the Easter duty is important, as are all the Easter ceremonies, he felt that he just could not go and receive Holy Communion with the rest of the congregation, that night, unless he had confession first. That would then do him fine for his Easter duty as well, he said.

'Easter what?' asked the lads, when I then suggested that maybe they might all like to go to town with their Dad. They are gone a bit beyond the stage when I can say 'Confessions tonight lads', and they meekly change their clothes and come along with me. Eoin was a bit shocked that they genuinely had never heard that they must go to both confession and communion sometime between Ash Wednesday and Trinity Sunday. A discussion ensued, which was only terminated when the sons with wheels said that they'd go themselves on Saturday, but only if they had time, and didn't have a date. In the end, Eoin Óg, his youngest, was the only one who would go with his father to town and confession.

That was Eoin's first shock of the day. The next shock was when he discovered that when the VAT was added on, his replacement part cost him more than the whole plough had done some years ago. The price quoted to him on the phone had been ex-VAT. And, to add insult to injury, he was told it would have been cheaper to have them put on the piece in there, than he coming in to buy it, with the different rates of VAT now.

This was a salutary experience for Eoin before he hit the city traffic at all. And boy was that traffic bad. For a full half an hour he cruised around trying to find a parking place. But it was no good. Each time he saw a car about to move, he was either on the wrong side of the street, or somebody else had spotted it first.

The wonder was that he hadn't turned for home at this stage, as I have seen him do more than once before, on hitting city traffic. But he was determined to get to confession. Then, finally, he saw a woman evidently going for her car, so Eoin parked strategically. And yes, the woman nodded that she was going to pull out.

But nothing happened. Your woman's car would not start. So, putting on his hazard lights, Eoin held his ground and went to help. 'All that was wrong was that she had flooded the engine, and needed to give it plenty of boot to get it going,' he explained, probably at my look of incredulity at his going to fix somebody's car that wouldn't start. I asked Eoin Óg, only joking of course, could she have been young and blond by any chance, since Eoin is not noted for his mechanical abilities?

Anyway, having helped to get her car started, Eoin returned to his own, grateful to have a place to park it at last, when suddenly, from across the street shot another car into that very parking place, almost taking the nose off our car in the process. 'And there he sat, grinning like a monkey,' said Eoin. That obviously was the final straw, and more than poor Eoin could take, quiet man and all that he is. And my youngest son was there to corroborate what happened next. Eoin was out of that car like a flash, and over to the other car, where he grabbed the driver by the neck through the open window, and told him to get to hell out of there, fast, if he knew what was good for him.

'And did he?' said I, half horrified. 'Oh, he blustered and he blew,' answered Eoin. 'But I told him that I had been waiting for that spot for half an hour, and that no one, big car or not, was coming inside me.'

'He wasn't a young fellow, then?' I asked again. 'Indeed no, Liz,' said Eoin, beginning to see the funny side of it at last, and he actually chuckled when he finished the saga of finding a parking space with 'actually he called me a right young pup as he pulled out.'

So that was how Eoin got his parking space. The next job was confession. With Eoin Óg in tow, he headed for Holy Trinity, it being the nearest. But when they got there, it was to find an excavator and a pick-up truck right in the middle of the aisle! Needless to say there were no confessions being heard while the renovations were going on. So, there was nothing for it but shank's mare across the city to the next church: he wasn't going to chance finding a parking place handy to there, after all his trouble getting the first one. In that church they joined the full pews outside the confessional box.

'See, boys', I interjected, 'everybody does still go to confession for Easter, if the pews were that full.'

'They were full all right, and slow moving along with that,' elaborated Eoin. 'But at least my legs got a rest.' I knew what he meant, because I don't know what it is about city pavements, but they make all our legs ache in a fright, which never happens here, even when we are on our feet, all day, in the fields.

However, while my mind was thus wandering, ever so slightly, Eoin was only working up to his punch line. Eoin Óg went into the box to make his confession. But as he came out, and it was now Eoin's turn at long last, the middle door opened as well and out popped the priest, with his purple stole. Without even a word to those still waiting so patiently, he went off up the aisle, taking off the stole as he went, genuflecting reverently as he passed the altar, and made his way into the sacristy.

Eoin, thinking the man only needed a small break for necessary bodily functions, waited, patiently enough. But the rest of those waiting, who obviously knew better, having seen the stole coming off, got up and disappeared. Eoin finally gave up when there was no sign of the priest returning, and Eoin Óg, after saying his penance, returned to point out the sign that gave the hours of confession. The priest had stopped on the stroke of time.

So there was nothing for it but for poor Eoin to get up and head for yet another church, on the off-chance that the confession times were different with the order priests. They were. But the waiting pews were also full again, among them being faces Eoin recognised from the last long wait. And you won't believe this, but as Eoin slid along, from seat to seat and bench to bench, this time, when he was third from the box, out came the priest again.

'What did you do this time?' we all asked. 'Have him by the throat?' chimed in one son mischievously. 'Not quite,' laughed Eoin with the rest of us. 'But I did get out of my seat to stop him. I was in a white-hot rage as I pointed out to him that this was my third church: was there any confession at all to be had in this so-and-so city, and that if the Church wasn't careful they would all finish up with empty pews for confession yet...'

'You didn't!' I exclaimed in shock. 'He did, you know, Mom,' said Eoin Óg, who was a bystander and an eyewitness to all this and thought it all great fun.

'And did the priest go back in?' I asked.

'No, he did not,' replied Eoin. 'But he curtly enough pointed out another box to me, where an additional priest had just started hearing. And where all those waiting had also gone, of course, in the meantime.'

So, after joining his third queue, again in the third pew, which was probably just as well since it gave him ample time to cool down and freshly examine his conscience, Eoin finally got his Easter duty done.

But when the two Eoins got back to the car, it had two parking tickets, for being way over time in a one-hour park! Now the one question I can't ask is, was the content of his confession worth all that hassle? (1982)

How much to pay the lad at home?

Tell me, what do you think that a son working at home should get paid a week? And before anybody says minimum agricultural wages, remember that he is also the heir, or at least the co-heir apparent, which must surely count for something.

It is all a bit of a vexed question in the Kavanagh household at the moment. Asking around, our usual way of gathering information, doesn't throw much light on the subject somehow. 'Too much money they all have nowadays,' says their grandmother, who points out that farmers' sons traditionally never got anything but the few bob they needed when going to a hurling match or what have you. 'And they were all so much happier then', she claimed, 'They worked away and there was no commotion about it.'

Eoin, however, who suffered under just such a system when he first came working for his uncle, still cringes when he thinks of the times he had to draw back from the crowd of lads if they decided to go to the pictures and he couldn't, because he wouldn't have the price of it in his pocket. He, of course, wouldn't admit that for the world at the time, so he always had to think up some excuse or other. He feels, as a result, that a son working at home should know what he is getting each week and then it will be up to him to budget accordingly. Otherwise they will just go and do as he, and many more like him, had to, to get the extra few bob unbeknownst.

The favourite way, and by far the easiest way to get money straight into the pocket, was taking just a dozen or so eggs every day, hiding them in the hay-barn, and then selling them once a week in the nearby town.

'And, until you sneak off on a bike with seven or eight dozen eggs concealed on your person, you don't know what dangerous living is,' he told his sons. And he made us all laugh when he told of the day he and his bike came a cropper and he finished up as the filling in an almighty omelette, since he had slung the eggs fore and aft, under his coat, and under his uncle's eagle eye.

Eoin had cousins who really were up to every trick in the book when it came to making the extra few bob. Their favourite dodge, when delivering hay or straw into town, where they had a contract, was to get up mad early in the morning to load it, saying to their father's delight that they wanted to be on the road early. But in reality, the reason that they got up so early was so that they could build their load with a hollow centre where, in season, they could conceal turnips, some of their mother's hens or even a fine fat goose. A fat lamb could also be spirited away, once its legs were well tied.

Then off they would go, singing at the top of their voices, and, since they were a musical lot, playing the accordion in accompaniment, in order to drown any protesting animal sounds. Only a mute load of turnips was completely safe. And I bet their mother saw them off, contented that she had such happy sons about her. Their hardest job was later to keep a straight face when she'd be complaining that the fox was at her fowl once again and could none of them shoot it for her?

The fox could be blamed for the missing lamb as well, for lambs were notorious for just upping and dying even when nearly fit for sale, and foxes could carry the carcasses considerable distances. But they were very nearly caught the time they took two fat pigs to market hidden under a load of straw. The squealing pigs made more noise than they did, as they set off. And, of course, they were missed from the pigsty eventually. So, even though the lads got their money that day, they never chanced pigs again. Their father eventually finished up blaming the tinkers for the missing pigs, since the lads swore blind they had seen some down the village, heading up their way, when they themselves were on their way to town.

But no way could the boys here do anything like that nowadays, with everything being sold only through official channels, and with everything both tagged and tracked. Though I did hear the talk going on about two of our sons' friends, who, last Christmas, sold several car trailer loads of blocks in the estates around the town, and their father never spotted the home timber supply slackening.

In fact, I myself heard that self-same father boasting that his lads were great with the chain-saw, and that it kept them gainfully occupied any bad wet day. But since we have neither timber nor chain saws, hens, chickens nor pigs, I can't see any alternative income for those lads of mine that we don't know about. And it is illegal now, isn't it, to go hawking milk, door to door?

So it is back to what is fair to both them and us, as well as to what they are expected to do on their money.

'Twenty pounds a week is what I give him,' one father told me when I questioned him. I thought that quite little for these times, realising too what a good hard worker that son is. From time to time I have held him up as a good example to some of my lot here. Then I discovered that not alone has he a car provided for his sole use, plus all the petrol he needs from the father's account at the garage, but his mother still buys all his clothes for him.

That would surely equate well with the forty pounds a week my sons tell me another friend is getting. He does not have free access to a petrol pump, and they are not sure about who pays for his clothes. Personally I would prefer to pay a few pounds extra weekly to have the hassle off me of them saying they have nothing to wear each time a new fad appears, their ankles or wrists are showing again, or they just feel like something new. Anyway, I swear each of them has twice the amount of clothes their poor father has, and he never complains.

But whatever amount we all settle on, unless they have all their tax forms, P's whatever they are and the proper PAYE paid, it is well to remember that their wages are not tax deductible, be they big or small. So they could be very expensive paying indeed by the time the tax-man is finished with you, and your claims, if all isn't in order.

Now, what I would dearly like to know is whether one can also claim for the food those sons eat, as one can for workmen. My lot are still eating us out of house and home. And the food they get at home is something they never seem to value. If I had my way, young men and women should both buy and cook all their own meals for just a few months and also pay for all the hot water they use. Then they'd know the value, in hard cash, of living at home, with a woman looking after all their needs. I have a mound of mending badly awaiting attention this very moment.

But since all that mending is not for the sons alone, there are a few husbands I know who would greatly benefit from that exercise too. The only thing is that they'd probably lie down and die of the shock, on the spot, and then what would we do? (1983)

The proper green wellies

I'm not with it at all. The colour of my wellingtons is all wrong. Mine have always been black. Like Henry Ford, it has never even occured to me that they could come in any other colour. However, if I am to have any pretensions at all, my first investment must be green wellies. Not only must I change the colour. I must also learn to call them wellies, and not wellingtons as I have always done.

My education in this matter came about when I had occasion to call to a relatively new bungalow in this parish during the week. Near the back door were two pairs of green wellington boots, his and hers. In my innocence, I commented on the colour. The owner, not engaging her brain before she put her mouth in gear, immediately said:

'John says black wellies are only for the dirty old farmers. All the right people wear green.'

'You silly bitch!' was my instinctive response. But of course I continued to smile sweetly while saying nothing. I always get annoyed anyway when women quote their husbands to me as the fount of all knowledge, the ultimate authority on all things. My annoyance, however, with the silly woman went deeper than her quoting her husband to me as some sort of oracle. I could have felt sorry for her, of course, striving so hard to fit into her country environs that even the colour of her wellingtons was important. However, she was symptomatic to me of that whole breed of urban dwellers who have run away from city life to find an impossible utopia in the countryside. This was by no means the first time I had come across this problem of urban dwellers chasing that impossible dream of a rural tranquillity undisturbed by the aforementioned 'dirty old farmers'.

My curiosity about this particular woman was getting the better of me, so, thinking of this week's column, I buried my annoyance in a show of friendliness. Then, my business done, I got myself invited in for coffee. Some discreet questioning soon led to her tales of woe, which were the old familiar ones, the result of that inevitable clash between the use of the countryside as a means of production for farmers, and its use as some sort of national leisure park by rural urbanites.

It is very hard for these people to accept that for the most part farming, up close, is noisy, mucky, smelly and pretty untidy. Only in books, and the visual media, is it pretty and picturesque. So when their dream gets a rude awakening – as when silage trailers rumble by their sleeping children half the night; beet lorries start up early in the morning; rats come by the dozens to eat the grain split on their boundaries by the trailers travelling back and forth for weeks on end during harvest time; slurry spreading means that smells are disgusting for the time being; silage pits opened for the winter scent the air for a considerable distance – some of the settlers then set about sanitising and prettifying the countryside. And this is when they make their presence felt a little too strongly for comfort.

The gardaí are the first to discover this. They get phone calls with demands for them to stop tractors working at night. The farmers concerned are also contacted by the irate commuters. It is the farm women who usually have to deal with such calls, since their men are out there working late to save the harvest or whatever. We also have had the gardaí make a special visit here because somebody living in the area made an official complaint of our cruelty to animals in having the cows' tails docked. I had to deal with that and explain why it was necessary in straight rail milking parlours when the milking machine is put on between the back legs, how it avoids the danger of the transmission of leptospirosis to the operators, and anyway it is done by means of rubber rings to them as calves, as is castration to lambs, and nobody objects to that, in what is doubtless a much more sensitive area. The two young gardaí were quite pink in the face before I was finished. They left, and we never heard another word on the subject.

The county council are another target for complaints, and not just about planning applications either. As to that, it amuses me hugely how people who disturb the countryside quite considerably, when they purchase their sites and build their bungalows, then want nothing whatsoever to change in their surroundings thereafter. Talking to farmers, who now must apply for permission to do every little thing, they tell me that the majority of non-farming locals, who have lived in the area for generations, are never the ones who object to their building plans. It is always the newcomers to the area who, not only object themselves, but canvass all the neighbours to join in as well in lodging objection to the local county councils.

I believe that the county councils get more complaints about the natural bodily functions of animals than about anything else. In England, I read recently, in 1990 there were 4,916 complaints about animal smells and a whopping 111,515 complaints about noise. But I hasten to add this also included urban noises; the complaints are segregated by content, not location. I could get no relevant figures for Ireland, but that is undoubtedly the way we, as farmers, are also evidently headed. A spokesman for the British Farmers' Union actually said that we now appear to be living in an age where farm animals are all right as long as they are 'mute and constipated'. I loved that, and if I thought I'd get away with it I would use it as my own. But doubtless I shall, some day! (1991)

A scene from hell

I just don't know how I'm going to write anything this week: we are still in a state of shock. Yesterday, at half past four in the morning, our nearest neighbour came banging at our door and throwing stones up at all the windows, frantically trying to wake us up with the dreadful news that our calf house and shed were on fire.

Eoin Óg was first down – he never stopped to dress. Eoin and I were down shortly after, struggling to get our wellingtons on. 'Phone for the fire brigade!' someone shouted, and my fingers failed to connect with the digits on the phone. I knew I had no hope of remembering where our local brigade's number was entered, but eventually I managed to dial 999.

It was answered immediately, but the appalling slowness of giving full name and address, and where exactly that was – coming from which side – my own phone number – and who I was – was impossible with my mind only on the shed. Were the animals all right? Would Eoin be careful of himself and not do anything foolish? I so badly wanted to be there to make sure, and yet I had to keep answering all these questions.

Eventually, I tore up the road and it was dreadful. Flames leapt sky-wards the full length of the shed, and half the roof did not seem to be there at all. Then there was the sound of an explosion and part of a wall fell out, showing me the inferno inside. Yet, for some reason, I then noticed the dawn starting to break, gentle streaks of soft rose red, over the trees, behind the shed; it was such an unbelievable thing somehow – dawn breaking, a new day beginning. And yet our calves had to be all dead – burned alive.

Almost in slow motion I took it all in. The men were at the shed doors and Eoin was shouting at Eoin Óg not to go in, that it was no use. 'No use; no use' my brain caught, and kept repeating over and over, while my legs, of their own volition, brought me to look in those doors with them. It was a scene from hell, not in the obvious flames roaring, devouring, destroying, but what was happening and had happened to the poor calves.

Frantic to escape, the near ones had tried to burst through their gates, and the flames had caught them there, as they got jammed between the restraining bars of the gates. Others did get through. But they had only got just a little way down the main passage, as their pathetic corpses clearly showed.

In the big pens, the weaned calves were all huddled together in the corners, dead. All this we could see near us, even if somewhat dimly, through the smoke. But far down along the shed, there was nothing but fire, hopelessly, helplessly, out of control.

'Are any of them alive in there, in the pens near the front?' I asked, not believing what I was only too obviously seeing. Eoin put his arm around me, just shaking his head. Words would not come. There were no words then, or even now, to describe the desolation of heart, spirit, and, of course, pocket.

Only somebody who has been through a bad farmyard fire, especially where livestock are concerned, can have any conception of what all this means. And, in some vague corner of my mind, I know, even now, that the full financial implications have yet to hit us. Those are, as yet, only dark menacing clouds above our heads, even though they are getting ever blacker and darker, and more oppressive, every hour that passes and the shock and horror recedes somewhat. The way those poor calves died is still more of a problem to us than the fact that they did die.

The fire brigade took forever to come, or at least that was how it seemed to Eoin and myself. 'Go in and ring them again,' he said. But then I looked at my watch and it was only a quarter of an hour since I had first rung them: that quarter of an hour must have been the longest of my entire life. There was no point in phoning them again anyway. What was done was done, and all the fire brigades in the world weren't going to be able to do a thing about it. The only hope now was for containment, and the sons and neighbours were already seeing to that.

They had moved the tractors and some other machinery well away into the field and were watching the next shed. It was an odd time to start counting one's blessings, but we did, thanking God that that shed, now on fire, was free-standing and the wind was blowing the flames away from it and harmlessly into the field. If the rest of the sheds had caught, the milking parlour would have been next, and so on and so on. This was how we consoled one another. We were talking about what could have been as a cover for what actually was.

We could not talk about our calves; those calves we had petted and minded all the year; the one Eoin Óg and his girlfriend were mad about and had begged off us as an extra Christmas present for her, so that it would not be sold. 'White Socks' Lisa had christened it, the very Sunday she had jacked it safely all by herself while Eoin Óg was milking. She was inordinately proud of having delivered such a big calf all on her very own.

Then I thought of poor old Harry, my pride and joy, the premature calf I had kept alive against all the odds. The family kept telling me that he'd be better off if I'd let them hit him on the head, because he would never pay for all the extra milk and medicines he was getting. Poor old Harry, he will never pay for his keep now anyway, I thought, dry-eyed.

My mind refused to take it all in, especially those twin heifers we had been so delighted with when the very best cow in the herd had them, just before Christmas. Every year up to this she had produced only bull calves. And there were all those other heifer calves, so carefully chosen for the sake of their dams – gone, utterly gone, irretrievably gone, all dead.

The fire brigade came, they told us later, in record time. Men in oilskins and helmets swarmed everywhere. Another fire brigade engine roared up. 'Anybody missing?' and 'Anybody in there?' I heard as they moved purposefully forward. Then, through the smoke, out of the shed, came one helmeted figure, with a live calf struggling in his arms.

The delight, the sickening jolt of hope, took hold as we strained our eyes to see others following in his wake through the smoke. But the fireman said that she was the only survivor they could find. All the rest were beyond help. That little thing, when he brought her over to me, staggered but stood. One ear was half burned off. Her coat on that side was badly singed. But she was alive, and I helplessly gave her my finger to suck.

A supply of water was the next problem. They discussed letting the fire burn itself out. But finally they went and rigged up piping from the river half a mile away. That really took a long time. But what did that matter now? In fact nothing mattered now. The lads went to do the milking. At least the power, water and all the rest of it were all right in the milking parlour, as were the cows. And the boys were better off doing something productive rather than just hanging around helplessly like us.

So the milking went on as if it was a normal morning. But I had no calves to feed. There was no milk to be taken up for the calves either, before the bulk tanker came, because there would be no calves to feed that night, or the next morning either. Eoin Óg's girlfriend had arrived by now – he needed her badly in his pain. My other son had his wife, and Eoin and I had each other after all. Lisa then did what I had not done: she fed the poor lone survivor, taking her down to the maternity shed, to a well-bedded pen. Lisa christened her Sooty as she made soft sounds of comfort to her, very similar to the sounds I had heard her make earlier as she put her arms around Eoin Óg. Dealing in a practical way with Sooty helped to console them both.

Sara was in the kitchen boiling kettles and waiting for the shops to open. Of course we did not have enough bread in the place to feed all those firemen and they must have been badly in need of a cup of tea by now. I couldn't swallow a mouthful but, when it came, I cut the bread, poured tea and tried to survive.

Sooty died in the afternoon. Lisa and Eoin Óg cried and cried as they told me that news. My tears are yet to come. Then, and only then, will the healing process start for me. (1992)

MAY

A fine feed of nettles

How many of you will be having a feed of nettles next
Tuesday, the first of May? Precious few, I expect! That is just
another one of the old customs that are being fast forgotten.
Long ago, tender young nettles were always gathered and
cooked for the dinner on May Day. When I first came here, the
nettles were gathered and cooked for me. So, naturally
enough, I ate them without fuss. And quite nice they were too,
especially since they had been boiled with a bit of bacon. They
are somewhere between cabbage and spinach in taste and
texture.

Then, as the years went by, I became the one who gathered
and cooked the nettles on May Day, just to keep all the older
generation here happy. This, of course, is the way that customs
are handed down from generation to generation – even though
the original needs or reasons for the customs are lost in the
mists of time.

I'm told that the original reason for eating nettles was that
they were known to be good for you. (In fact they are
extremely high in vitamins and iron.) Don't forget that in my
early years of marriage, not to mind bygone times, there were

no supermarkets and freezers with year-round supplies of fruit and vegetables. Nor were there convenient chemist's shops with their multicoloured vitamin pills or bottles of different tonics to pep you up. And how far down people must have got, in terms of their health, by the end of April, with their few stored turnips gone soft and their potatoes running out.

The new potatoes, with their high vitamin C content, were still over a month away: the new sowings of cabbage and turnips only just well above ground. Weren't they the wise ones then, to go for the nettles? There were precious few vitamins, minerals or iron in the Indian meal which was all that many had to last them out until the new potatoes came in. What a long way we have come from those days of Indian meal and nettles? Still, even if our tastes now run to exotic foreign dishes, it is no harm to be reminded, on just this one day a year, of the times when maize, or 'Indian meal' as it was then called, was the mainstay of our ancestors for the month of May. So on Tuesday I'll pick my nettles, and even if modern young noses are turned up at them, I'll tell them all of their history, and of reasons why too, to foil their usual taunt of 'Don't be so old-fashioned and downright superstitious, Mom!' when I try to preserve any of the old customs of the place.

Of course custom can so easily turn into superstition when the reasons are not passed on with the practice. Last year we found a very interesting example of that here in our old farmhouse. We were doing a bit of reconstruction on the kitchen chimney, which, I would safely say, hadn't been touched for hundreds of years. There was no need ever to sweep a chimney that wide, the soot just fell down, on and off, especially after a lot of damp weather. It was actually an ideal chimney for a corpulent Santa when the boys were very young. They, as small children, never had any problem with the concept of him coming down it, bag and all.

Anyway, up this chimney, above one of the ledges, we found what we first took to have been a fine ham which was put up there to smoke and, we decided, had been forgotten all

about. But when we tried to get it down, it wasn't simply on a
hook or anything like that. No, it was securely wired on,
somehow or other. Curiosity then made us get it down
carefully, to discover it was not a ham at all, unless from a very
long-legged pig indeed: it looked more like a haunch from a
leggier beast. We next thought of smoked venison, but
couldn't say, as we are not in the venison class, never having
seen it in our lives, not to mind having tasted it. And I doubt if
the past generations of Kavanaghs were either, unless it was of
the poached variety!

The haunch from the chimney was remarkably well
preserved. The fibres of the meat were still clearly visible as
such. The dog might even have got it, there and then, if our vet
hadn't chosen that moment to walk in for help to catch a sick
cow. He was called over to see our find, and, as always, was a
fund of information. He confirmed that it was not a forgotten
ham. Neither was it venison, legal or otherwise. It was, in fact,
the hindquarter of a weanling bullock or heifer.

What once happened, he explained, was when an animal
was found dead of black-quarter, in the autumn, as animals
are prone to die, even now, if they haven't got their proper
inoculation injections in the springtime, a hindquarter of the
dead animal was hacked off. It was then brought in and put up
the chimney to preserve it in the smoke of the fire for the
winter.

'It was nothing more than pure superstition then?' I
interrupted, fascinated by the tale, 'for what on earth good
would that do for anybody?' But that, the vet explained, was
precisely what happened over the course of time in many
places. It became pure superstition, when, in the last century,
farmers hung up those diseased hindquarters, and thought
that that alone was the cure for black-quarter disease in their
animals. They had forgotten, or indeed had never been told,
the real reason why those haunches were cut off in the first
place, and then smoked to preserve them. That reason, as he
then went on to explain, was simple, logical, and as modern as
today.

Originally the haunch was to be left until the springtime when the new crop of calves was ready to go out to grass. In the early 1800s there are documented cases of the dried haunches being taken down, a cut put in each young calf's backside, and a few fibres of the dried flesh of last year's, or even the previous year's, casualty put into these cuts. And there you were, early inoculation, all those hundreds of years ago. They got the same result from the kitchen chimney that we do today with our syringes and the bottle from the chemist. It was just unfortunate that, over the course of time, a good sound practice turned to superstition and shadow replaced substance once again.

The vet took away the haunch with him. And I am wondering ever since should I have left it go. And what I can't get out of my mind is what on earth did the first person think he was doing in the first place, to accidentally discover that this method worked? (1978)

Youngsters know more than their prayers

Aren't youngsters today something else? I suppose it is all this thrashing everything out, on both radio and television, with no holds barred, that is to blame. They know a lot more than their prayers now, and that's for sure. And they are not afraid to express their opinions either. This week, in spite of all the usual stresses and strains of silage making, we are still laughing at what our youngest son said to us before we got started into the job at all. A new expression has entered, permanently, into our silage-time jargon.

Every year, the list of Eoin's worries at silage-time is endless. So, it is no surprise that he gets a little edgy with us all, especially when the silage circus is overdue here and yet he can hear no sound of them coming up our hill, when he was promised, faithfully, that they'd be there, first thing in the morning.

I was nearly as bad in the kitchen that day, wondering whether I'd have them all for dinner or not. The meat was cooked, and would hold one way or another. I was just debating to myself whether the usual pot of potatoes would do us, or should I put down a lot more, when Eoin stuck in his head to me to say that there was still no sign of them, so it was nearly safe to say they would not be here, for this dinner time anyway.

Then Eoin Óg came in to borrow a knife. It wasn't altogether surprising, all things considered, that he got a kind of a swipe of the tongue from the two of us on the spot: Eoin, because the lad was obviously skiving off from whatever job he had been given to do, and me, because my best vegetable paring knife is still missing from the last 'borrowing'.

However, instead of being suitably cowed and abashed, didn't our brave bucko say, in his best Miley of Glenroe accent, 'Well *Holy God*! Isn't it enough to have Mom there, wicked out with her P.M.T. and biting the head off everyone, without having you even worse, Dad, with *your* P.S.T.! I don't know what to make of the pair of you, *atall, atall, atall!*'

I thought I'd explode, with laughter fortunately, not with temper, for the lad was so right on both counts. What did I tell you about the youngsters of today knowing more than their prayers? Eoin, being of an older generation, had to have the joke explained to him, when his son was gone, that P.S.T. evidently stood for pre-silage tension and he should know that P.M.T. was pre-menstrual tension. Then, in spite of his P.S.T., for that is the expression now in our vocabulary for ever more, fair dues to him, Eoin laughed too. He first had a sideways glance at me, however, to see how the land lay. He too must have been aware of my condition, although he would never mention such a thing in a month of Sundays, to anyone, least of all to a son.

Still, how else could anyone take it but with laughter: the lad had hit the nail on the head so neatly, on both counts. Eoin worries. He worries about everything. He is just particularly bad when it comes to silage time. He worries that the crop may be poor and we'll be short of silage next spring; that the rain may destroy the crop; that the contractors will get badly broken down and the crop lie there for days losing feed value; that the forage harvester will pick up something that was carelessly left in the silage field, iron fencing stakes, lumps of concrete blocks, or anything else either that accidentally went out in the dung.

'And they won't listen to me, ever, when I say that every field stopped for silage should be walked in April when first closed up for silage. You and I always did it, Liz...' He always seems to conclude his present litany of worries with comments of how things are not done now like we used to do them ourselves. However, while it is true enough to say that we walked every paddock, every April, and gathered up heaps and heaps of rocks and rubbish, it is precisely because we did that, that the boys no longer have to. We hadn't concrete absolutely everywhere then and an awful lot of stuff did go out with the dung each autumn.

Well I remember compelling all my sons to walk the paddocks with me, during their school Easter holidays, all of us in a long line, picking those stones and rubbish. It was a job they just hated. They could never understand where those stones all kept coming from, year after year after year. They swore that they must be being dropped on us from aeroplanes. But, of course, what was really happening, besides any brought freshly out in the dung, was that we had missed some the year before and stones were also gradually working their way up from the ground. That was why I had each of them carry an old iron fencing post, and was killed roaring at them to prise up the half buried ones whenever I saw them skipping those. I was also never done pointing out the fact that, of course, no grass could grow where a big rocker of a stone was, and we were in the business of growing grass. Then, I also had to watch those iron stakes of theirs because it was precisely that sort of thing which played havoc with the silage harvesters.

We were once sued, many, many, years ago, by a contractor who picked up a lump of metal which had been lost off a machine of ours, in the grass swathe. He, successfully, held us legally responsible for the damage done to his machine, and the time lost by his men. Fortunately, our public liability insurance covered us totally at the end of the day. But we were not to know that at the time, when the bill was pending.

Those were worrying times for us, which our sons were too young, then, to remember now. But of all that could go wrong, very poor crops were the worst. More than once we ran out of silage and faced hunger for the animals, when there was nothing but concrete for them inside, and conditions too terrible underfoot to put them out. There is nothing worse than fodder shortage, especially when there just is not the money there to go out and buy. It is memories like these which now cause Eoin to suffer so badly every year from his P.S.T.

His sons do not suffer, precisely because he does. Neither do they understand each other's attitude of mind, despite my best efforts at explaining one to the other. Tell me, do all mothers feel, like me, a bit of a pig in the middle at times? I get cross words from Eoin, complaining the latest from a son 'How on earth can I be expected to run this farm when...' he says. Then, often within minutes, I am asked 'What on earth is the matter with Dad today? He nearly bit the head off me when I just asked him...' A more frequent complaint will be from Eoin, saying 'You couldn't tell him anything, and the damage they do... it doesn't seem to cost them a thought either, the cost of repairs... but will any of them ever listen to me...?'

Now, what is a wife and mother to do? Agree with one side always, and it is the worst of bad news for either the husband/wife or son/mother relationship, regardless of who is in fact right or wrong at the time. Then again, when I do point out which side is right, and why, as often as not, they combine against me and say I just do not understand the situation at all! 'Being just a woman...' is left hanging in the air, unsaid....

Anyway, since there is usually no clear-cut right or wrong in most of the problems that arise here, I find that I usually finish up making soothing noises and more or less agreeing with whoever has my ear at the time. But I take care to put in a heartfelt request for understanding for the other side of the story as well. I just don't know what I will do when I will no longer be able to say to Eoin that it's the boys' age group, they'll improve with time and marriage, and in the meantime let me talk to them! Equally, I will be lost when I can no longer say to the sons that it is hard for a father to hand over the reins, but that he will in time, and, in the meantime, let me talk to him!

In actual fact, I rarely, if ever, do talk to either side, since the spots of bother are usually all over nothing at all and blown over before I get around to having my few little words with anybody. It is just at the time that they are bad, like Eoin's P.S.T. this week caused him to lash out more than the situation warranted. Doubtless, I will have another lot of smoothing over to do with Eoin's P.H.T., come harvest time, not to mention his next dose of P.S.T. for the second cut of silage!

Now, I know quite well that time and the menopause will rid me entirely of my P.M.T. The really serious question to be answered, however, is whether handing everything totally over to sons, if that day ever really comes, will totally cure Eoin's P.S.T. for good? I personally await with relish the day when Eoin Óg's behaviour will allow me to ask how is his P.S.T. today? Because, mark my words, if that young man really chooses to be a farmer, the day will come when the buck finally stops with him, and then we'll see how *he* behaves under pressure! Of all his sons, Eoin Óg is the one I often think is most like his father, although right at this moment that is the last thing either of them would want to hear. (1979)

Counting the flowers on the wallpaper

Well, after all my long years of dreading it, it finally happened last night. My son crashed the car coming home from a dance. I have been expecting this night, every night, ever since the first of them started driving. I could not possibly count all those nights over those years that I have spent, between waking and sleeping, listening for the sound of the son who was out, and not settling down properly until, finally, I'd hear the welcome sound of the car coming up the avenue.

It is a very real dread, that awful gnawing sensation at the pit of one's stomach, as if something in there had tied itself in knots, as the apprehensive hours wear on. Fruitlessly, I'd wonder what could be keeping him and the dance over for hours. Always, of course, I pictured the worst, with him dead or dying, in some dyke or ditch, and no one to find him, as his life blood ebbed away. And then, the marvellous relief at the first faint sounds of his homecoming car, followed by an intense annoyance, at both him and myself, for the torture I had needlessly endured.

No use, of course, saying anything the next morning to any son, because I'd only get an impatient 'Ah, Mom! Didn't you know I'd be all right? Don't I always drive carefully? Quit worrying for once and for all!' And all eyes would be thrown up to heaven at the foolishness of women, but particularly mothers. But it is as a mother that I know the statistics about young men and cars. I also listen to the radio each morning, so often giving the toll of the night before. I read the papers, the news items and the inquests. I know the carnage caused by road accidents to the flower of Ireland's youth. And always, I am afraid, deadly afraid, that the next time it will be one of my own sons.

What is now killing me is that at one time I had no sympathy whatsoever for a particular friend of mine whose children, one after another, crashed cars, when they got to the age of driving. 'Why do they give them their good cars?' I said to Eoin, after their youngest son wrote off his Dad's new car, and we learned that the parents' comprehensive insurance had not covered the earlier two crashes either.

Then, our own sons got to the age of driving and we discovered just how difficult it was to get any kind of insurance, not to mind comprehensive insurance, for seventeen-year-old boys. Obviously, the insurance companies know their statistics and read their papers too. We also discovered just how impossible it is to hold young men at home at night once they have well and truly caught their inevitable dose of 'road fever', when they have to be on the road, practically every night of the week, whether allowed wheels or not.

The one thing we did do, however, on that friend's advice, since they had learned their lesson the very hard way, was to keep the good family car just for ourselves. We let the sons have at it in the most dilapidated of old bangers, which we insisted they bought themselves, and where another dent or two would make absolutely no difference. They could also get some car repair and maintenance practice in that way, we reckoned, plus being more careful when it was their own money they had spent.

This worked well for the eldest, as he commuted from home to his first job: I pretended not to notice a damaged fender, when that happened. And Seamus, the next lad, looked as if he was going the same road with his beloved wheels, for which he had paid all of £400. I often wondered was his C.B. radio equipment worth more than the car? But he took great care of his car, washing it and fitting it up with carpets from off-cuts in the attic.

Then last night he had a heavy date, or so he told me, and wheedled our car out of me. 'That fellow can wind you completely around his little finger!' grumbled Eoin, with some justification I may add. I know and he knows that that son has his own particular soft spot in my heart, from birth practically, even though I try very hard never to show it. Anyway, Eoin did not say no either, when Seamus put his arm around his shoulders, turned his big blue eyes on him and said 'Ah go on, Dad!' The wretch knew he was as good as there anyway when his mother had said yes to him.

So off he went in style to his date and dance. We, as usual, were heading for bed as he was heading out. Quite ridiculous, isn't it, the hour dances start now? But we commented idly, as he drove off, that at least they weren't going to the pub first which is where we hear more and more young people are beginning to congregate. I, as usual slept and woke, slept and woke, until finally, at a quarter to five I was fully awake, because there was no trace of him home yet.

'God, I'll kill him!' I'd say to myself every so often, as I distracted my thoughts by counting the flowers on the wallpaper, which I could now see clearly since dawn had well broken. 'That's the last time he will ever again get the car from me...' I'd continue in temper. But then, dread and tiredness gripping me again by the stomach like a vice, I'd take refuge in prayer, the rosary even, interrupted every so often with 'God, please God, let him be all right, whatever about the car!'

Finally, of course, I just had to wake Eoin. He, I have no doubt, would have done for his son there and then, if he could only have laid hands on him. But when the temper wore off him, and infected no doubt by my desperation, he got worried as well and back and forth we tossed the possibilities and probabilities. We then wondered should we start phoning the hospitals and the gardaí. It was now half past five and we decided we would start phoning at six. I kept saying that if he was in an accident the hospital would surely have contacted us: he was still a minor after all.

Then, at almost six, we heard a car coming up the hill and turning in the avenue. The relief was such that I felt physically sick. But Eoin said, when it stopped outside, that it wasn't our car. And the footsteps coming to the door weren't Seamus's either. We fairly hit the floor then, I can tell you. Outside was a young man we knew well, a neighbour's child, who, he told us, had come across our car in a dyke, when on his own way home. He had taken Seamus and his companion to hospital.

'But you are not to worry, Mrs Kavanagh!' he kept assuring me. 'They are just keeping him in for observation. There is nothing broken, just some cuts and bruises... and I took herself home as well, because nothing at all happened to her. It was his side of the car hit the wall... she has a few marks, that's all....'

We thanked the young man for his good Samaritan efforts, but knowing quite well that a few marks was not all of the story, for either of them. And so that young man left, with our profuse thanks, and the wry aside from him that he had better get home fast before his own mother started checking up on all the hospitals. I knew that she too was wide awake by now, and worried out of her mind. But she, at least, would have the relief of having him home, quite safe, in every way.

An immediate phone call to the hospital gave us some relief to hear our son was very comfortable, and, depending on what the doctors said later on, might even be allowed home later that day. Then, and only then, we thought of our good car – where was it, and in what condition? I thought of the girl too – what state was she in? – and of the state of insurance cover our seventeen-year-old had. Did ours cover him, or did the insurance from his old banger transfer to our car? – questions to which I hadn't given a moment's thought when my dearly-loved son was using my great love for him to get his own way, against my better judgement.

Eoin was asking a much more practical question. How could the car have hit a stone wall on only the driver's side of the car? That must have meant that the car crossed over to the wrong side of the road, entirely! There are going to be a lot of hard questions asked this day, after the doctor has been. I am not looking forward one bit to the answers, I can tell you. The dreadful anxiety of the night is now worse in a way. I know that neither he nor his girlfriend is hurt. But I foresee nothing but trouble ahead. (1980)

The only love that does not have to be earned

One of the many advantages of having reared our own replacements is that Eoin and myself can stay in bed, these mornings, and it is our sons who, in turn, have to get up to milk the cows. And being able to turn over and stay there, just another little while, is all the sweeter because of all the years when it was we who had to get up first. 'Thank God for sons' is our feeling as we snuggle once more under the blankets.

But then, you could not even look at the same boys when they come in for breakfast, or they'd eat you alive without salt! And as for asking them any questions about the work to be done that day, or work that was done the day before, you'd be taking your life in your hands to even try! I wonder, is any other house in the country so full of morning grouches as this? And it isn't just one or two of our sons who are so violently anti-social in the mornings either – it's the whole blooming lot of them.

Eoin Óg didn't put a tooth in it this morning when he told me, straight out, that he would much prefer if we'd leave him strictly alone until after he had eaten.

'Don't even try to talk to me,' he said crossly. 'You must know by now that if there is anything that you really must know about the farm, I'll tell you – so please stop going on and on... is this all right and is that all right... You ask the same questions, and go on and on about the same things, each and every morning... so is it any wonder I get cross?' He then continued on with asking me, in no uncertain terms, to please get the same message across to his father!

So once again I am being used as a go-between, a sounding board. He obviously has been dying to say all of that, to both of us, for quite some time, but never had the courage, or rather the opportunity. Lack of courage would imply that he was afraid of us, which is far from the case. In fact, since he is basically a very kind boy, I would say that he was really afraid of hurting our feelings, especially his father's, and I could quite understand that.

I know there are quite a few things that, at times, I would like to say myself to my sons, and indeed to Eoin as well. But I never do, not because I am afraid to, but because I don't want them to feel hurt in any way. The annoyance they cause me isn't that unbearable... yet! And I had given Eoin Óg his ideal opening, after all, when I innocently asked him what was the matter with him this morning?

However, did he but know it, my question was not all that innocent either. He was so sour that I guessed that the trouble was not entirely to do with us, or the cows – but with whatever it was that had gone wrong for him the night before. Things obviously had not gone quite to plan since I last saw him waltzing out the front door in a cloud of after-shave. When something goes wrong with any of their love-lives, we, their parents, are the first to suffer – just as when they are newly in love and the girl of their choice smiles on them, all is sweetness and light about the place. Then they come in from the cows singing, and even I might get a quick hug with my good morning salutation. I know then that they are feeling just great.

I say they, but I really should say he. I doubt if I have ever seen them all happy like that at once. When it is 'Big Love' for one of them, it never is for the rest. And my trouble is to read the signs correctly for each one of them, be it love coming or love going.

But even when the nights before have gone to plan, they still don't want to talk at breakfast. Silence reigns supreme in our kitchen at breakfast time. Or, to be more correct, noise, from the radio, reigns supreme. There are times when I think our sons put on that radio as a barrier of sound against Eoin and myself. And it is put on so loudly that we won't even try to talk to each other over it – as if anybody could talk over that dreadful 'boom-boom' music from RTE 2 anyway!

So what do we do? Do we take the easy way out and try to have our breakfast at a different time to the boys – and, if we have anything to discuss, wait until they are just finished – and then turn the radio off and try to come directly to the point?

All this is in the name of family give-and-take, which all the experts are worn out from telling us is so important. But sometimes, I feel that it is we do all the giving, and they do all the taking. I said as much to them the other day, when I really wanted to say a lot more: I was really trying to manufacture a suitable opening. But my quiet son took me quite aback with his answer.

'Of course it is that way, Mom – you have to love us! Don't you know that a parent's love is the only love that doesn't have to be earned? You have to love us – but we most certainly do not have to love you. You must earn that love...!' And then he was gone, out the door, leaving me silenced, with my mouth still open with shock.

While the boy was probably right – I'd never have expected that bombshell from him. He was the very last of the five that I would have suspected of such deep thinking. He, after all, is the one who is not in the least demonstrative and he never was.

Even as a baby, and a small child, he used never to care for much hugging and kissing, unlike the rest of them. And he hasn't changed since. Moreover, when he wants something, he will never try to coax it out of us, as some more of my sons do, with great skill. He is so self-sufficient that at times I worry if he will ever show enough feeling to attract a girl for keeps. And then, out of the blue, he came out with a statement like that, showing that he is at least aware of the nature of love, and that he will have to earn the love of a life partner, himself, someday.

He also gave an explanation for that vague feeling I often have, as I said before, that it is Eoin and I who do all the giving and never get much in return. We plan treats for them, from a simple bar of chocolate in our pockets to a major purchase for the house or farm. We studiously avoid overt criticism, and in fact, lean over backwards to preserve peace. So, is it the way that we are, all the time, sub-consciously trying to earn their love? They, in turn, do not feel any such need, they are so sure of our love that they do not see the necessity to reciprocate in any way. They know that our love is as unchanging as the sun in the sky, and doesn't have to be bought – so why bother? And, above all, why bother at breakfast time when they just do not feel like it? (1988)

It isn't safe to be alive at all these days

There was great commotion and excitement here this past week, but it is not the kind of commotion and excitement anybody would care for and that's for sure. It all happened at dinner time on Tuesday when the word came to us that our neighbours had been robbed. Eoin, leaving his meal after him, went off up to them on the spot, grabbing up a stick as he went. He said for me to get the gun but I said no. Whatever about using a gun to defend your own property, I'd say defending a neighbour's, after the fact, mightn't stand up too well in court. There wasn't time to go up to the bedroom and get it anyway from where it always stands, ready, as Eoin says 'to blow the legs off anybody who comes near us at night'.

Naturally enough I was all curiosity waiting for Eoin to return. You know that it gives one quite a shock to hear of such things happening in one's own area: we always were sure it would never happen here. But this now was only one field away, two brothers, no longer young, living on their own. And one had come to answer the door, just before dinner time, the other being out, to a man who said he was there about the hunt passing by on Sunday next and how they were closing off the road, putting up notices of warning and would he just come out for one minute to see if the places chosen for these notices were all right. And he had some big story about owner's liability and if the notices were not put up and anybody following the hunt hurt themselves, then a farm of land wouldn't pay the damages, and they would be responsible in law...!

You know quite well what was happening at the same time of course. When this 'Good Samaritan', with his talk of warning notices, left, and our neighbour went back into his house, he found it was ransacked, turned upside down, and while I have no idea what was taken, since that is none of my business, I suppose the robbers hardly left empty-handed.

The gardaí, of course, were called for on the spot, and in the meantime Eoin went tearing about the place to see if there was any trace of the two fellows and their car. Another neighbour, there too because the news travelled fast in the country, reported having noticed this car with 'two right hardy chaws' in it earlier that morning up and down the hill twice. And last week there was another bit of a scare when the same neighbour reported having seen a car backed into a field opposite for a couple of hours and he didn't know what on earth they were doing there. It was hardly the weather for picnics.

The local guard was told of this and came to talk to all of us to be on the watch out, that it could have been someone watching the habits of people with 'nefarious intent'. These robbers, of course, always go for the old, the weak or the defenceless, the house left empty, the working wives who take their children with them, and so on. None of us had noticed this car at all as near as it was to us. But the tyre marks showed how it had been tucked in under the road ditch in our field. The local garda told us to have an eye out in future, to note anything at all out of the usual.

But nobody had anything to report for that morning. Eoin, in the meantime, had gone tearing off down the road and up the road to check on everybody else living alone, and the empty houses. He came back all excitement because there was a strange car parked near one of them; there was nobody around, but he had the number. The squad car immediately phoned back to headquarters and in two seconds flat, the owner of the car was given. But once Eoin heard the name he knew who it was, a visiting relation to that house, and we heard afterwards that his car had broken down and that's why it was left in such an odd spot.

So the euphoria of the chase turned to despondency again. That is, until Padraig came back after his dinner and on being told what was going on said, in a most matter-of-fact tone, 'I have the number of that car' – and he reeled it off on the spot, plus the make, colour, dents, and a description of the two men driving. The rest of us were looking at him goggle-eyed, including the gardaí. But they got back on the phone again and yes, the car number and description fitted a known offender.

Of course we all wanted to know how on earth Padraig had taken such precise details, and remembered them as well. And he told us that he has just got into the habit of noting every strange vehicle and the occupants, and memorising them. 'You told us to, after all...' he commented to our own garda. Padraig, actually, came on the pair of robbers shortly after they must have done the job. He was on the way home for his dinner, with the tractor and a trailer, and met this car which wouldn't back up on our narrow hill. And since, years ago, when the same son gave way to a car and he reversed back and in the process managed to dyke himself, burst a tyre and damaged an axle, at that very spot, nobody here with a trailer will give way to anybody. It is so much easier for a car to reverse back to the nearest gap or wide place. Anyway, the pair of bucks objected strongly to being made to back up. So Padraig, with the easy confidence of youth, dropped the loader on the road and just sat there and then they had to, eventually. But they were so mad that he took particular note of them and he had all the time in the world to study their car, while studiously pretending to be unaware of their threats, high up in his tractor cab.

Within an hour of Padraig having given the number of the car suspected on good grounds of being involved, the possible perpetrators were identified. Within another few hours they were arrested, and that very night Padraig was in to identify them. We were all dying of curiosity to know all about the identity parade. Of course none of us had had any experience on either end of one of those. Padraig went off very willingly too, he was so convinced he would know the men.

'Aren't you nervous?' I asked, but again, with the confidence of youth, he said what was there to be nervous about. But you know anything at all to do with officialdom, be it gardaí, courts, tax offices, whatever, and Eoin and I are quaking in our boots without having done anything wrong at all. Even consultants in hospitals can make us feel like that. It is the helplessness of the individual against a bureaucratic system, I suppose, that disturbs. But Padraig felt nothing of that.

It was a different story when he came home, however. He said it was the most nerve-racking thing he had ever done in his life, way worse than a driving test or even an exam. He was brought into a room full of gardaí and had to give his statement all over again. He had already done so during the afternoon. Now he was reassured that everything was in order, but still he had to do it all again. The gardaí have to be sure they are sure, I suppose, before they take any action.

But the net result of all that officialdom was that Padraig said he would sure as hell hate to be on the wrong end of the law, that being on the right end was nerve-racking enough for him. He also had the idea that he would be behind a screen, or window, or something, while the parade was going on, like we always see on the television. But here he was face to face with the line-up. And suddenly he was no longer sure he could remember the men in the car. And making a false identification would be terrible. He said he was afraid of his life of putting his hand on the shoulder of a garda in a civilian suit standing in, or on some poor innocent who was just having a quiet drink in a pub when called on to stand in line for an identity parade.

And faced with the line of men it was even worse. He just couldn't be sure. He thought it could be this one man all right full face, but there were differences. So he asked for them all to turn sideways, and then, in the turning sideways, this man threw up his head in exactly the same way he had done, when forced to reverse on the road, and suddenly Padraig was sure. It was your man. He put his hand on his shoulder. And then he said the man called him every name under the sun, making him most decidedly sure. He had the accent and the same choice expletives as earlier that morning at Padraig's road-block. But the second man was decidedly not in the group.

Which he wasn't, nor was supposed to be. He had done a runner when the pal was arrested. Now there were other jobs pulled in our neighbourhood the same day so identification wasn't entirely down to Padraig. But it was his having the number of the car that speeded things up so much. Such a simple thing should be possible in every area. And if the word went out that everybody in rural areas, as a matter of course, took note of strange cars, especially those seen more than once on a road, there might be a slow-down in such robberies.

Very few of them are opportunistic, I'm told. Most of them have their ground well prepared, and those are the ones to watch, the cars stopped somewhere odd for too long. Although, in our case, the way the car was tucked under the ditch opposite the house they were targeting, in our field, made it impossible to see it, except in the going in and the coming out.

Now, while things have quietened down a bit since the day of the robbery, it has changed all our lives, even those of us not directly involved. We, surrounded by youth and strength and numbers, are now watchful. So what must anybody alone and old be? Wouldn't you love, though, to catch one of them at it? I was not joking, you know, when I said that Eoin keeps a legally-held shotgun near him in the bedroom. And I have seen him load it up whenever he hears a queer noise downstairs or outside. And, as well as that, we now have one of the calving cameras directed on the road, now that the calving season is over. So we are only too horribly aware of the change in society since our early days when we never locked a door in this house, day or night.

Indeed, for many a long year we actually were unable to lock our front door. The lock on the door no longer functioned when I first came here, and, as the door was also badly warped, we used to put a half-hundredweight – you know those heavy lumps of iron for the old weigh scales – against it at night, to hold it shut. So we never had a front door key in our possession.

Indeed, Eoin frequently joked that this fact put him at a decided disadvantage, in the event of a wife-swapping party. If the men then really all threw their front door keys on the table, nobody would ever pick up a half-hundredweight! Anyway he never did, in the times that he could... throw a half-hundredweight on the table, of course, is what I mean! (1995)

JUNE

Little tin gods!

It's a good thing for my sanity that I found a few sheets of paper in my handbag, because now I really can let off steam. Otherwise it's in a very different kind of doctor's waiting room I'd be sitting, possibly being forcibly restrained as well!

You see I'm cross, and is it any wonder? I had an appointment made with this back specialist, and all of two months I had to wait for it. The time designated was 2.45 p.m., and I was here just after half past two, lest I keep the great man waiting. However, the waiting room was full when I arrived. And now, almost two hours later, I reckon there are still four to go before me, so I could be here for a good hour yet.

Is there any sense at all to it? Surely to God that man in there is long enough at his trade to know whether it takes him ten minutes or half an hour to see each patient, and to arrange his appointment book accordingly. Or is this room full of people meant to impress us, to show us to how lucky we are that he deigned to see us at all? I, for one, consider it the height of rudeness to keep people waiting like this. Do doctors and the like think they are little tin gods or something? Or have they the effrontery to consider their time that much more valuable than ours, that it can be of little consequence how much time we have to spend waiting here?

The milking, for instance, is now going to be very late at home, as I said I would be back in time to do it. And that should have been no bother after all with a quarter to three appointment. The woman next to me, looking at her watch every few minutes, got only an hour off work to come here, as she rather pointedly told me and the others before her, twice. I think she is angling to get in before her turn. But she has another think coming to her if that is really what she is thinking!

The woman opposite is also very uneasy in herself. Earlier on she had volunteered the information that her son and daughter-in-law are waiting for her downtown, to give her a lift home. Judging from the worried frown that is deepening all the time on her forehead, I gather that all is not sweetness and light in that relationship. She had also told me earlier that she doesn't drive, and since her husband died, two years ago, she is dependent on her daughter-in-law to take her wherever she needs to go. 'She is very good about it, really,' she hastened to assure me. But now that frown speaks even more eloquently to me. God grant me independence in my old age, whatever else, was my one thought.

We were, most of us, on our first visit to this particular specialist. Yet an old habituée was obviously amused at us as she knitted away, quite happy, sitting well back in her chair. 'It was almost seven o'clock I got out of here one night,' she told us, almost proudly, as we in turn grumbled and fidgeted. No wonder she came prepared with her knitting, I thought, as I went rummaging in my handbag for paper and pen, to fill in my time usefully, getting a start on this article. The only magazines available on the centre table were nearly as old as myself, and of as little interest, being mainly yachting magazines and the financial supplements.

I also had got all I was going to get out of the other patients, since there were too many of them there anyway to get any real conversation flowing. It is hard to get people to talk freely with too many listening in. However, if there are only two or three it can be great crack, with strangers wittingly, or indeed unwittingly, giving me, a complete unknown, a great insight into their lives. Eoin says that I must have a face like a mother confessor, otherwise why do these total strangers tell me the most intimate details of their lives. Nobody ever tells him anything, he says. But then again, as well as having the disadvantage of being a mere male, he also never would dream of striking up any kind of conversation, not to mind asking leading questions.

With sexist thoughts like that in mind, I wonder how do women specialists treat their patients and clients? Our dentist, a woman, runs a tight shop: I was never more than ten minutes waiting, for myself or any one of the sons. Our solicitor, also a woman, is good about appointments. But so was the solicitor we had before her. He did not keep us too long waiting for an appointment either. It was because he delayed too long about everything else that we finally left him. So, really, I cannot be too sexist about waiting rooms.

Maybe it is something about the medical profession that makes them like to keep us sitting around waiting? This even applies to the more humble GP, who may profess to keep an appointment system, but who invariably operates on a first-come-first-served basis, regardless.

I've heard people say that it would be cheaper to pay for medical house calls than spend their valuable time in waiting rooms, when they are not actually desperately ill. But, of course, that system would never work. These specialists would never stand for a taste of their own medicine. They value their own time too highly, even if they place no value whatsoever on ours.

Well, anyway, I'm finally the next in. The woman with an hour off work has long gone. And no, I am not going to tell you what is wrong with me. But doubtless I shall, depending on the diagnosis I get. (1978)

It wasn't really my fault

Eoin was furious with me one night this week, as though it was in any way my fault. I had nothing to do with the whole affair – well, maybe I had in a way, but only remotely, as I'm sure you'll agree when you hear my side of the story.

You see, I was having a garden walk at the time. Yes, a flower club from another county had actually requested a visit to my garden. So of course I said yes. This was one of the most flattering things that has ever happened to me. I quickly covered my tracks, however, by telling them that I was only an ordinary farmer's wife, lest they'd be expecting a big estate garden or anything like that. It's much easier to impress people, don't you find, if they aren't expecting too terribly much, even though their preconceived ideas may drive you mad in the process.

Nothing irritates me more than being told by somebody that I don't look like a farmer's wife, when they think they are paying me a compliment. I have been known to reply tartly enough, 'No, he's quite an extraordinary farmer,' when somebody tries that one on me. And they think I am just being witty. But it has really come to the stage that I think I shall designate myself as a 'plain farming wife' in future, and leave Eoin out of the equation entirely. And they can take whatever meaning they like out of the word 'plain'.

Anyway, that night, while I was being a gardener and not my usual farming self, my extraordinary farmer was unexpectedly at silage, the silage circus having come in a day earlier than expected. So I was only started in on my welcoming address, telling them the history of the garden and the house, when Eoin came in and pulled me to one side, to tell me that the silage trailers could not get up or down the road with the way the cars were thrown everywhere.

Eoin, as is usual at silage time, was a little het-up, to put it mildly. So it was just as well he had pulled me to one side, out of earshot of the ladies, since I had to put his message into more parliamentary language before I delivered it, asking anybody who was blocking the road to please move their cars. A few of the ladies duly departed, and presumably rejoined the group later.

There must have been up to fifty people there, as I went on with my spiel about how mulching with straw on the borders both kept down the weeds and kept in the moisture. I demonstrated this fact by lifting a lump of it to show how damp the soil was underneath, despite weeks of drought. Being on a hill my soil burns out very quickly, so then not only do I have the chore of watering, but I have to watch my times carefully too. The cows' needs come before the needs of my garden at all times. I can never use water in the evenings, when the milking is on and the cows are grazing near home. How I wish we were on mains water, so the supply would not be rationed. Wouldn't I just love a sprinkler system to keep my lawn emerald green all summer.

My lawn was not at its best anyway this week, as my lawn-mower has finally packed it in, admittedly after years of hard work and it was second-hand when we bought it. It was a ride-upon model, so the cost of a replacement has frightened the life and soul inside of me. Therefore, with all these ladies descending on me, Eoin had hired out a lawn-mower for me the day before. But no firm would hire out one with a grass collection box. So, between the jigs and the reels of getting the silage pits ready, it was only that very morning that I gave up hope of help and tackled the job myself. It is extraordinary how, with a sit-upon mower, cutting the lawn becomes a man's job, but it soon reverted to my work with a lesser model.

It is always the same anyway. When cows were milked by hand, that also was exclusively women's work. But once the job became thoroughly mechanised, the men took over on most farms. But fair dues to Eoin, he was up to his eyes with work, but he did get back to give me a hand with raking off the grass. However, the thought of raking off two weeks of growth over the whole area quelled even me.

Then I had an absolute brainwave and told Eoin, who was worrying on my behalf, to go about his business.

'Leave it, love,' I said, 'and I'll tell them that my lawn burns up so much in dry weather that I am leaving the cut grass on as a mulch, to preserve the moisture, to prevent my grass being burned off entirely, and they'll probably believe me too!'

'There's no doubt but you can't be bet, Liz girl,' said he, thankfully laying down the rake. 'But how are you going to manage to keep a straight face while telling such a barefaced lie?'

I must have managed it, for several of the women there agreed with me, saying how well it worked, and that it only stood to reason anyway...! So my garden walk went merrily along, with me showing them how to take cuttings of young delphinium and lupin shoots, or the side growths of dahlias, as well as the more usual soft wood cuttings.

All the time I kept on snipping off pieces of this, that and the other, to keep them all happy. At garden walks everybody just loves to get something for nothing, and the bits cost me nothing anyway but earn me a whole lot of good will. Also, I find, if one is generous with garden visitors they are a lot less likely to attack plants themselves, yanking off bits without the proper tools, and doing untold damage in the process.

I admired the woman who came, unabashed, with a basket to carry her booty. And I advised the rest that they should never, ever, travel without a plastic bag, to keep their cuttings in perfect condition. 'You can line it with wet newspapers before you start, if possible,' I told them. 'But there is always the loo, and loo paper, which can be added to your bag in wet lumps, and then your cutting, or little rooted plants will be safe for a least a couple of days.'

I had them all eating out of my hand at this stage, since they told me that they had been at a much more famous garden just before they came to me, where they daren't touch anything, and the owner hardly gave them a kind word, never mind endless samples.

But then Eoin was back again to me, very agitated entirely at this stage, and in a bog of sweat from running.

'Liz,' he said, 'will you for God's sake get all the cars out of the neighbour's yard – they are there backed up to his front door, and three of them across his gate, and he can't even get in...' He did not have to fill in the rest of the story for me. How would you feel, and react, if you came home from work and couldn't get into your own yard for cars? I know that Eoin, for one, would be heard across the countryside, giving vent to his frustration!

So I once again made my suitably censored announcement and once again a few women detached themselves from the group. I carried on the walk, and then marshalled the lot in for tea. Several had been into the house already, as visits to the loo were requested very early on. And I did have the downstairs loo all cleaned up and ready for the invasion, complete with lots of extra toilet rolls.

All went merrily along, over the tea. They had brought their own biscuits, all I had to do was provide the tea and enough cups and mugs. Then I went up to my bedroom to get an address in England for seeds for one of them. That was when I found the door locked against me. A very cross Eoin let me in.

After all the commotion about the cars, and coping with the silage, he had gone for a quick shower, and lay down on top of the bed, as he said, for just two minutes, with the *Farmers' Journal*, which he hadn't a chance to look at all day. The safest place for him, he had decided, was in the privacy of his own bedroom, away from everything and everybody.

But shortly after, didn't two of the ladies open the bedroom door and walk right in on him. Which might have been fine, but he didn't even have the benefit of a towel as he lay on top of the bed after his shower. Looking for the loo, the two said they were, as they hastily backed out, having seen the apparition on the bed. But, of course, what they were really looking for was a quick look around to see all that there was to be seen. They surely got more than they bargained for, in their curiosity. No wonder Eoin had then locked the door. And he was simply furious with me when he let me in.

I really paid for it. He said it was all my fault, interestingly enough not so much about the curious women, but he went on and on that all the cars had not been cleared from our neighbour's yard. That was an easier target, as was the ultimatum that never again must I have a garden walk here. He was gone far beyond any apology from me, which I was quite willing to give. But I did agree to his ultimatum, on a temporary basis anyway, in order to hush him up – and all those women still downstairs in the kitchen, within possible earshot.

I heard the key turn in the lock again as I left the room. But to make doubly sure, I put a small table at the bottom of the stairs to block off anybody else from heading up that way again. Then, when all were finally gone, I decided to take Eoin up a cup of tea and some of those nice biscuits that had been going the rounds, and which I had been far too het up to eat. However, those who brought the biscuits evidently had taken them all away again, for their next garden visit no doubt. And how am I to tell Eoin that two women had asked if they could bring their own clubs here, that they were only along as guests that night? And I had said yes! (1984)

God doesn't think much of women

I'm tired and kind of fed up in myself. Everything is wrong somehow. I seem to be getting nowhere fast. The sons are annoying the hell out of me and indeed Eoin isn't that much better!

I could burst into tears right now, except that I know from bitter experience that that would do me no good at all, and only make things worse. And do you know what also strikes me so forcibly? God does not think much of women! Otherwise He would never have inflicted the menopause on us.

So there are no prizes for guessing that I think I am well and truly menopausal by this stage. Of course, for the past ten years I've put everything possible down to that. I could hardly get a pain in my big toe without wondering if, perhaps, that was the first symptom manifesting itself. *Waiting for Godot* had nothing on me.

I watched for each and every symptom, and, God forgive me, I watched all my friends, relations and acquaintances too. The more I read about the condition the more I expected to see. I had a sharp eye out for hot flushes, irrational behaviour, patches of brown pigmentation on their faces, sudden signs of ageing, etc. In my own mind I became an expert on the lot. I'd think, on seeing a lot of weight going on an acquaintance, 'Ah! she's menopausal' – forgetting, perhaps, that self-same woman was always a little plump anyway, mainly because she was a perpetual nibbler.

However, it wasn't all guess-work, because I can't begin to tell you the number of times I was backed into corners, at the country market or elsewhere, while the sufferers told me of all their symptoms, one by one. And it is only now that I am wondering was it the way they had spotted a fellow sufferer? Did they know something was up with me too, long before I did myself? – and me thinking, all this time, that it was just my sympathetic ways!

It is hard to admit, even to oneself, that that time of life can be really upon one. Instead, we keep feeling all of that menopause stuff is still some way off, even if vaguely hovering about there, somewhere in the distance. But take it from one who knows, the nearer it looms, the more sympathetic and interested, fatally fascinated, one becomes in such recitals by others.

Then, this Friday at the country market, there was a change in the normal state of affairs. Up to now my shoulder was the one being wept upon – but there I was, being offered a shoulder to cry on myself, and some totally unsolicited good advice as well. Then, to add insult to injury, that very same evening, a friend, of whom I am trying very hard not to feel resentful, dropped in casually, and she gave me the exact same advice: that I really should be on hormone replacement therapy.

And her I had to listen to, because, while I know quite well she is only seven months younger that me, anybody looking at the two of us would say that there is at least seven years in the difference. And it certainly is not in my favour. Now, isn't it hard not to be ever so slightly resentful of anybody like that, always so full of energy, with both a full-time job and a perfectly tidy house at all times?

Her children, who are all daughters, are, like my own, grown and gone. But unlike me, she seems to always have time to do all the extra things, like popping in to see her friends once in a while. She also never seems to put on an ounce of weight, and her hair is still an immaculate soft blonde. So, if I did not like her so much, I could positively dislike her!

I had no choice anyway but to listen to her, as she went out of her way to tell me that she has been on hormone replacement therapy for well over two years now, and has no notion of coming off it in the foreseeable future either. She pointed out to me the very practical point that I, like her, am a very good subject for H.R.T. since we are both fully paid up members of the womb-less club of Ireland! I had only to interject a few 'Really's and 'Is that so?'s to hear all of the side benefits, and also a fair list of mutual acquaintances who, she informed me, are already on that treatment. And I had never even guessed that they had arrived at that stage in life!

Absolutely fascinating information it all was, including the fact that one of those mutual friends, who now lives in England, wears something resembling a band-aid on her thigh and absorbs her oestrogen thus, only changing it once every so often. 'But watch it, Liz,' warned my friend. 'Be careful where you put the patch, keep it well away from any erogenous zone, because all that oestrogen does stir you up a bit, especially in your night-time dreams!'

All this heart-to-heart took place out by her car in the garden, as she was just leaving. So we were well out of earshot of Eoin. And, as he said afterwards, it was a wonder we didn't both catch our deaths of cold, with that dew falling. 'It'll be your own fault if you're in bed for a month,' he concluded. I kept my thoughts on the subject we were discussing severely to myself, no point in counting chickens...

And what really fascinated me was how that whole conversation had got started anyway. I'm positive I did not initiate it. So, had she taken one good look at me and said 'ah-ha!' and out of the kindness of her heart decided she must really do something about me? I do know that the conversation earlier that morning, with my country market friend, had started off with me complaining, as we did cash-duty together, of always feeling tired lately, and of never feeling on top of things any more.

'Of course you're feeling miserable, Liz,' said she, in quite a matter-of-fact tone. 'You are menopausal, aren't you?' – as if it was the most obvious thing in the world to anybody with half an eye to see. But I am not exaggerating when I say that I felt as if she had just delivered a solar plexus blow to my abdomen. The wind was clear knocked out of me, hearing it put so baldly. And me thinking I was still fine really, only a young one.

So watch out and see if you see any improvement in my weekly reports, because I am off to my doctors this evening, and presumably from there to the chemist for either pills or a patch. As for Eoin, I'm going to tell him nothing, just see does he notice the difference, both in and out of bed! (1987)

I'm not a funeral-goer

This week I went to a funeral. So what, I can already hear the regular funeral-goers thinking. What is unusual about that? they may well say. Ah, but you just don't know how badly I personally rate as a funeral-goer! In fact, I often say to them here, and I am only half joking about it, that they will have to put 'Strictly private' on the papers after my funeral notices, or otherwise I will be disgraced entirely with the poor turn-out for me, on my last journey.

Not that that would matter much to me, then, of course. But still and all, having a big crowd at one's funeral still does mean something. A big crowd, or a very small crowd, are the two extremes that cause the most comment after funerals. And funeral going is very much a case of tit for tat. Well, maybe not quite a case of 'if you go to my funeral then I'll go to yours', but it is certainly a case of if you go to my relation's then I just have to go to yours'!

Some people, however, obviously enjoy going to funerals. Otherwise they just would not go to quite so many. They certainly do not go because burying the dead is one of the corporal works of mercy. One man, who is a great funeral goer, told me a few Sundays ago, as we came out from Mass, that we had missed a great funeral entirely the day before, that there was a great old sing-song in the pub afterwards and he himself didn't get home until well after one o'clock in the morning. 'Sure 'twas better than a wedding any day,' he concluded, 'since there was no call to give a present to anyone!'

I know the death notices are what an awful lot of people look for, first, in their daily papers, before they plan their days. In a way, having a husband to look after one side, and a mother the other, quite spoils me. I know quite well that if there is a funeral to be attended to, from his side, he'll go, and my mother will tell me quickly enough if there is one from my side of the house that I absolutely must attend. So why should I put myself out? I never, ever, read the death notices for myself.

You know, it is quite true that while you have a parent living you never feel old, or fully responsible either, no matter what the years or the mirror says. You still have the feeling that death, by rights, belongs to another generation, and not you. There is always that something there between you and the end. I know I am not alone in this feeling, because a friend of mine, who lost her mother only last year, tells me that she is now, for the first time in her life, reading the death notices regularly herself. She is the eldest of her siblings, and feels it is now up to her to keep them all informed of their duty, in a way that even a year ago she would have dismissed as impossible. In fact, at that funeral this week, she told me that she is never off the road now returning the compliment to so many who went to her own mother's funeral.

Eoin is no great shakes at funeral-going either, since he said he got his belly full of it when he first came to live here, with an ailing uncle. Now that same uncle was a champion funeral-goer in his day and could see no good reason why his nephew and heir-apparent should not follow in his footsteps. Never mind that the young fellow had only a bicycle, and was not a whiskey drinker. In those days Eoin tells me that the chief mourners' car always went up to the graveyard gate. And the boot would be filled with quite a few bottles of the 'hard stuff'. This was distributed to all and sundry as they passed. But he himself always passed it on since, as he explained, there'd always be plenty of bottles, but never more than the one glass. So it had to be drunk quick and neat and the glass passed on to the next hand waiting. And poor Eoin hates whiskey at the best of times.

Eoin also says that he often had to cycle maybe twenty miles to the funeral of someone he didn't know at all, and then cycle back again in the cold and wet to report to the uncle warm and snug in his bed, with his whiskey bottle beside him. 'And I always had to count the number of priests for him, and how many of them had the white sash on,' he explained to his sons over supper, as we all discussed the day and 'my' funeral. The boys, of course, didn't know what he was talking about. And indeed I had quite forgotten myself the custom of the priests, who were paid to attend the funeral, wearing this ornate white pleated linen sash, and the great demand there was too, from the priest's housekeeper afterwards, for this fine linen to make up into sheets and pillow cases. And, of course, the more priests at a funeral the more important it was – as well as being more expensive when the undertaker's bill came in. Priests who attended out of friendship, relationship or respect were expected not to wear this sash. But as Eoin remarked dryly, they nearly all enjoyed the contrast of the white with the blackness of their coats!

There that conversation ended. But I suppose naturally enough, thinking of those times and changing customs, reminded me of wakes. Now there was one particular wake I went to as a child that I shall never forget. Among the very many things we used to do, on the way home from national school, which parents really never got to hear of, was to go to any house where we heard there had been a death and so there must be a wake on. We would all set off in a troop to view the remains. We had absolutely no fear, as I recall. It was just part of the entertainment of the long walk home.

Anyway, this afternoon, we made our long way home even longer because we went via this house where we had often been before. There was the best chestnut tree in the parish nearby, and, despite what I now realise to have been great poverty, the woman of the house always had a piece of bastible cake and jam for every child going the road. Her small house, under the road, was just the one room, with the 'tester' bed up against one wall, *sugan* chairs, and a beaten earthen floor, where dogs, hens, cats, and all human callers as well, were made thoroughly welcome by this great-hearted woman and tolerated by her husband Jamesy.

Well, now Jamesy was dead and laid out in the bed, in the middle of the room, with lighted candles all around the corpse.

I was full of curiosity because this was the first person I actually knew alive, who was now dead. Before, at wakes, we just scampered into the room, and out again almost as quickly, having just blessed ourselves at the door and no more. There may have been just a little nervousness mixed with our childish curiosity.

But this time my curiosity was my downfall. My companions were all going but I stayed. Not being quite sure what to do, up close, I carefully fell in behind this other old man who was just in the door that minute.

He flung himself on his knees beside the bed, so I followed suit. He blessed himself. And so did I. He then launched into a Hail Mary and I thankfully joined in the familiar words. But that Hail Mary was interrupted for him by a big glass of whiskey being put in his hand. The next Hail Mary, for I think he was set on a full decade of the Rosary at this stage, was interspersed with loud swallows from the glass, and frequent 'poor Jamesy – sure God be good to him!' throwing me completely off track.

But worse was to come. He got up, and leant over 'poor Jamesy' for a better look. Still playing follow the leader, I attempted to do the same. And, to this day, I still don't know quite how it happened but I jogged the old man's elbow and over went a candle – and the half glass of whiskey: 'poor Jamesy' caught fire, as did the bedclothes and bedding. Such 'mila murder' then you never saw, with the enamel bucket, full of water for the kettle on the hob for the tea for the women, being thrown on the remains. Then some resourceful person reached under the bed and pulled out the pot – there was only the one room, remember – and emptied that as well on top of him.

That completed the fire-fighting exercise, and we were all, young and old, cleared out the door, while, I suppose, they repaired the damage. I struck for home – and kept silent to this very day. (1989)

Mothers' Day nonsense

Michaella came in to me on Sunday last, all importance, with a bunch of flowers wilting in her tight little grasp. She had her self-important face on and her mother behind her, urging her, 'Go on Michaella... tell Diyee what we were practising all the way over... Happy...? Happy... what?' But Michaella went all shy and not a word could be got out of her. She dropped her flowers on the floor and went, instead, to the fridge to see was there anything in it for herself.

Her mother was very disappointed because she had rehearsed and rehearsed her to say 'Happy Mothers' Day' with the flowers, and to give me a big kiss with the box of chocolates. But what would a two-year-old know about anything like that? She does not believe I was ever a mother, I'd say. Grannies, such as I, are always old in her eyes, naturally enough. And, anyway, I am not her mother and I doubt that she even knows that I am her Daddy's Mom. She does call Eoin Dad-Dad all right, but I think that is more by accident than knowing that he is her Dad's Dad. Still, it is a nice name for her grandfather and he loves it. Besides, she was not in the least interested in the fuss her mother was making of her grandmother for Mothers' Day.

However, I was thinking how that child already is being socialised into thinking that all mothers get all sorts of fuss made of them on this day every year. Therefore, she will grow up expecting the same in her turn. Now I never heard of 'Mothers' Day' when I was young, and my mother certainly did not have the day marked for her in any way whatsoever when we were all children ourselves. 'A lot of nonsense,' I can hear her saying at the very idea. And maybe that is why I was never big into this Mothers' Day stuff myself when my lads were young.

In the meantime, big business took over, and cards, flowers, presents, meals out, etc. became the expectation of all mothers on that day. Eoin, last year, was all apologies for not thinking of me, when he heard what day it was on the radio while we were having breakfast. But as I said to him, I am not his mother: so what had he to be sorry for? My sons only began to notice the day when, at national school, they had a teacher who always got her classes to make lovely little cards and write their little messages of love on them for their mothers. Those I treasured and still have.

That was the only way our sons were socialised into making a big fuss of the day. Therefore, it is not surprising that more often than not the day goes unmarked for me now that they are grown and I find that after all I do mind not being made a fuss of on the day. They never get reminders from their father and that's for sure. He, like me, said that there was no such thing in his home long ago, for his own mother. However, my daughter-in-law is quite the opposite. Her dad brought both flowers and chocolate to her mother and always took her out to dinner on Mothers' Day. So the poor girl can't understand us at all here. She has her work cut out for her to make a romantic, in that sense, out of my son, and that is probably all my fault.

However, I must remember sometime, if the opportunity arises, to ask her whether she'd prefer the couple of dozen of red roses delivered to her door, or the cost of them in her pocket? That is what Eoin said to me once when I commented that he never brought me red roses by the armful. 'I would then,' he swiftly replied, 'to have you ask me how much they cost us!'

That, I think, is the difference between farmers and a lot of city men and women who are into this big romantic gesture. Those women get their housekeeping money every week of their lives and the red roses do not come out of that. Thus, the grand gesture is welcome because it is something extra, like bringing home a bar of chocolate, unexpectedly, to a child. It is not instead of something else, or out of the communal purse. I myself heard a husband of my acquaintance say of his big bunch of florist's flowers last Sunday, 'Sure I have to keep the little woman happy at all costs.' Wouldn't you swear it was a child he was talking about keeping happy?

Now, we are not all that averse here to special occasions. Birthdays and anniversaries are always remembered properly. The sons check in from all over the world on those days, and we expect them to do just that! Their reception might be a little on the frosty side, next time, if they didn't. When they were quite small I always encouraged them anyway to make a fuss of us on our birthdays, the same way we made a fuss of them on theirs. As a result, over the years, I collected the greatest load of rubbishy bric-a-brac, the most useless lot of little ornaments going. Yet I never would part with one of them, despite the constant calls on me for jumble sales, and the like, ever since. While I no longer have them all on display, because the job of dusting and cleaning the things became too much for me long ago, they are all safely wrapped up and put all together into a box in the attic. There is a comfort to me in that, in some strange way, although I never see the things. But think of the fun some grandchild is going to have some day when he or she discovers that box of little treasures there.

There are all sorts of things in it, little brass ornaments, animals, ships, and what have you, yokes that change colour when it is about to rain, souvenir ashtrays for a mother who never smoked and a host of other childish fancies. Even then I suppose I was training my sons not alone to give presents but to give the kind of presents that last: they never were ones to bring me edibles. We always put our values onto our children unwittingly.

So my daughters-in-law will give their children the values they themselves got from their own mothers. But what's the betting that I won't be there somewhere in the background as well, for the ones at home anyway? And the box of chocolates Michaella gave me, I passed on to my own mother, for the day that was in it. (1992)

Daughters-in-law

This week some of my preconceptions about daughters-in-law took a bit of a hammering. Actually, the last time I was pulled up short that way was when a certain son of ours, over the phone, said that Dad was living on borrowed time. Then he pointed out what I already knew quite well, how much longer women live than men, and asked had I really taken thought of my own future? This was about the time that yet another son was getting married.

For some reason the rest of the sons were quite uptight about this, knowing their mother too well I suppose. This was that particular's son way of showing he cared no doubt, but talk of Eoin living on borrowed time went down badly with me, as well it should.

And anyway, I already had a wise mother and good friends who advised me about the teething problems when a son marries. One friend, who is a fair bit older than I, and had all her sons married before mine ever started, gave me the best bit of advice of all, years ago now. She said to me to always watch out for that notice on their backs. 'The what?' I asked in mystification.

'Well,' she answered, 'each and every one of my own daughters-in-law was grand before the wedding day, no problem at all with any one of them. They courted me as well as my son. But then, each one of them without fail, when walking down the aisle after their wedding, put a notice up on their husband's back for me, his mother.'

At the time I laughed heartily when she told me that this imaginary notice said:

'Don't you even look at him: he's mine.'

But I remembered her words later on. Because she was dead right. Once they walk down the aisle things are different. You can no longer dust down *their husband's* suit for dust, comment on *their husband's* choice of a tie or lack of polish on his shoes. You cannot even comment on his comments, and that was the hardest of all to take. My biggest investment when each of my sons got married was a zip for the lip.

But the notices up on their backs do gradually come down. Now it may take a long time or only a relatively short time. But nothing you can say, or do, hurries the removal. This is because that notice is nothing to do with how good or bad a person you are. You are a *mother-in-law*, full stop.

Years ago, before I grew accustomed to that position, I was talking to this young mother I know at the country market. She seemed a bit tired and not her usual cheery self. So I asked her what was wrong. She thought for a while and then said 'Nothing much, really, except that I have my mother-in-law with us this past week...'

So I inquired first of all if her mother-in-law was interfering with the way she was bringing up the children, the usual bone of contention between the generations. But Honor just shook her head. Then I asked if her mother-in-law was taking over the kitchen, criticising Honor's cooking, talking too much, too little, or what? But each question was greeted with a little shake of the head. I genuinely wanted to know, so I finally asked the direct question. 'What *is* the woman doing wrong, so, if it is none of those things?'

I have never forgotten the answer, because Honor put her head on one side, gave me a half smile and said wistfully, 'Nothing really, I suppose, Liz. She is just *there*.' And there was no answer to that.

But you know, I had already been given the answer – if I had only been clever enough to pick it up – when she said that her mother-in-law was 'with us'. Her mother-in-law was not part of them, she was excluded from the 'us'. Each family is complete in itself. Just as Eoin and I are. And I must get it firmly into my head that I have no right at all to expect anything more, just so long as Eoin's borrowed time holds out.
(1995)

JULY

Liz takes refuge in the garden

I just don't know what I'd do without my garden. However, I strongly suspect I'd go raving bonkers without it – or else drive the rest of my family that way fast! There I was this morning, extremely cross, worried and upset, all at once, over something that has happened here, this week, with our farming son.

The worst of it all is the helplessness. We are totally unable to do anything at all about the situation we now find ourselves in. Now, and only now, with this son of seventeen, do I fully understand what people mean when they say that when your children are little, so are your troubles. To the poor mother harassed with broken nights, nappy mountains and crying children, it may not seem that way at all. They feel things just have to get better. But at least at that stage, the parent is in control. A hurt child can be kissed and made well, its troubles are soon surmounted.

Then, if a toddler misbehaves really badly it can be coaxed, coerced, or even up-ended into more acceptable behaviour. It is just up to the parents, then, to make their child conform to their ways. The parents hold practically all the power.

However, the balance of power has pretty well shifted by the time your children are in their late teens, as was brought home to me very strongly this week, when I felt like both walloping and comforting my son, at one and the same time. However, I can do neither at this stage. He now has to climb out of the mess of his own making, as best he can.

So, after tempers had run high and he was finally gone, it was quite a few days before I headed for the garden at all, with the sick taste of a family upset still robbing me of all pleasure in life. My mind stayed in turmoil for a period. Then – gradually – peace crept in around the edges. I found I was aware of birds singing, the lovely condition of the soil after the recent rain, and what a magnificent size, shape, and perfume my *Lilium regale* clumps now had, as I gently pulled some weeds from around their now considerable girth. By degrees I regained a sense of proportion.

By the time I had the wheelbarrow full of cut-down lupins and delphiniums (most of them now well past their best), I had decided that maybe my son was not in danger of turning into a hopeless lout after all, and surely he would come to realise, some day, that words spoken in anger don't really count.

I worked down my herbaceous border with its ugly remains of the once stately lupins, now untidy with brown seed pods, spoiling the symmetry of the whole. Bearing all that seed must take as much out of the plants as taking care of our children does out of us! However, there is a very easy cure indeed for the plants. Just cut each and every stem down to a few inches of ground level, and both the lupins and delphiniums will soon grow a neat little mound of greenery again, as well as rewarding you for your attention, with a smaller autumn display of flowers as a bonus. More important still is the fact that the lupins will then last for years and years and not flower and seed themselves to death within a short few years, as is their wont.

That is one thing I have learned in gardening: one must be both selective and severe to be successful; have lots of everything to start off with and then keep only the best. But to do this, one must really harden one's heart. Because you grew a plant from seed, all by yourself, or it came from a dear friend, or even because it was so expensive to buy in the first place, none of these are good reasons to keep plants that disappoint.

However, just think of the hardening of one's heart there would have to be to get a perfect family by this method – having lots and then keeping only the best, discarding the rest... As much as this thought has attracted me from time to time, the possibility of employing such a system, successfully, is only on a par with ever having even the one perfect child, through all the stages of its development.

Now, some of my crowd, who had better be nameless for the sake of the remaining peace in the house, were pretty awful when small – trouble every waking hour – or so it seemed at the time. Yet one son in particular, who once broke our hearts, as we thought at the time, is nothing but a pleasure and a comfort to us now. He slid into well-adjusted manhood, seemingly while we weren't looking. Others, however, who really were good children, are now making heavy weather indeed of adolescence.

So, at what stage would one discard? Even in my garden not all of the plants are as straightforward as the lupins, where what you get the first year is what you have for their lifetime. There are other plants which are poor and insignificant for years, like my Black Dragon wisteria: but I am content to wait, in the hope that, some day, it will live up to its full potential, even if in the meantime I have to keep it well pruned several times a year.

So thank God for my garden, and the sanity it brings me when all seems hopeless. There I can see the richness of maturity achieved, so doubtless I shall see the same in all my sons some day – even though my friends, with children in their middle twenties and even thirties, tell me there is still a fair bit of rocky ground ahead! (1980)

My young entrepreneurs

At last the end of a marvellous fruit season is in sight, and I won't be sorry really to see the back of it. I know that is a funny thing to say but my Puritan conscience is the problem. I can't just let the fruit rot, which would be the sensible thing to do, since there is no way we are going to use up all that is in the freezer already. Still, I keep packing it in, just because it is there. I have offered free fruit to I don't know how many people, but very few actually took me up on the offer. They are delighted all right, and thanked me very much as well, when I give them picked fruit, which I do rather than see it wasted. But picking it themselves seems to be too much to ask!

The picking of fruit, and not the growing of it, has always been the problem here. My mind goes back to when my sons were all young and in theory at least I had plenty of pickers as well as consumers of fruit. But then there was many a row on that subject. Payment per pound picked was not really effective since their demands were such that I would virtually have to buy my own fruit back from the little Shylocks. Therefore, I had to fix a daily quota that each had to pick... or else!

And if they wanted to go somewhere, I then upped the ante and said I would drive them when, and only when, they had brought me in so many extra pounds each, depending on where they wanted to go. But they had to be watched, forced and cajoled every step of the way. There was the famous day that they came in with their full quota of raspberries in punnets, extraordinarily quickly, and said they were done and ready which didn't suit me at all at the time. But a promise is a promise, so I got them to put the lot in the freezer, just as they were, while I went to make myself respectable enough to go out. I also pointed out the lesson of application, of how capable they were of picking quickly, once they put their minds to it.

It was days afterwards, when noticing that those raspberries had shrunk terribly in the freezer, that I discovered that there was only a top dressing of raspberries in punnets packed with lawn-mowings and covered by leaves. The whole lot was fit for nothing but the rubbish bin, and I had to pretend to be extremely cross while privately amused at their initiative.

However, the funniest incident of all was the year that the phone started hopping one morning, with the boys unusually quick to answer. The phone then was in one fixed spot in the hall. The calls were not for me, was all I was told each time. So it was later, when all had gone out picking, and of their own accord, that I had to answer the phone to a lot of people ringing up about fruit of all kinds. To the first caller, seeing a chance to make a bit of extra money, I said OK, while wondering how on earth she knew I had fruit. However, when the second and the third call came, all was made clear. My wretches of sons had put an advert in the paper advertising fruit for sale, by the Kavanagh brothers, and giving the phone number here, and their expected prices per pound.

I went out hotfoot to the orchard to find what on earth was going on and what they thought they were doing. 'But Mom, when you were giving out to us yesterday for not working harder, you said that all that fruit was there so why were we not doing something with it?' they justified themselves, in quite an aggrieved manner. 'Now we are doing something about it and you are still giving out to us!' There was no answer to that.

Right then they went back to picking with a will and told me to write down any orders and/or phone numbers for them to ring back. They were very happy boys that day, calculating their profit per day and per week, before it ever was made. They were onto a good thing of course, selling my fruit for top price, having contributed nothing whatsoever to its cultivation.

That went on for years, actually. At times, we scolded and swore when they took more orders than they could manage, and Eoin and I found ourselves picking fruit for them, so as not to have irate customers on our doorstep. Secretly, however, we were quite pleased with our little entrepreneurs. I even extended my fruit-growing operation to give them still more scope for enterprise.

So for most of their teenage summers they were gainfully employed. They earned themselves quite considerable sums of money and bought bicycles, cameras and many other things, as well as all they squandered on sweets and chocolates and soft drinks, the sort of things we never kept in the house. If my lot said they were thirsty or hungry I always told them that there was plenty of water in the tap and bread in the bin, exactly the words of my mother before me.

It is only now, with so many young people getting into all sorts of trouble as teenagers, that I realise how useful was the work ethic our sons developed, by accident almost. It was a form of self-preservation, for us anyway, to keep them working hard, so that they would then be too tired to fight. I also had a thing about seeing great big lads lolling about the place, watching television in the daytime, while their father was up to his eyebrows in work.

Therefore, if we had no work for them, we invented work. One year Eoin had them paint every single fence post on the farm a pristine white. It looked magnificent against the green of the grass, even if it had no practical function at all and merely took money out of our pocket. But the reward to us all was real, even if not in monetary terms.

It is also a fact that the first time Padraig ever set eyes on a certain girl was when she came with her mother to buy fruit from the Kavanagh brothers. She says she does not remember him at all, but does remember quite well being stung by a wasp, here in the garden. Perhaps it was Cupid's dart she was experiencing, even at that early stage? (1990)

Puppy love

I am nearly afraid to tell you about the bad case of puppy love that has broken out in this house, lest the more knowledgeable of you start lifting eyebrows. I've been careful myself, from time to time, never to ask about possible children, if and when you see a young pair lavishing undue love and affection on a dog. But it is a grandchild I should be doting on by now...

Nevertheless, it is quite extraordinary how many young couples get a dog first. We did it ourselves, long and merry ago, with a red setter pup called Maeve. And Maeve reigned supreme for quite a while as it was a longish period before our first son appeared on the scene. There is no doubt at all but I spoiled that dog rotten. She went everywhere with me. I showed her off with such pride and she was a picture to look at, with her red glossy coat gleaming from all the good feeding and grooming. I would nearly take the bite out of my own mouth in order to give it to her.

With the benefit of hindsight, of course I can recognise her for what she was, a pure and utter child substitute! That seems to be the pattern for all young couples, first each other, then the house and next something small and cuddly on which to lavish care and affection. And what better for that than a small pup all soft, warm and trusting.

Our young pair were just running true to form, therefore, when they got Odie, a golden Labrador puppy. Well he is mostly that anyway. His very blue-blooded mother had a fling with an unknown father one moonlit night. Then, because the resultant litter had no papers to back up their breeding, Odie was under a death sentence. My tender-hearted daughter-in-law-to-be couldn't have that. And so Odie came to us, to be reared here, where he would be living. But the fact that he was to be their dog – and not mine – was firmly and frequently stressed.

My attitude for years anyway has been that the only place for dogs is in the yard, and for cats even more so. And that rule has been firmly imposed ever since they grew up. When they were little lads the house was full of dogs from time to time, because young boys need something to lavish their affections on, at a certain period. My sons, however, still have no idea how soft I once was about a certain red setter!

So Odie started out strictly on those terms. But sure, who could resist and confine outside a beautiful bundle of fur and fun, with the most appealing face you ever saw on any dog? In no time flat that dog was everywhere. Everywhere I went in the house and garden, he tagged along as well. And when he couldn't quite make the stairs, he cried so pitifully that I just had to go back down and bring him up with me. But in no time flat, he learned to negotiate them for himself.

Now, at the first sign of life from anybody in the house in the mornings, he is around scratching at all the bedroom doors, to tell us that it is time to get up and start another fun-filled, attention-giving day. This is great all right for getting all the sons up: but I do wish that someone would explain to Odie that Eoin and I are now semi-retired and just don't want to get up first in the morning any more.

Very early on, Odie learned that when the boys put on their wellingtons that means that he cannot come too. Padraig was insistent, from the very beginning, that Odie had to be trained to keep away from the farmyard: otherwise he could not go visiting his real mistress without first having a good bath. I don't want him back in the house either when he is smelling of silage effluent.

Odie loves his bath, however, it is kind for labradors to love the water. And when our engaged son has his bath before heading off for the night, Odie hops in now, as a matter of course, once his master gets out. So both of them leave me every night, smelling mighty fine. Though the dog does not go every night by any means. I think it is all very well him having 'accidents' in this house, but it is a different matter entirely if he does so in her parents' house, or in his master's beloved car. Then I'm asked, somewhat petulantly, when will he be fully trained, as if this was something I was neglecting to do, house-train this dog which isn't even mine!

However, I know that it is as useless expecting a puppy to be house-trained before they are ready, as is putting babies on potties too young, thinking that will hurry up the process. Both do it right, in their own good time, and not a moment sooner. All any of us can do in the meantime is to keep a watchful eye out, and lay out plenty of newspaper. There is great soaking in newspaper.

Though Odie is good enough now about going out with his water, the other is liable to be found just about anywhere as yet. I forgive him even that, since he is always so glad to see me. He becomes nearly hysterical in his joy in seeing me again after even the shortest of partings, passing by everybody else in the line there to greet him so as to get to me. Such obvious affection, even if it is only from a dog, does make one feel good. And I must admit I do enjoy playing with him, even to the extent of rolling around the lawn with him.

But I have to be careful, even in that. It does not go down too well with his real owners when it is obvious where his real affections lie. I am the one who always feeds him: so of course he comes to me. It only stands to reason. Puppies always form an attachment to the one who feeds them. Children are no different, they always like best those who give them something. I know my sons divided all their relations into two main categories, those who stood to them and those who didn't. And I'll tell you another thing too, in that category of good relatives, they had more value on the relation giving them a little and often, than the ones they only saw occasionally, yet who gave them really generous amounts of money as a stand.

I have gone on quite a bit about that dog, haven't I? So, before you say it for me, yes I am quite well aware that Odie is my grandchild substitute. When the time comes, and I have the real thing, I will tell you all about that too, probably *ad nauseum*. But in the meantime I am learning one very important lesson: I now suspect that it will not go down too well at all were the real child to become as fond of me as has the child substitute! (1989)

The shift in power

'Aren't you blessed with two fine sons farming away with you and you all get on grand?' is something often said to Eoin or myself as a half-question. But as with everything else in life, it is no way as clear cut as that. Blessed we most certainly are: but that blessing did not just happen. And it comes with a hefty enough price tag attached, let me tell you. The price is that I, and especially Eoin, have to accept a somewhat subservient position in the order of things, and what's more, be publicly seen to do so!

All the years that a family is growing the father, with the mother, is the supreme authority on the farm. They decide what is to be done, practically every minute of every day. Then the son or the sons grow up, and take over the farm, with all the power shifts that implies. At some stage the parents have to take the position formerly held by the son in the hierarchy of power. If he does not then the son will always be 'the boy' and there will never be peace. It is not enough for the son to be boss, he must be seen to be boss in a myriad subtle ways.

We have just finished our formal monthly directors' meeting, which we always have in addition to whatever number of ad-hoc meetings arise with the everyday problems of the place. Once more, even though contentious matters were aired, Eoin did not have to use his casting vote. Many years ago, when our farming partnership first started, that was one thing which was made clear on all sides. It was written down, in black and white, in the partnership agreement we all signed, that our arrangement was a partnership, and that there could be no unilateral decisions. Any major expenditure, or changes in work practice, had to be discussed before being undertaken. A majority vote would then carry the day in the case of any disagreement. However, if there was a tie, Eoin could then, and only then, use his casting vote. That of course was designed to keep the balance of power firmly in our hands since he and I combined could always out-vote the sons. Therefore, he would still be boss if it really came down to brass tacks.

But never once, in almost ten years, has it come to Eoin having to use his casting vote. I have often wondered why. Today, when things were amicably resolved once more and all were in a relaxed mood, I asked the question why. 'That's simple, Mom,' said Padraig, as he relaxed back in his chair. 'If I want something, and Eoin Óg does not, I get you on my side, knowing you will talk Dad around, or vice versa. Then, and only then, will I bring it up at a meeting. Of course, if I can't talk either of you, or Eoin Óg, around, then I just forget it – until another time!'

We have been aware, of course, for many's the year, that the sons come to our meetings having already reached private agreement beforehand, especially when it is anything to do with the spending of money. Today, the necessity of buying a new tractor came up for discussion and quite honestly Eoin and I could not state categorically whether it was a justified expenditure or not: the sons are the ones using the tractors and not us. The best we could do was to use delaying tactics, and suggest that they wait for the Ploughing Match to buy, while I had a word with our accountant re leasing or buying. It should be all right because milk prices have been very good this year. We also had our clear herd tests so we should have a lot of calves to sell. And, most importantly, there is nobody with his hand out at the minute. The tax man in October will be the next big pull.

But look how completely power has shifted away from Eoin. The last tractor we bought was the year before the two of them were home for good. I remember much discussion about make, horsepower, etc. But we finished up with Eoin going off and buying *his* tractor and not the one the sons wanted him to buy at all. Today, however, there wasn't even a real discussion on the matter. They told him what they had decided was the best buy. And he said no more about a good second-hand tractor, or even alternative manufacturers.

'There was no point,' he said to me afterwards. Eoin has long ago accepted that he is no longer the sole boss. He is still in there with his point of view, but he no longer can push that against combined opposition. Moreover, this situation suits him just fine. In a way, he is having his cake and eating it. He wants to know everything that is going on, without having the hassle himself of making sure the wheels keep turning smoothly.

Most of the problems we see between fathers and sons is when the father still acts as complete boss, even when not actively involved. In one case we know, where there are regular fireworks, trouble always erupts because the father, when he needs help for anything, just goes out and takes away the farm apprentice, without as much as a by-your-leave to his son. Then the son comes back, sees that the apprentice hasn't done what he was set to do, and blows him out for that, until he discovers that his father called the lad away to paint high windows, cut up timber, clear the roadside, or whatever. The son then goes to complain to his wife. She has a sulk up on her when she sees her mother-in-law and maybe even goes as far as to deliberately keep away the grandchildren from the grandparents. So, because the father cannot accept that authority has shifted, everybody finishes up being both cross and upset, and all for the want of sitting down and discussing the whole situation. (1991)

Dead money

What makes money comes first, that motto is deeply engraved in most farmers' minds and pockets, and woe betide any innocent young girl, from a non-farming background, who thinks it will be any different once she marries her farmer. It won't, you know!

Now, I am not advocating that any farmer goes anything like as far as the man in our parish who, in 1961, when electricity first came to this corner of Ireland, sank a new well and laid on water to every single field on the farm and to every farm building and shed in the yard as well. Then, when all that was finally done and finished, he brought a pipe as far as the back door and put a tap on it there, for the use of his wife in the house. I'm not joking you. Not one drop of water was laid on to the house, not even to the old earthen-ware kitchen sink. His wife had to bucket in all her needs and he thought he was doing her a real big favour, that she no longer had to go to the spring well, half a mile away, with a bucket swinging off each hand, as she had done all her married life up to that.

I dare say he never once even considered the installation of a bathroom in the old farm house. That would be a case of complete 'dead money' to him, and what was wrong anyway with the daily emptying of the pots from under the beds, onto the dung heap in the yard? But that same man was able to set up each of his five sons on five farms before he died, and I dare say his daughters did not go fortune-less onto their big farms either!

And then he died, out in the fields one fine summer's morning, all by himself, quickly and quietly. And who is to say he wasn't a happy man, with his life's work done? His widow, however, had no bother about putting in more than the one bathroom into the house, before her year's mourning was up. And she bought herself a fine new car too, the blessings of God on her.

I am reminiscing away like this because this week the ESB was off for the whole day. They were working on the lines or something, because we got plenty of notice that the power would be off all day, so we took action to ensure that the cows would have access to water for the full day, by putting them into a field with entry to a stream.

My daughter-in-law-to-be was wondering how I'd manage in the house, not realising that cooking the dinner, or washing the clothes, would come quite so low in the order of my priorities. I explained that the cows and their needs always come first in this place. And I also explained how even one day without water would cause a severe drop in their milk yield, and that a drop in yield at this time of the year, and at this stage of their lactation, was critical, in that they would never recover properly again.

That is why we always hate it when we have a herd test in the summer, because, no matter what you do, their yield drops permanently after their routine is disturbed so much by the pulling and hauling of the test, with their heads being caught to read their ear tags, the injections for the test and the drawing of blood from each and every animal. While all this is going on they also have to be away from food and water for hours on end, when normally they go back out straight to grass after milking.

Lisa listened, and I think understood. Soon enough Miss Lisa will find out that the routine of the cows will govern her life, as it has done mine, until a daughter-in-law also takes over in turn from her.

'Home for the cows' has always been the refrain for me as a child, and as the mother of children, whenever and wherever we were out for the day. Always, especially at the seaside, we seemed to be packing up to go home to the cows, just when everybody else was arriving there for a leisurely afternoon of fun. We were always going home to work.

Now, the same day that the power was off, we heard the good news on the radio that we are to get a price increase of 2p a gallon for our milk, due to a green pound devaluation, and with possibly more to come. So there was jubilation all around at that kind of good news, with the calculators out working out what it would mean in a year in hard cash. Then Sara, my daughter-in-law, came over. They had no electricity either, but I do have a gas cooker, on which she said she'd get Padraig's lunch. I started to tell her the good news and, God love her, she immediately commenced to reel off all the things that I knew she genuinely needed in her house.

She wasn't here earlier in the day, of course, when all the male farmers in the place had decided to spend all that money, and a good deal more as well, on a new slatted house for the extra beef animals they had held onto in order to establish a beef quota for themselves for the future. Claiming the headage payment in December and then having to hold onto them for at least a further two months meant that accommodation for the full winter period was needed for those bullocks, and it had to be good accommodation too, so that they would thrive. So poor Sara's dreams of improving her own personal accommodation were about to evaporate in the heat of their plans.

I did not want to be the one to dash her hopes, although she is now coming to realise that anything which makes money always comes first, and who knows but a beef quota might yet be as valuable as a milk quota in years to come. We still wish that we were milking even more cows that one important year, 1983, which determined so many people's real chance in farming profitably by having a good milk quota. We were extremely lucky to have got as far on the road to development as we had then, before the EEC rules put a stop to our gallop. But, of course, there is no such thing as enough when it comes to milk quota! As everybody keeps saying, the farmer with a big milk quota is the one with a higher quota than yourself, just as the big farmer is the one with more land than yourself! That sentiment, however, is not confined to farming alone. What is a rich person but the one with more money than yourself?

It is at times like this that I think such thoughts because I also remember being in the exact same position once as I suspect Sara is now – when just about everybody we knew had modernised their houses, put in new fitted kitchens, holidayed abroad, and goodness knows what else – and we could not afford even one of those things.

We had invested a lot of borrowed money in cows, and all that goes with them, and we were finding the monthly repayments tough going. So I tasted jealousy quite often in those years, a jealousy so bitter that I can almost still taste it on my tongue, a jealousy of all the people with similar farms or even less land than us, but who all seemed to be so very much better off, with their fancy cars and their children in the best schools, here and abroad.

I remember especially the night we met up with a man at a meeting who was just about to take his whole family off to the Canaries, for Christmas, for a fortnight. That self-same year, the cost of Santa Claus for the boys was a bother to us. But this man told us, quite seriously, that he owed it to his family, because he had been working so hard all year he hadn't been able to spend as much time with his family as he would have liked, and as they deserved. So before the cows started to calve again, they were all off to the sun for Christmas and the New Year festivities.

How marvellously generous he sounded to my ears. And I was positively jealous because I knew that nobody worked as hard as Eoin, and myself as well. I wanted to know just what was it we were doing wrong, that we were finding life a struggle for just the bare necessities of life when everybody else was doing much better. I knew this man well enough to say as much to him. And to this day I will always remember the answer he gave. He said that our trouble was that we did not borrow enough from the banks when we were about it!

In my envy, I even wondered could he be right? Fortunately Eoin would have none of it, pointing out the undoubted fact that our repayments were only just within our capacity at the time, so why on earth would we borrow more for such things as fancy holidays, the deadest of dead money! And now, many years later, with the wonderful wisdom of hindsight, I see that those years of struggling and waiting were the making of us. We had built up to a decent number of cows, by that important year of '83, which we would never have done if we had not deferred everything else so long.

My children were then over the fierce damaging stage when we did tackle the house and I also knew by then what I really wanted. No young girl does, as we saw when those who did all the changes earlier were quite dissatisfied again and wanted still more changes; that is, those who could afford it this time round. So many of those who spent so freely, on personal matters and on buying land, all those years ago, hit troubled financial waters later. Some even sold part of their farms, or were sold up. Their income just did not justify their standard of living.

Now I wanted to use all my accumulated knowledge to prepare Sara for the disappointment that was inevitably coming her way. But I was afraid that she might shoot the messenger, her mother-in-law. Better her husband to be the one to explain properly to her all about 'dead money' in this farming game, how up to a point any money that does not make money is essentially 'dead money'. And how a farm is just like a sponge. It holds an awful lot of liquid assets before any drip out for the use of the farming family. And if that sponge which we call a farm isn't kept good and wet, all the time, it just breaks into pieces and is gone with the wind, no matter how hard anybody works. The trick is to make the right decisions at the right time. We did with cows in 1983. But now, in 1992, we really have no idea where beef is going. So much in farming is nothing more than a calculated gamble! (1992)

Whose dream is it anyway?

I have to go off to the races in a minute, all dressed up so that Eoin will be proud of me on his arm, and I am not looking forward to it one little bit. I hate races only marginally less than I hate point-to-points. All that standing around and trying to look interested is worse than a day's work for me. Form means nothing to me, and I hate losing money, which I invariably do when I bet on any horse of my choice. And Eoin's choices don't seem to work that well, either, on the day.

But Eoin loves his horses. The first page he turns to each day in the newspaper is the racing results. Then he looks at the death notices, and only then the general news. And by bedtime he will have read every small ad as well. I never saw anybody get such value out of a newspaper.

He is the one who gets all the value out of the teletext too because every single day he has the teletext racing pages on and spends ages decorating the racing page of the newspaper with all sorts of hieroglyphics as a result. He tells me that these are how the horses actually performed that day and their final odds and how that compares with their form. But even after all these years, form still means nothing to me because doesn't it all depend on whether a horse is really trying or not on the day?

Still, Eoin surely loves his horses, regardless, the horses running around this place as well as those on the teletext. The sons, however, just like their mother, have very ambivalent feelings. A new one arrives every year to Eoin's brood mare, and then we all ooh and aah over how sweet it is. And Eoin stands by, practically the proud father, ready to receive all compliments.

But when the stud fee cheque is paid, etc., and the non-horse-loving partners see those cheques, as see them they must, because the brood mare is a farm enterprise, it is more a case of oh-oh! Or the sons say, when the cows are due to go into a paddock in which the horses have left their mark rather too well, that we are now in very serious danger of having a flock of them about the place shortly, if we don't do something about it.

The unfortunate thing in a way, for me, is that we only have a brood mare on the place because of my dislike of races and my unwillingness to go racing with Eoin as his earlier racing friends dropped out, through death and disablement. So, in answer to an ad, Eoin joined a racing club where a whole load of men owned one horse, a two-year-old filly, Corcaigh. It was all just a bit like the Coronation Street nag, except that this filly did eventually win quite a few races, and was also placed several times. Eoin and the gang travelled the length and breath of Ireland, North and South, when Corcaigh was on her winning streak.

'She broke down' was an explanation which, each time I heard it earnestly discussed as the reason she had not done as well as expected on the day, always made me visualise her crying bitterly, out there on the track, because she could not keep up with the rest. Sometimes her owners, in the bar, as I, on the outskirts of the conversation, listened on, did not seem a great deal more composed in their disappointment. I'd idly wonder could this particular breakdown mean that she, and others, were heading fast for nervous breakdowns!

However, the main reason why she did not live up to expectations at any particular race, a reason the men could not empathise with over their pints and small ones, was usually because she was just coming into season, or was it still going out of season? I'm not sure which. But it was always one or the other, or even maybe both! I don't know. Perhaps I'm getting too cynical in my old age!

What I do know, however, is that the outlays on Corcaigh, except during the odd exceptional winning period, always exceeded the income. Still, what price can one put on friendship and companionship? And they could have been doing far worse on their days off. It was quite extraordinary, though, how the times I went to see that horse race were the times that she didn't win, so much so that the word 'jinx' hung, unsaid, in the air. Punters and owners alike are the most superstitious lot, and it suited me fine not to follow her fortunes on the track.

Consequently, my once vague hope of a public moment of glory leading in the winner never came to pass. I do have a lovely photograph of Eoin leading her in one of her winning occasions: the club members took it in turn to do that. They did also have great days out with her, and great camaraderie. Having a horse run is always most exciting, I was constantly being told, as telephone calls flew back and forth. But to have one gallop up to a win, however, is a dream come true for the owners, a dream so regularly rehearsed in the forward planning that you'd have to move smartly out of her way as waving hands demonstrated just how it was going to go, this time.

Anyway Corcaigh really 'broke down' when she damaged some bone or other in her leg, and was no longer fit for racing. So the club tried to sell her, but this was when the market for racehorses was as bad as for beef right now. The sheiks had stopped buying then too, it appeared. So it was the knacker's yard for her, or for Eoin, the farmer, to take her on.

'Sure you have plenty of land. One mare isn't going to eat that much grass. She won't cost you anything to keep,' said some urban members of the racing syndicate. 'And that way we can all hold our interest still.'

'No bloody fear,' said Eoin privately to me. 'I'll make them an offer for her, because I'd be waiting for my money for her upkeep and yet they'd all have their hands out when it came to selling the foals, and how would we agree on sires anyway?'

They'd have a long wait though, to put out their hands. It is now five years later and at long last the first of the progeny is off to the sales in August. She is a filly by Torus, who, Eoin tells us, has bred a lot of winners. And you know, sometimes when I see Eoin out in the field near the house, with a faraway look on his face, and his horses all around him, some resting their heads on his shoulders, and the others nuzzling him gently with their soft mouths for their share of attention, I know he is dreaming impossible dreams of Gold Cups winners, or one of his darlings storming past all the opposition towards the winning post at the Grand National!

And while they stay untried, he can dream away. But think of the real interest he will have if Corcaigh's eldest goes into training and starts running in races. And if she starts winning, think of the increased value of her full sisters and brother, and they might even be sold at an earlier age. But who is dreaming now, tell me? (1996)

AUGUST

Almost berserk in the kitchen

The drought has really been hitting us hard, this long, hot, dry summer. Grass is vanishing before our very eyes. And, instead of being forty shades of green, we now seem to be turning into a uniform grey-brown.

The silage pits are still far too empty for comfort, especially since the fields, which had been earmarked for their filling, have either already been eaten by the cows or dry-stock, or else their yield is frighteningly low. It is heartbreaking, at the present cost of harvesting, to see the big machines fly over our poor second crop and clear the fields too quickly – and without the silage clamps inside rising much as a result.

At least the machines were flying at top gear until about 11 o'clock this morning, when the harvester swallowed a piece of itself, and came to a shuddering halt. Frantic phone calls produced mechanics. Nuts and bolts flew in all directions and repairs went under way, watched, knowingly, by all the men who were now standing idly by, smoking.

Meanwhile, back in the kitchen, I had cut up what seemed like the best part of a side of beef for the stew, prepared mounds of vegetables, scrubbed buckets of potatoes and counted heads. 'Eighteen in all for dinner' was the information percolating back to me, which did not, of course, include myself. 'What am I to a Christian anyway?' I asked myself somewhat bitterly.

I got hotter and hotter as the stew simmered away, the pudding was made and the two big pots of potatoes went down. As I counted out the cutlery and crusted mustard jars, I thought, crossly, why do I have to feed all these men? In any other business do the men who come in to do a job expect to be fed, as they do in farmers' houses? It's not as if we had free food and scores of willing helpers to both prepare and dish it out.

I did put down my foot, with a strong hand, some years ago when I got fed up to the back teeth of forever feeding just about anybody who happened to be on the farm at the time, as was always the custom here. I then made the firm rule of no dinners here for mechanics, electricians, builders, calf buyers, salesmen and all the rest who had, for generations, put their legs under the table here. Most of the men who came for the day had their own lunch with them anyway. But if I was fool enough to feed them, then they would happily eat on the double.

Don't think that I am completely hardhearted. I did make exceptions where there were unusual circumstances. But never was my kindness reflected in the bills when they came in. They never got lower because of good feeding. The men were grateful, sure enough. But thanks is cheap. So, for the most part, I stuck firmly to my new regime and only regretted that I hadn't put it in place years before. But it is well nigh impossible to change the status quo without giving offence.

The silage contractor, however, was just as firm as I was, and the ultimatum was 'no food – no silage cutting'. As his is a big concern, in an area where contractors are as scarce as hens' teeth, that meant that there was no real argument. So that was why I was there, in a hot kitchen, on a boiling hot day, counting out eighteen of everything.

At one o'clock the trek in began. But it was soon obvious that something was wrong. All the chairs were occupied. But there were still four men standing. So it was a case of family hold back, as I made room for that four. My two eldest boys were luckier than Eoin, who went away with nothing.

The four interlopers turned out to be the three mechanics who were repairing the forage harvester and somebody – I think a German – who was something to do with the manufacturers, none of whom had any right to be there at all. They had hearty appetites, praised the stew mightily, and one of them then asked, 'Is there any more of the powerful mate in the pot, missus?' I felt like throwing the remnants in the pot over him. But I restrained myself and got on with my role of patient provider.

When they had all gone, leaving behind them a mountain of unwashed dishes and the usual aroma of waste oil, silage effluent, or worse, I never wanted to see them, or food, again. However, for my starving family's sake, out came the frying pan and on went the rashers and eggs and lukewarm left-over potatoes. Those at least smelt good. But any appetite I might have had disappeared when I realised that, with all the delays, tomorrow would see a repeat performance in the kitchen.

I vowed, though, come what may, only eighteen are going to be fed tomorrow, even if I have to stand guard at the kitchen door with a rolling pin. So if you see a headline on the news, 'Farmer's wife goes berserk – batters hungry men to death,' you'll know the full story behind it. (1977)

Peer pressure brings success

We were mighty busy here all week because Eoin's discussion group was due to call, so there was a mad dash on to get everything reasonably respectable in time. That meant inside as well as out, because, or so I was informed, the whole group gathers first, in the house, for a drink and 'little bits and pieces'.

'What do you mean – little bits and pieces?' I asked. 'Will I make tea and coffee and a plate of sandwiches as well as the drink?' Of course I was anxious to do the right thing, as always when people call.

'The sandwiches might be all right, some of them do do that, with the drink and the other bits and pieces... But nobody gives them tea or coffee; they are all men and I don't want to be the first one to start...' mused Eoin, half to himself. I smiled to myself at the idea of grown men still responding to peer pressure just like a pack of teenagers. I resolved, since the meeting was in mid-afternoon, that of course I would make a pot of tea. I know full well that quite a few men, Eoin included, would much prefer a nice cup of tea to all the drink going, at that time of the day.

It was my sons who were the last to tell me what I could and couldn't have in the line of refreshments in this house, when their friends were calling. Once I was ridiculed for suggesting jelly and ice-cream for dessert, which, to them, was now just too childish for words – and which they never got in other people's houses anyway! That was the important point. Peer pressure is such a terribly strong force, especially in the teenage years.

However, I am convinced that the reason for the great successes of farm discussion groups is exactly because of the self-same peer pressure. And the greater and more vocal the pressure, the more successful the group. There is no use in the world in telling your fellow discussion group member that he is doing great, when exactly the opposite applies, now is there? The object of the group is to lift the performance of everyone in it, and not to act as a mutual admiration society!

Eoin still tells the story of how, some thirty years ago now, his first group, a very local discussion group, came to visit, and he took them all over the place. We were only doing very fair, financially, and were genuinely anxious to improve matters, especially our cash flow, and thus what was finally left in the heel of our fists at the end of the year. I did not go along with them on their grand tour of inspection. It wasn't done in those days for a woman to appear to be too involved in farming matters while she had a husband living. There now, I was responding to just the same sort of peer pressure then, when I would not, inside or out, do anything that the wives of the other discussion group members were not doing on the walk.

There were too many jokes and innuendoes for comfort then, about any woman who dared put her head above the parapet of the male bastions of power. One wife in the area used to attend the mart with her husband and go into the auctioneer's box with him, to make the decision of when to put the animals on the market. Her husband was then described to Eoin one day at the mart, while all this was going on, as 'a nice poor chap, who would have been all right, really, were it not for the fellow he married!' All the men present thought this remark hilarious, so much so that some, at least, brought it home to retell, whether or not with malice aforethought! And I wouldn't mind but she was twice the farmer that her husband ever was, able to turn her hand to everything, as subsequent events proved in her widowhood. She stood up to a lot of peer pressure along the way to successfully safeguard her farm, home and children.

Anyway, Eoin's story is not about what his group said along the way, as they looked at his grain crops, his sheep and his grassland. It being early spring, the beef bullocks were still housed. So, the whole line of men stood by our one and only shed, and looked and looked, in silence, at what we considered to be our fine strong bullocks, our *pièce de résistance* of the whole farm walk. Nothing was said for quite a while, until one man found his tongue and in a loud clear voice said 'Do you know what, Eoin Kavanagh, but you are one tight, mean, lousy f....r when it comes to feeding animals!'

There was a stunned silence for a moment, while everybody, and especially the agricultural instructor who attended each meeting, watched Eoin to see how he would react to that outburst. Fortunately, Eoin just laughed and said something like 'Now, that's more like it, lads! Maybe now we will get somewhere at last...'

And, true enough, the floodgates were immediately opened and advice and criticism flowed freely for the rest of that visit.

We were put right on several matters, including the fact that we really should be milking cows and not buying in beef and growing a bit of this and a bit of that... We hadn't even one cow in the place at the time, but dabbled instead in about everything else in farming, including early potatoes and vegetables for the sugar company.

So, of course, Eoin found it hard to be generous with meal to his beef bullocks, when the cost of every ton bought at that lean time of the year meant a little white envelope in the post from the bank manager. Therefore, the discussion member's description of Eoin being a tight, mean f....r when it came to feeding his stock was true, but only in as much as his overdraft would allow. Nevertheless, the point was taken and accepted and that day was one of the turning points of our lives. You know it often takes an outsider to come in and point out the obvious, that one can never see oneself, when the mind is clouded with extraneous problems. Actually, when I say an outsider, that term also includes good friends, because they are the ones who can feel free to make their points forcibly, as our friend did that day. He was, and is, still one of Eoin's best friends, even if he hates, to this day, to be reminded of the good turn he did us that day of our first farm walk.

Still, every discussion group needs at least one member just like him, willing to call a spade a spade and really spell it out in forceful language. If Eoin had been asked if he would, perhaps, consider feeding more meal to fattening bullocks to improve his profit margin, I doubt if he would even have properly heard the question, convinced as he was that he was doing the very best he could in the circumstances prevailing. Later, that evening, over the tea and whatever 'bits and pieces' I provided in those days, a whole strategy was worked out, on paper, for how Eoin should approach the bank manager in order to increase his overdraft, with hard facts and figures to back up his feasibility study.

No one suggested that the woman pouring out the tea, and passing around food, should be sitting down at that table as well, since it was also her future that was being discussed, and certainly nobody suggested that she accompany Eoin to beard

the lion in his den, when he went to see his bank manager.
Those days were still a good way off in the future.

There have been many visits from discussion groups and
others here, since that fruitful day. That original group fell by
the wayside, mainly I think because it was too small, too local,
and most importantly did not have a regular intake of new
members. All the members eventually got to know each other,
their farms and their problems, only too well, and not all were
as ready to listen and benefit as was Eoin. I don't care what
group it is anyway – country markets, ICA or IFA – any group
that keeps the same people in charge, year in and year out,
soon stagnates and starts to go backwards and not forwards.
New young blood is so necessary in every concern in life.

That is why I was delighted, when the present discussion
group did arrive there that afternoon, to find so many of them
new faces to me since their last visit here. That was over four
years ago, they told me, even though I would have sworn that
it was only late last year, or the year before at the most. I
missed many of the old friends who have left the group for one
reason or another.

But then Eoin would be long gone too if it wasn't for his
sons coming after him. At times he talks about giving over his
place in this group to one of them, the only real question being
which. It is only natural that Eoin does not have the same
interest that he did twenty, or even ten years ago. Then, every
night, when he got home from a discussion group meeting, if I
wasn't awake he'd make sure to wake me up, no matter how
late the hour, to tell me all he had seen and heard discussed,
and what did I think? Now, even if I am not asleep, I pretend
to be anyway, because if we start talking it can go on for ages
and then it is hard to go back to sleep. So, basically, I am not as
keen now, either, as I used to be. Maybe it is high time Eoin did
give over to a son – the first member of this particular group to
do so.

Yet, when all those men were here, I enjoyed the whole
thing very much indeed, just as they did their tea and coffee,
which got many more takers than the drink tray. Apropos of
nothing, there has never been a woman invited to become a

member of that discussion group! But at least now, after all these years, I am not in the least shy or embarrassed about admitting that I am very involved with everything to do with our farm. Therefore, I too went along on the full farm-walk, contributing my little bit to the general discussion, as did Eoin Óg. (Padraig is still on holidays.)

But Eoin is still the main man, make no mistake about that. He was the one all wanted to question, as I discovered when I heard Eoin being asked the self-same question Eoin Óg had just answered. Fortunately, if our veracity was being cross-checked, both answers that man got were identical. Having excellent hearing, I then deliberately eavesdropped on the verges.

Suddenly, as I stored up tit-bits to tell later on, for no reason at all the memory of a certain Grassland Association meeting came back to me. Eoin and I were sitting about three rows back when a couple of men in front of us started to discuss, of all things, Liz Kavanagh, and was she real or what? Of course my ears were out on stalks immediately, as I nonchalantly leant forward and beckoned Eoin to listen as well.

Shamelessly we eavesdropped as one man said that Liz must be real, since she talks about things like the way the crubes of calves come during a calving. Then they went on to say a few more things. But the best piece of all was when one turned to the other and said, quite clearly, 'Do you know who I feel really sorry for always? I feel right sorry for Eoin – that quiet poor hoor!'

Only that it would have spoiled all that was yet to come, I would have tapped him on the shoulder and set him straight on that score. Instead we both leaned forward, just that little bit more... just as I did for the rest of our farm walk. (1990)

Poor Eoin gets nettled in the chemists

Eoin is making slow but sure progress every week now after his sojourn in hospital following his accident. This is great, but I can tell you that I will be very glad indeed when he gets back to driving himself again. As it is I am never off the road, with physiotherapy and the regular trips back to the hospital for check-ups, x-rays and the like. And every second day it seems that he wants to be driven about the farm too, just to make sure the place hasn't gone to rack and ruin in his absence. Which, needless to mention, it hasn't. But he still has to fuss over small things, even every bit of ragwort he sees under the paddock wires.

'Why don't they give them one good yank out as they see them, all year long, especially when they are soft after the rain and then they wouldn't be in flower now, making a show of us,' he fumes, with a certain justification. I can well see his point as the ragwort is a particularly vivid yellow weed, visible from quite a distance. Also, if they are not pulled and carted away soon, in the near future, we are going to have an almighty crop of them all over the place when they seed. It is the same with the thistles and the nettles. The topping of the grass in the paddocks keeps them reasonably clean of weeds. But without yearly attention the edges get disgraceful.

We well remember when you could hardly walk into a field here without getting lost in the nettles, thistles and ragwort, noxious weeds all, and the height of ourselves in their luxuriant growth. But, of course, the sons do not remember that, or the width of nettle groves which could take huge sections out of a field at this time of the year, which is something that can still be seen in far too many parts of Ireland right up to the present moment. That, thankfully, was only the case here when we were starting and times, and the farm, were rough. So the sons do not understand the grief that a weedy farm, even if it is only under the wires, causes Eoin. He probably does not fully understand himself that, to him, it is symptomatic of the whole place going to rack and ruin, without him in charge. The fear of farmers, and others, whose power has weakened, is that things will not be as good without them, despite any evidence to the contrary.

Still, Eoin himself is getting better and better all the time. Today, for instance, after our visit to the doctor, he said that he would go into the chemist to get his prescription filled, by himself, while I went to the supermarket for our few bits and pieces. We agreed to meet back in the car-park. I got there, and when he wasn't in the car before me, I went off to the chemist to see if he was all right. However, when I got as far as the chemist, I met Eoin coming out the door in what seemed to be quite a hurry for a man on crutches.

'Whoa – slow down there,' I said to him. 'You're not fit for the 100-yard dash yet...' But he grabbed hold of my arm, abandoning a crutch, and said, 'They might think I am fit for far more than that... For God's sake, Liz, get me out of here fast!'

And then I noticed he was in great difficulty all right, but it was really with trying to keep the laughter in. Once we were safely in the car he sputtered 'Do you know what, Liz? You are married to the greatest eejit going. A child of five would hardly have done what I have just done in there...' He exploded again with laughter with the memory, and no sense could I get out of him again for quite another while. In the end I had to threaten to stop the car, there and then, if he didn't tell me what it was all about.

So eventually I did get the whole story. He had got in fine to the chemist, even though he was much delayed by meeting some neighbours waiting their turn at the counter. They, of course, had to tell him how great he was looking and how good it was to see him up and about once more. Finally it was Eoin's turn to hand in his prescription.

'Why don't you sit down in the armchair there while you are waiting, Mr Kavanagh?' said our chemist to him. But he, feeling that to sit in the one and only chair there would be only drawing further attention to himself, or, perhaps more pertinent still, be making an old man of him, declined her offer. He stayed standing at the counter where he was.

'Was it the way she thought I was too old and decrepit to stand for a few minutes?' he protested, confirming my suspicions of his paranoia on the subject of his not being fit for much, at the moment, as he even became annoyed once again in the midst of his laughter, that anybody might think him old enough to be automatically offered a chair. That is why I did not waste time by pointing out that he was, after all, on crutches!

Anyway, while he was standing there, he looked idly at all the bits and bobs on the counter top. Then he noticed a box of stuff he did not recognise at all, all sorts of colours, and with a big M blazoned across them.

'They were right there, Liz,' he explained, 'where they usually keep all those lollipops and sucky things and stuff. So, naturally enough, I picked one up to see what on earth these new things were and whether they were some sort of novelty I could bring home to Michaella, as a treat from her Granddad. There was a big sign up all right, "Your Mates are here", but sure that could have meant anything. So I started reading down the fine print. I had to hold the package up real close to get the thing in focus for my bi-focals. And then the word "condom" jumped out at me and I dropped it like a hot coal, out of my hand and back into the box, and then I literally fell back, with shock, into that armchair I was just after refusing a few minutes earlier.' He stopped for breath, as I so clearly visualised his collapse...

'And I wouldn't mind but the shop was packed with people,' Eoin continued, 'including all those locals still waiting for their prescriptions! So what must they all have thought of me? I kept my eyes firmly on the ground, until, finally, ages afterwards, a young one came up to me to tell me my prescription was ready. I swear she was dying laughing at me and my Mates... Out of there I thought I'd never get... Did you ever in all your life see such a stupid eejit as I am?' he concluded with a completely rhetorical question.

But a few seconds later, while I still wondered how best to reply, Eoin really put the tin hat on it for me, when he questioned, this time in a completely non-rhetorical manner, 'And I still have no idea, Liz... Would you have any idea what on earth were they all different colours for?'

Then I was free to laugh too, because I could just see him, with the packet of condoms in his hand, and he appearing to be studying the fine print with exaggerated care. I bet he will avoid that section of the counter like the plague the next time he goes to the chemist, so he will probably never find out the reason for the colour coding.

I had to laugh again, even more heartily, when on our way home we took a detour to see the outside farm. Eoin, fuming once more about ragwort in bloom under the fence wires, suddenly laughed again and told me that the packet he had inadvertently picked up in the chemist was the exact same colour as 'that line of ragwort under the wire there!'. So maybe it was nothing more than ragwort in bloom that was really on his mind at the time he picked up his Mates in the chemist. (1993)

The new arrival

'Diyee, Diyee! It's out! It's out! Come! Come quickly!' Michaella shouted, no, Missy Michaella shrieked at me, from the top of the stairs. I had just come in the hospital door. She hooted and screamed with delight in that lovely way she has, and kept on telling me that it was out, it was in the room, and all this despite her father doing the best he could to hush her. The girl at the reception desk was just bent over laughing. Every other patient in the place must have heard the commotion, but Michaella's news was just too stupendous to be held in. The long-awaited event had happened. Her baby was born. It has always been her baby, you know, all these months. And now she was dragging me along the hospital corridor to show me my new grandchild, our new baby.

Of course I already knew all about it. Wasn't Michaella delivered over to me the night before when things started to really happen? Grandparents near at hand are a tremendous advantage to any young couple: the last thing a child needs is to be woken up in the middle of the night and left somewhere strange because a new baby is on the way. Michaella is well used to spending nights here. But before she would settle down to sleep, Michaella told me that she was going to have a baby sister very very soon, and she demonstrated with her doll how she was going to mind her new baby sister. 'Maybe it will be a little baby brother,' I countered, because I am never quite sure how much she knows or is supposed to know. But no, she insisted that it was going to be a girl. 'I'se a girl,' she said, 'you'se a girl; Mommy's a girl; Daddy's a boy and Dad Dad's a boy...' and she went on to tell me what everyone is, including the dogs, cows and bulls. So isn't it early children have an awareness of the differences in the sexes and what their own sex is?

But then, too, she might only be repeating what she had already heard, because it all came out so pat. She is fast coming to that dangerous age when she is likely to repeat anything and everything that is said in her hearing. So I don't know whether she knew more than I did about the sex of the coming grandchild, or whether she was just expressing a preference for her own sex in everything.

I never ask any questions about things like that because quite honestly I don't want to know. Knowing the sex of a child beforehand is a bit like knowing what Santa is bringing. I love the surprise element. And whichever it is will be welcome when it is there. Though, if I was quite honest, my preference would be for what I haven't got, the long-awaited grandson. But then again we couldn't ask for anything better than another little Michaella who gives us unstinted love.

We do spoil her rotten. Even that night, as every night, we let her watch her favourite videos when we put her to bed. There is nothing like an electronic baby-sitter, after all. I turn on *Bambi*, *Peter Pan*, or whatever her choice falls on that night, turn off the light and she settles down no bother, lost in a magic world, and generally drops off to sleep very quickly.

But no magic could possibly compare to this real magic that had happened this morning. The excitement was killing her but I had to hear all: she has a real live baby sister; it was there in the cot beside her mother in the bed; it was going to wear her dolly's clothes; it wasn't crying yet. And she'd run over to the cot and look at the little thing, all neat and tidy and sound asleep making gentle little sucking sounds and the odd grimace; then back to me again. Remembering all the mistakes I made when my second son was born, I didn't make too much of the new arrival, just let Michaella take complete and utter charge of me, as usual. I sat down and she sat firmly in my lap, all set to stay and totally monopolise me. 'Oh-oh!' I thought, is she feeling just a little bit funny despite her expressed joy at the new arrival?

Jealousy of the second child can be a quite appalling thing, you know, a real physical pain, just as she will doubtless feel later on when some horrible fellow or other lets her down for another, or even before that when her friend at school wants to play with another little girl and not with her any longer. You know you hear that expression, about somebody not having a jealous bone in their body? Well, I for one don't believe that's possible. Jealousy is part of the human condition. It is only when it gets out of control that there is trouble. Jealousy taken to extremes shows a most terrible corrosive lack of self-confidence. And I wonder how far back this goes, perhaps to the birth of a sibling. So I tightened my grip on my little girl, to show her just how secure she was.

Of course, things are much better managed now than when I ran into the worst kind of sibling rivalry. When my second child was born there was a notice up on the ward door that children were strictly forbidden at all times. Such strictures were noticed with my eldest, but then we really only see what interests us: I had no other child whom I might want to see. But when Seamus was born, as soon as I was on my feet, we planned that Eoin was to bring Michael in downstairs, so I could go down in the lift to see him and so circumvent that notice.

Eoin, foolish man, happened to mention this to the nun in charge on the way out and she said bluntly that he couldn't. In hindsight, we shouldn't have accepted this so meekly, for God knows I was never one for accepting things quietly. But then again I didn't know any better and thought my missing my big son was the only pain being inflicted. I did not look at things from my little son's point of view. There he was, abandoned by his mother: I went off in the middle of the night and just wasn't there for him in the morning. Then he didn't see me for an eternity, which is what seven full days is to an eighteen-month-old child. Finally, which was my biggest mistake of the lot, I arrived home and came in the door to him with the new baby in my arms and so I wasn't able to pick him up immediately and renew our loving bond. He ran away from me, down the garden, and Eoin had to go after him. But he only did so when he had me settled in and the cot brought in, and doubtless Michael had not run so far that he could not see all of this.

My poor little big boy, although he was brought back, made much of, and things seemed all right, must have felt the new baby was now a usurper of his Dad as well. Michael was coaxed to look at the baby, whose cot we had put down on the floor so he could get a good look in. Then we all left Seamus sound asleep – the little cherub, he was always a bonny placid baby – to allow me to renew my acquaintance properly with Michael, who was anything but a placid child, from the very moment he was born, and for us to have a cup of tea after the journey.

At some stage Eoin took a notion to go back into the dining room to check his new son and to his horror saw Michael with a poker in his hand about to bring it down full force on the baby's head. Eoin just managed to get his hand in first and took the full force of the blow. I shudder to this day when I think of what could have happened, and deeply regret the jealousy which endured all their childhood, because so much of it dates back to that incident, the result of our mismanagement. Plus, of course, the stupid rules of that hospital.

How grand it is now, in comparison, with my grandchildren: hasn't that a lovely ring to it, 'my grandchildren'? Once Sara and Padraig had somewhat recovered from the birth – needless to say, Padraig was there all the time – the proud father came out to tell his elder daughter the news and bring her in immediately to her mother, where the baby would not be in her arms. Neither did we even whisper a word to Michaella – the great news was to come from her father – and that was the hardest part for us, once we ourselves had heard the news.

Waiting for Michaella was a beautiful new doll inside the hospital, so she would not feel left out. She has a new baby as well: in every way the young couple are managing it beautifully. Yet when Eoin picked up the little one, Michaella suddenly planted a kiss full on my lips, quite unsolicited, and hugged me close, with a tight grip on my dress, the new doll carelessly abandoned on the floor.

So I have yet to hold the new arrival, which I ache to do. She looks the absolute image of Michaella when she was born. And I suppose she will invade my heart too, just as her sister did, the very first time I held her close. As I once read on a car sticker:

My grandchildren are so wonderful – I should have had them first.
(1994)

Are farmers their own worst enemies?

Do you ever wonder if farmers are their own worst enemies? Three things happened here this week which gave me cause for comment. The first one was yet another troublesome calving case, and on a Sunday too, surprise, surprise! Despite his best efforts Eoin Óg could not budge the calf in the cow. It seemed to be totally upside down and wedged. So, knowing his limitations, he did the wise thing and sent for the vet.

Our usual vet, however, was not available, so the call was diverted and we got a new young vet we had never met before. But he was fine, got down to work and only after trying his best, decided that it had to be a caesarean. This went fine too, quick and efficient, and a good-sized live Simmenthal bull calf was handed out to Eoin Óg in due course.

'Good man yourself!' said Eoin Óg, delighted to have a perfect live calf when he was positive it was some sort of a deformed thing in there, because he couldn't knock even a shake out of it. Then, shortly after, he was handed another, equally good, live Simmenthal bull calf, which he hadn't suspected at all. So, naturally enough, he commented that he was delighted altogether with this.

Then the young vet, without stopping in his sewing-up job, said in a surprised tone, 'Now I know I am not that long in general practice, but do you know that you are the first farmer ever, in all that time, to say well done to me? No matter what I do I can't seem to please farmers. Instead of being pleased with a live calf they give out about the cost of a caesarean, or give out about the cow, calling her a bloody bitch, or worse, for not being able to deliver the calf herself. Or they go on about how well it wouldn't be to have two heifers, or bulls, or whatever it is they didn't get... I could understand if it was a dead calf, or the cow was a write-off... but...'

That nice young vet didn't finish up by saying that there was no satisfying farmers. But did he have to? I suspect farmers can carry on as if it was the vet's fault that a caesarean is sometimes the only chance to get a calf out alive.

Eoin Óg, while telling us the outcome of the calving case, also told us of his surprise at those comments about farmers. But you know it was far from the only time we have heard this sort of thing. Another vet, years ago, thanked Eoin for taking the news so well on one of the occasions we found ourselves with TB reactors. Eoin, at the time, looked at him in amazement since he was hardly likely to attack the vet as the bearer of bad news when it was nothing to do with him personally that our cows had those big neck lumps staring us all in the face. It never does make sense to shoot the messenger.

But that vet told Eoin that, after many years in practice, he absolutely dreads a positive test, purely because of the tongue-lashing he regularly has had to endure as a result. And once he was even run out of a farmer's yard at the point of a pike when he broke the bad news.

Talk about killing the messenger! And it isn't only vets who suffer. Department officials get attacked as well when they come bearing bad news about herds having to be locked up as a result of lesions found in factories. I also think I told you about the time a pollution officer called on us and leant over backwards not to accuse us of anything, so much so that Eoin commented on the fact. Then Eoin was told that he gets attacked so much by farmers, when he has occasion to call on them officially, that he tries to be as inoffensive as possible so as to escape the worst of it. But surely the boot should be on the other foot and it is the farmer who should be trying to placate the official and not the other way around? But I don't know. Some people, from childhood on, act as if indeed attack is the best method of defence in all circumstances.

Dear God above, will people never learn? What was it that Mary Poppins sang about a spoonful of sugar? And, from one who always uses that method whenever possible, it works a heck of a lot better than attack, I've found. Then, yesterday, I heard Eoin using the spoonful-of-sugar method too. There was a rush on to get a couple of loads of filling so that the bulldozer could continue working at the new shed complex we are about to start. But when Eoin got onto the office in question, he was told that there was no way he could have even one load of filling that day, that every lorry was out, and all were booked up for days ahead since 'all the farmers in the country seem to have gone mad building, not that we are complaining, mind you...'

So what was Eoin to do but spin a yarn about how the bulldozer would have to come to a full stop if the filling didn't come, and he finished up by saying:

'I'd be awful grateful to you if you could see your way to send me out a load before dark, and I'd be twice as grateful if you'd send two! And sure the lorry would know exactly where to go if the same man delivered both loads, and then it wouldn't matter how late it was when the second one came.'

The chap in the office laughed heartily and said:

'T'would be hard to refuse that. You know,'tisn't often I get farmers talking to me like that.'

So Eoin got his two loads of filling because he was nice. Wouldn't it be lovely if Eoin Óg equally got his two calves because he was nice? That would soon change farmers' tune to their vets! (1996)

SEPTEMBER

Sunshine & our sanity is saved

This past week here we have been in a sort of a limbo, not knowing whether we would find ourselves in a heaven or a hell of a harvest. For days Eoin seemed to settle to nothing at all. He was like a hen on a wet sop. Every day he would first test the grain in the heel of his fist, then between his teeth, before finally pronouncing, 'No... Not yet!'

Nevertheless, almost in the very same breath, he'd have second thoughts and wonder whether he'd be wiser to phone John to bring on the combine anyway, since he well remembered John was three days late coming last year. However, indecision struck again with the thought that if he came immediately to the call, and the grain not fit, we'd be crucified entirely with the high moisture content of the grain!

The poor man couldn't even settle down in peace to read his paper after supper. He was forever jumping up if he heard a machine in the distance, for fear any of the neighbours were harvesting, out of turn, before him. He was worried too about the straw and spent hours each day fiddling around with the knotters on the baler, which, like ourselves, is growing older and less inclined for hard work.

Would the weather hold? Would the baler hold together? Would we, with just our own help, be able to manage all the straw? These were the rhetorical questions flying past me time and again. But when I said to him, and repeated it over and over, that 'everything will be OK – wasn't it every harvest now, for years back?' I was told, curtly enough, that it was easy for me to talk. 'But...' – he always added another possible problem pessimistically.

I didn't dare join in his pessimism, or we would both be stuck in the mire of depression. I think the sons thought that it was just their Dad acting up again, and for no good reason. They had their own thoughts on the coming or not of John and his combine. The older sons were secretly hoping that the corn would not be cut before they had to go back to school, while the two youngest were hoping to God it would be, or they'd be the only ones around to deal with all the stacking and the drawing of all those bales. So each lot was all the time asking when the corn was going to be cut, each hoping for a different answer.

Each cluster of men, be it at the creamery or at the church gate, also had but the one topic of conversation – 'how was it going?' Still, as Eoin came home with glowing reports of two-tonne-plus crops, he always added: 'But who'd believe that anyway? Sure you couldn't believe daylight from Tom or Joe, or any of the rest of them either, aren't they all condemned liars?'

Finally, John and the combine were sent for. When he did not come on the day that he said he would, or the morning after, tempers were pretty badly frayed all round. The forecast, at five to one, was listened to in deadly silence, with just a deep exhalation of breath when there seemed to be no rain in the offing. Then, at the dinner, when the boys were bickering as usual, I was told to get them out of Eoin's sight fast, or he would hang one of them as an example to the others! So they left for the garden, clutching their pudding bowls and the custard jug. It was easier to make more custard for Eoin than to go after them.

In due course, however, John arrived to save our harvest and our sanity. All was sunny again when the harvester had to turn frequently to empty its full bin into the waiting grain trailers. The two-tonne-plus crop was definitely there all right. They were not all condemned liars outside the chapel gate after all!

I took the tea out to a golden world, a deep yellow combine harvester devouring vast golden swathes and golden grain cascading down the spout. The old baler was rapidly kicking out glistening golden bales, and at well over a hundred bales to the acre too, or so its clock said. The golden sun beat down on the gold brown backs of my sons, and lit up the glints in their hair, as they willingly loaded up the bales on the tractor and bale trailer.

Now all was laughter and fun. I too was glad that I had gone to the trouble of making that batch of scones and a really big apple cake. I lay back on the unbaled straw as they all tucked happily in, closing my eyes against the sun, only half listening to the chattering voices. We were all content again. Our state of limbo had given way to a heaven of sorts. I still had to go home and face the cows by myself. But wasn't it worth it, to linger awhile, with the smells and sounds of a good harvest, and the sun warm on my face? The cows would get done too, in the cool of the evening, because, while this weather held, everybody would be working late anyway.

Relaxing with my own thoughts, I realised that our worry and nervous anticipation, in the days just past, which the sons just do not understand, must be nothing more than a residue of all the bad harvests of the past lingering in our sub-conscious. We remember, only too well, those years when we anxiously watched and counted each bag as it fell from the old combine, needing each sack to be two.

When the corn was gathered in those old jute bags which we hired from the sack merchants in town, we knew our yield immediately, as the sacks slid down the chute, when the rope was pulled at the end of each row. In 1959 we barely cut the seed off all the fields. As the combine moved on without even one bag dropped per run we panicked, with thoughts of the bank manager, and no further income for the year. This immediate knowledge of exact yield, for good or bad – because there were good years too – is now no longer possible with grain in bulk. But I daresay someday some bright spark will find a way of measuring that too. Now at least I have this hiatus of hope before the official weigh dockets are all calculated.

Thankfully, now that we have the cows as well, the need to know, to count every sack as it falls, while still necessary, is no longer vital. We survived. But will our sons ever understand the scars left in our psyches by the desperate struggle of those years? And, even if times stay good, will that background worry ever fully leave us until the day we hand the lot, worries and all, over to them? (1977)

Bad harvests & moving statues!

It rained again last night. I woke up sometime in the darkness, hearing the merciless rain on the roof, and I knew, instinctively, that Eoin was already awake beside me. Yet what could I say to him in his misery? It has gone beyond simple words of comfort now. I have given up saying 'It must improve soon, didn't it every year – even the worst yet? Maybe the rest of September will be fine?'

The continual rain has gone well beyond the tolerance level of both land and people. What words of comfort can one find for a year's work going, going, gone, down the drain? That is the worst of all: the total feeling of helplessness, as day after day it rains down mercilessly upon us and our crops.

I have heard people say, with quiet conviction, that God must be very angry indeed with the people of Ireland. Many flock to the moving statues: they, and the pubs, are doing a roaring trade as the papers tell us what we already know, that this is the wettest summer this century. It was one of the wettest years on record, too, when Our Lady appeared in Knock. Weren't religion and drink always most in demand in really hard times? There was always more ways than one of drowning your sorrows!

Now, don't get me wrong. I am not, by any means, equating drink and religion as means of support in times of trouble. I do believe, however, that either, carried to extremes as an escape route from misery, is not a good thing. But it is a hard thing indeed to look ruin straight in the face and not try to find solace somewhere else.

And I am not exaggerating when I say ruin for some. The grain cut around us was so bad that when the trailers were tipped up at entry point the grain stayed in them, in a congealed lump, sticking to itself and also firmly to the sides of the trailers. It is hard to believe but the local co-op grain dryer here has a man stationed there, full time, whose sole job is to climb in and start the grain moving with his shovel.

It is no surprise, therefore, to anyone that such grain should test out at 33 per cent moisture, plus. And, at that, it is lucky to make the £70 a tonne. Now, at that price, the simplest calculation shows that it won't even pay for the seed and fertiliser, and what is the poor unfortunate, totally dependent on grain, to live on for the rest of the year? I don't know. It just does not bear thinking about. There will be a lot of unpaid bills gathering interest until this time next year and that's for sure. And I know some who, last year, bought mad expensive land in anticipation of continuing good harvests.

Now, we will survive, because we are lucky enough to have cows as our main enterprise and comparatively little grain at this stage. And the rain keeps the grass growing well. We also make all silage and no hay. I do not know how animals are going to survive this winter with the blackened cocks of hay we see still out, all over Ireland, cut in season but never properly saved. I fear a severe fodder shortage in places this winter.

Silage is different to hay, because if it isn't cut today it can be cut tomorrow, or even next week or next month. The quality suffers, naturally enough. It rots a bit at the base and the feed value decreases with every day that passes. But with sufficient acid to preserve it, even if cut in the wet it ensures a full belly, at least, for the cows for the winter.

I know that the cost of having it cut, and laying the concrete to put it on, is horrific at times. But then again, isn't the cost of not having it even more horrific! We did not always have enough concrete to put it on. A few times in our career we made the silage on the bare earth, when we just had not got the price of the concrete. And although the mess was fearful, we, and the cows, survived those winters, just about.

However, as the months went on and the dry cows ate into the pit, there was no way one could walk through the quagmire they made of the earth. It was pitiful watching the cows struggling to the silage face for food and a little firm, untrampled ground under their front feet. I have just remembered too the time we had to bring in a JCB to lift out two cows, sunk in the mud in front of the silage face. And I do mean sunk: they were so badly bogged down that they had given up the struggle. But the JCB got them out and cleared a passage up to the silage face as well, so we were able to feed the rest of them by laying down planks and carting the silage in wheelbarrows, most labouriously, to them, huddled in their tight concrete yard. The tractor just would not travel in the depth of mud. It didn't do the cows, now heavily pregnant, much good. As for us, it was a really major chore for days already too long with sheer hard physical work. But they survived, as I keep reminding everybody, we also survived the dreadful harvests of the late 50s.

Eoin and I got married on the strength of just two good harvests, 1956 and 1957. Then, the very first year of our marriage, it rained all summer long. Our harvest was cut by a tractor-drawn combine harvester, a bagging machine. Eoin nervously counted every bag that fell. I stood at his side, not fully comprehending his nervousness. But his gradually whitening face and his growing apprehension that the first round was a true indicator of what the yield was to be, is something I shall never forget.

Things did not improve as the machine worked inwards. Yet hope revived, in me at least, that the next field might be better. But rain stopped harvesting in that very first field, so the sword of Damocles stayed suspended over our heads until the next break in the weather, two weeks later. Then it fell with a vengeance as yields did not improve and the wheat was now accepted only at feeding price, because it had sprouted in the ear while still standing.

The last field, in the reclaimed bog, was cut on 17 October, and that day the final seal was put on our year's hopes. There we were, a young couple starting out on the rocky road of both farming and marriage. And I can remember, only too clearly, the reward we gleaned for that full year of hard work and worry. Our total return from our harvest, our only farm enterprise, was eleven hundred pounds and some odd shillings. But we owed the co-op, on our harvest account, just over two thousand pounds. That was some return for a full year's work. But we survived, as I keep on saying, just like a mantra against the clutching hand of anxiety.

Indeed, with hindsight, I can now see that it was the making of us, as we clawed our way back to solvency. However, if anybody had even whispered then about blessings in disguise, not alone would I not have believed them, I would probably have hit them, hard, where it hurts most. A harvest like that, and this present one, is enough to make grown men cry, or take to drink, or to say endless rosaries waiting for the statue to move at Ballinspittle. And then, to add insult to injury, this is the year our Government is introducing Land Tax! (1985)

Cutting up the frillies

There is no doubt about it but I'm getting soft in the head in my old age: I spent most of yesterday afternoon, Thursday, and all of last night, right up to bedtime, doing something I haven't done for the best part of fifty years. And you needn't laugh when I tell you that what I was doing was making dolls' clothes for granddaughter, my Missy Michaella. She loved every minute of it. And to tell you the truth, so did I. Michaella was absolutely fascinated at the way that a piece of material could be turned into something quite different as, for her, I cut into a perfectly good piece of underwear, all frills and lace. In that act the memories came flooding back, and I was a little girl once more dressing my own dolls.

As a child I really loved making dolls' clothes. Not that I had too many dolls, I can assure you, not like my granddaughter who has a whole shelf piled high with them. Yesterday she came over with a couple from her collection in tow and little on them besides their smiles and their curls. The rain was also pelting down once more. So there was no hope that my stint at baby-sitting could be done out of doors in the garden. And God love my precious child but she does demand my full attention when she is with me. That was when I got the bright idea of dressing the bare dolls for her. How I then regretted that I no longer had a rag-bag, or even that spare room wardrobe full of dresses and things which I'd never wear again but which were still too good to throw out. However, when we gave over most of the house to the young pair all sorts of things got dumped, as I had to stop spreading myself all over the place.

And Missy, when I asked her what sort of clothes she wanted for her dolls, said she wanted pretty party dresses. But a quick root through my own wardrobe showed nothing suitable that I was definitely finished with and could cut up. Missy, my shadow, was with me, looking into everything, and she it was who pulled open my hospital drawer and fished out a white shortie nightie, all frills and flounces, and not worn for years, if ever. Definitely it was not the thing for a woman of my age, with varicose veins on both legs, if, or when, I ever do find myself in hospital again.

It was, however, just the thing to make the most gorgeous wedding dress for Michaella's biggest doll, and a matching bridesmaid's dress for the other. Missy's eyes went all big with wonder when I draped the doll with the material, with the flounces to the ground and a train to the back. I had not the least compunction running the scissors through the material; that will show you quite what a doting grandmother I am. Nothing mattered only the fun the two of us had for hours, me showing her how to thread a needle, and trying to show her how to sew, tacking the pieces together before I set about running them up on the sewing machine, and she, endlessly questioning me on all sorts of topics.

Most of the time I had to keep on telling her stories, non-stop, about what I used to do when I was a little girl, just like herself. Michaella never seems to tire of my stories of long ago, any more than she tires of my telling her about how, when she was just born and only so big, I came into the hospital to see her and she was crying and crying and nobody could get her to stop. Then I picked her up and she immediately stopped crying, opened her eyes, looked up and smiled at me. All at once I really loved her on the spot, this child of my child, and I have loved her to bits ever since. Which is true enough, God knows: that immediate bonding between us two really occured, whatever about her smiling at me the first time I saw her and she not yet two hours old. However, she really did stop crying that day, more secure in my practised arms.

One story, however, I could not tell Michaella, for my daughter-in-law's sake. My activities as a doting grandmother this wet day brought back to me a similar dressing of a doll, once, a very long time ago, also on a wet Thursday possibly in November too. That particular day both my father and my mother were gone on their regular weekly trip to town, selling the butter and the eggs, so that is why I know it was a Thursday. I was bored and bold and occupied my time poking about my mother's wardrobe, forbidden territory as I well knew. And down in the very bottom drawer I found a box with baby clothes just the right size for my dolls. So I succumbed to temptation and took the lot over to my own room to make babies of my dolls.

One of the dresses, however, which was wrapped in white tissue paper in a box of its own, was way too long for any of my dolls, or for a baby either for that matter. However, I got the bright idea that, by cutting off the top, I could make a First Communion outfit out of it, with the dress down to the ground and a full-length veil as well – the kind I had really wanted for my own First Communion, a year or two before, and hadn't got. So for hours and hours I laboured, pricking my finger often and spotting the whiteness of the silky lining and the fine white lace with specks of blood.

But I was so proud of the end result. It was perfect. The veil was even held on by a piece of elastic just as mine had been. I checked out carefully how that was done, in the box on top of my parents' wardrobe, where my First Communion finery, also wrapped in white tissue paper, awaited its second use by the next sister in line. I had only got to wear it once, that morning at Mass, so I suppose it didn't really matter that much that I hadn't got the one I had liked best in the shop. On the morning of my First Communion, as soon as I got home again from Mass, it was an immediate case of off with the finery, and on with the old clothes and pinafore. I don't even have a photograph of that dress, or that day. The last in line of the girls was the only one to be allowed to wear it out. But then she got everything anyway!

When I trespassed once more and opened up all the tissue paper to check how the First Communion veil was kept on, I knew, on the spot, that a piece of the waxy wreath was just the thing to finish off my doll's outfit. All of it would be much too big, but a piece off the side of the those waxy white flowers was just perfect, as so it proved.

And so proud of my work was I that, as soon as I heard my father and mother coming in, I rushed downstairs to show off what a clever girl I was. My poor mother – she must have come home tired, knowing that the cows were still to be faced, and then to be confronted by her daughter proud as Punch of what she had done with the old family christening robe, all those yards and yards of handmade lace. Was it any wonder that I went back up those stairs with a sore bottom, no comic, and minus my doll?

But later that night, when they came to tuck me in, that doll was tucked in with me too, and she still had her First Communion outfit on. But sure, what else could they do at that stage? (1994)

Our yuppie farmer

This week Eoin Óg arrived out in the yard sporting a mobile phone in his waistband. Of course the teasing started immediately about our young yuppie. But in the midst of all that, Eoin and I looked at each other, knowing precisely that the other was suffering the same feeling of unease. That feeling of unease is one that often strikes us. You know that kind of unease that you can't quite put your finger on, but still it lingers and niggles away at the back of your head. It comes especially when you see your children doing all sorts of things that you personally could not afford at their age, or even felt were not for the ordinary farmer like us. Mobile phones seem to go with free-spending yuppie business types, but are decidedly not for the likes of farmers.

And it isn't just us and this mobile phone. We were out the other night and I heard tales of new carpets and curtains when what was there would do fine, and of new machinery and sheds. 'It's great to see them doing so well – but...' prefaced all these remarks, and I knew exactly what they meant. Having come up the hard way themselves they felt uneasy that the next generation have so much so soon.

Some years ago the EEC did a survey of the value systems of all the member states and one surprising result was that the Irish put poverty very high on the list of things they most valued for their children. No other nation came up with that one. But I know precisely why people answered that way in the survey. Knowing the value of money, and really appreciating things, only comes when they have been hard to achieve. We, as a nation, do have a pessimistic gut feeling that 'easy come easy go' is one of the truisms of life. We feel, therefore, if our children have to struggle a little they will be all the better for it, and their prosperity is earned. We feel that a good standard of living should be hard-earned, not just given.

And our children most decidedly have it a lot easier than we, who farmed pre-common market. All our generation had so little in the 50s that when affluence of a sort came for dairy farmers with the Common Market we all had that awful feeling that it was not going to last. And that fear is at the root of much of our unease now. Our generation can't really believe that things have improved so much and the worry is always there that the whole thing may blow up in all our faces. We know that we could cope again if that happened but we doubt very much if this soft new generation could. Of course, we have absolutely no proof that this is so. It is just a gut reaction of ours, really without rhyme or reason.

I can imagine how cross all our respective children would have been if they had overheard us parents talking the way we were that night. The old feel that the young do not make provision for the inevitable rainy day and the young feel that nobody gets anywhere without taking a few risks and anyway everybody gets only one life to lead, so why not enjoy things now. Our main concern at their age was sheer survival.

Our generation always prepared for the future, and dare I say that we are all ever so slightly jealous that our children now have all they have, mainly as a result of us stinting ourselves when we were their age. While we say that we do not really begrudge it to them, I wonder if this in fact is true. Do we just cloak our begrudery by feeling and saying that they lack any appreciation of what we went through just so that they could be so well off?

None of us went anywhere or did anything when our children were young and undergoing education. But this generation grew up in affluent times and it shows. They do seem to want to have their cake and eat it too. They are quite prepared to go into debt for what the older generation consider non-essentials or 'dead money', on the assumption that things are going to get better and not worse. They see no reason whatsoever why they should not have things as good, or even better, than their urban counterparts.

We were precisely seventeen years married before we did anything with the old house here. Every penny we earned and borrowed went into the farm and cows. The farm was a sponge that kept soaking up everything. Which, with hindsight, was a very good thing since it meant that we finished up with a reasonable milk quota, and the sons were able to expand when they joined us in farming. I well knew the craving to be able to make big changes in the very fabric of the house here and have a fitted kitchen, a bedroom with a bathroom *en suite*, and all the rest of it. Which I did acheive, eventually, nearly twenty years later.

However, I was very mad when one of the visiting relations on Eoin's side passed the comment that it was all very nice, but it wasn't the old home any more with all the modern changes. That dislike of any innovation must come with advancing age, because our first reaction to Eoin Óg's mobile phone was all wrong. It has since proved to be one of the best things that ever came into the place. And it doesn't cost the earth either. Eoin Óg has it on what is called the personal service system in which it costs him little more than the rent if he confines his outgoing calls to off-peak hours and uses it mainly to receive incoming calls. Then the callers have to pay the extra charge, not us, so that's all right. And I don't know how often it has spared us bother, personally. Having the phone at his hip, no matter where he is, anybody can contact him, whatever the reason. And the reasons have varied from lost lorrymen looking for directions to Eoin having a heifer in trouble calving and being able to ring up that son to come home quickly, which saved that calf and a lot of wear and tear on our nerves. If we are to get cute, from now on, instead of trying to deal ourselves with the day-to-day emergencies that arise, we should just take advantage of that mobile phone on our son's hip, and always call for help.

There is no doubt but that one generation's luxury is another's necessity, so we may as well get in on the act as well. And isn't it a good thing that things are generally improving for farmers? So why am I still waiting for the other boot to drop? (1995)

Calves & Civil War politics

The first calf of the new calving season is here already, now that we have switched to an autumn calving herd. The calf is small, a bull, and a few weeks premature. But it is quite hardy for all that. Sputnik, Lisa has called it, God knows why. She, however, is the one who has the perfect right to call it whatever she wishes, since she is the one who is feeding it four times a day so that it will survive.

Last night, as I was settling down for my first sleep, I heard the back door bang, and I knew she was headed for the calf shed: she had said she would feed it yet again the very last thing. Now whether she got up to it in the middle of the night as well, I'm not sure. But I wouldn't put it past her. She takes incredible care of the baby calves. In fact they bring out a very strong maternal instinct in her, but of course I daren't say that out loud.

I'd prefer her to be all about the calves anyway, than the other latest additions to the menagarie here. My young pair arrived home one day during the week with two potbellied black Vietnamese pigs. I kid you not. They are incredibly ugly things. Lisa has named them Itchy and Scratchy, for obvious reasons. 'You didn't get those for their beauty anyway!' commented a passing neighbour, when he passed them on the road. The wretched things couldn't be kept out of my garden for the first week and I needn't tell you the good that did for family harmony! Now they have one of the horses' stables, with a run out to the horses' field. And all I will say is that the horses at least are beautiful to look at.

Our little calf is a beauty too, for all that he is premature. So if it dies it is just as well he is a bull. An A.I. heifer might be worth the rearing. I really put the cat among the pigeons when I told Lisa she was only keeping it alive for the slaughter scheme, the Herod policy, when that scheme is up and running here as well as in the North. I think I also asked if Sputnik would ever pay for all the milk it would drink in the meantime, but that was really naughty of me.

I was probably being naughty too, when at a wedding party during the week I brought the conversation around to the slaughter policy of calves in the 1930s, which I always heard came about as the result of the economic war. But I could get very little information on it, and what information I got was quite contradictory. There was major commotion, however, at our table, and all over calves and politics because I asked what really happened back in the time of the economic war.

One person told a horrific tale of a pet calf which his Dad, who was then a child, had been allowed to keep secretly when all its companions were killed. But a neighbour, 'a blind follower of de Valera', explained this wedding guest, thus showing his political hand, informed the authorities. Then, again according to him, an official came out, killed the calf in front of the child, and what's more, refused to pay the compensation of the measly half-crown which was all they were to get anyway for each hide.

However, this man was hardly finished his tale when an older man at the table flatly said 'Nonsense! There was never any such thing as a calf slaughter policy... and anyway it was ten shillings per calf. And that is more than it would ever have made as a dropped calf at the fair in those days!'

The contradictory nature of that statement quite passed me by as I hastily got in my tuppence-worth about my father telling the story of how they themselves had to kill the calves, thread the tongues on a piece of wire and personally take them to the barracks to collect the bounty. But that was just my memory and not necessarily fact either. We were all going on anecdotal evidence of our parents only, since none of us were actually old enough to remember those times.

Eoin wasn't at my table. I then commented, harmlessly enough as I thought, that although ten years older than I, he has no memory whatsoever of ever hearing anything much about the effects of the economic war on farming, or the calf slaughter policy. And it was then that the naked politics came to the fore. To my utter amazement, and with a certain shock, I was verbally attacked by one gentleman for evidently having 'corrupted a good Fianna Fáil household... and that I myself was nothing but a Fine Gael git anyway!'

There was momentary silence at the table, before all hell broke loose. In the middle of the hubbub, for and against, I said that, for his information, during my lifetime I had voted for four different parties, naming them out, so how could it be known what I was, or what Eoin was either, for that matter? That will show you how naive I am politically, and what chance the North has when a simple comment about the forthcoming calf slaughter policy here brought old Civil War animosities tumbling about my head. I'll admit that some of the people concerned were even older than I. However, some of my own age group, or even considerably younger, were also quite vitriolic in their political opinions.

I always say that I love a good argument, which is what you may call what ensued, before we exhausted the topic and got on to more innocuous topics. Some days later, talking to my hostess, I idly commented about what a lively debate had arisen at our table, what fun it was, and said, in a throwaway remark, that I thought I had won the argument with that particular gentleman anyway.

'That's funny,' she replied. 'He has just said precisely the same thing about you!' So doesn't it just go to show that there are some arguments that nobody wins? And I still don't know the full story. Somebody, and possibly everybody, must be at least half wrong. But I do wonder what will future generations say, in retrospect, about the wholesale slaughter of calves predicted for all of Europe, including Ireland in the season to come.

Poor old Sputnik is safe, as are most of our calves, because our calving season now commences in autumn. By the time the bureaucracy is in place here my bet is that we will be well into spring. Sputnik will either be too old to qualify, or dead anyway of natural causes by then. (1996)

Is it good news or bad news?

Eoin came over to me in the plastic tunnel today to tell me that he was almost certain that the mare was in foal after all. 'Is that good news or bad news?' I innocently asked, uncertain of how to react. But as he turned on his heel and stormed out, capsizing a seed tray of just-sown sweet peas and three pots of cuttings in the process, muttering as he went, I knew that I had said the wrong thing once more. I just do not understand the horse business.

So, only stopping to repair the damage he had done, I made my way after him to make amends. And there he was, with his arm around his brood mare Corcaigh, talking to her. The two-year-old had her head resting on his shoulder. The foal was nuzzling him for his share of the petting. And the other ladies were trying to get in on the act as well.

I dare say he was telling them all what his awful woman of a wife had said. And, quite honestly, when it comes to those horses I am forever putting my big foot in it, no matter how supportive I try to be. I just don't see the attraction of the things. All I do see is the grass they eat, the stable room they require each winter, and the regular bills arriving for service fees and the like.

And now, if foal number five is truly on the way, that bill for the service fee to Supreme Leader cannot be ignored. Each time I saw it with the rest of the bills I have been repeating my mantra of 'no foal, no fee'. And there was, as well, all that talk of leaving her barren for the year when she did not hold to that first service and after there was some cock-up about the vet not coming to scan her when requested, so that she missed the next heat period as well.

So the added expense of another scan was not undertaken after the next service, not only because of the cock-up, but because the year was much too far advanced by now. Horses are far harder than cows to get to reproduce within the twelve-month period. Their gestation period is eleven months. And, if our lady is anything to go by, they think nothing whatsoever of going two, three and even four weeks over their time on top of that. So, if Corcaigh wasn't in foal this time, all the horsey men concurred, it would be better to skip this year so as to have her served real early in 1997.

Though, whatever about all that, this year's foal is going to need a new stable when weaned. And, talking of stables, one of the existing stables is already occupied by Itchy and Scratchy, those pot-bellied pigs of Lisa's. So any one of these days now, I can see a head-to-head occurring when a really cold and wet spell occurs and something has to stay out of doors.

Although, come to think of it, perhaps they could share stables quite happily. Corcaigh, in her racing days, was one of those peculiar horses who always needed a companion, to prevent her sweating up with tension in strange surroundings. So, the trainer gave her a goat – a white goat – which shared her box at home and travelled to each and every race meeting with her.

The only trouble was, at race meetings, when Corcaigh was all saddled up and ready to go, the goat knew quite well that she was going to be left behind and would start bleating long before the stable lads took away the horse. Then, given half a chance, that goat would be out the stable door like a piece of greased lightning. And then the job was to catch her.

There was one famous day in Roscommon, while Corcaigh was doing her thing in the parade ring, that somehow or other that goat got loose. Eoin, with all the rest of the racing syndicate members, was enjoying the importance of being in the parade ring, as co-owners, and being seen by all outside the rails as apparently giving last minute instructions to their trainer and jockey. Their gravitas, however, was totally disturbed when the goat came bounding in, bleating loudly, the stable hands in close pursuit, as she hopped up so close to her stable companion, and thus the massed owners, that she just could not be ignored.

They all tried to lay hands on her. But she easily outwitted them and did her own lap of honour of the parade ring with all those men fast in pursuit. A cheer went up from the onlookers and Eoin, for one, was deeply mortified. Think of his mortification, however, were one of his darlings to develop a fixation on Itchy or Scratchy, if, for lack of room, they were all stabled together. Then those pigs would have to go into training too. I could just see Itchy and Scratchy, in all their black, potbellied ugliness, insisting on joining the horses, and of course the proud owner, in the parade ring. The mind boggles at the thought!

But it is others, hopefully, and not Eoin, who will be preening themselves in that parade ring that day, if Corcaigh's first born is sold at the sales. But I did not say any of this to Eoin, as he testily explained to me that the sire is only the best horse at stud this year in Ireland. So how could it be bad news that Corcaigh was going to have a foal by this paragon. And any progeny should be really valuable with the dam having won those six races (including that one in Roscommon) and having been placed I don't know how many times... And if the first of the progeny could only make a name for herself by winning a race or two, not getting much for her would not be that important, since then he'll have no bother selling the rest of the mare's progeny. Extra noughts were being added to the imaginary cheques before the first one was even in his fist, as his enthusiasm grew wings.

Peace restored, I finally left him to his dreams, and I returned to my equally vainglorious dreams, over in the plastic tunnel, where I was potting on all those Abutilon plants I grew this spring from last year's home-saved seed. This particular strain of supposedly tender Abutilons I originally grew from seed, at least ten years ago, as potential houseplants. But some I planted out in the garden, while still in their pots, temporarily, to show off, before a garden walk. I never got around to bringing them back in, and some of them survived the winter, and each winter since. Many is the cutting of these five foot high shrubs, which they now are, I have given away. But then, after the heat of last summer they set copious seed. My dream is that perhaps, when they flower next year, I may have bred a winner... a totally new colour, or form, which would make my name...

I then found myself talking to my plants, just as Eoin had been talking to his horses, wondering what the Latin form of my name might be. Though, to be quite honest, Eoin has a much better chance of seeing his dreams with his horses come true some day in the future. Still and all, you never know. And, after today's little episode, despite the odds of breeding a significant new cultivar of Abutilons, I now have a better chance of having a plant called after me than a race horse! And I do have a strong claim there, you know, because the first-born filly arrived on my birthday. Also, when I tried both names out loud *Liz's Birthday* did run more easily off the tongue than did *Abutilon Kavanaghensis*! (1996)

OCTOBER

Professor Kavanagh's first night

The family are treating it as a huge joke, me going off to University to try for a BA degree by night. As I was heading off that first night, Eoin Óg and his girlfriend Lisa produced a going-to-college present for me – a clip-board for a 'Hiley Edukated Purson', full of coffee cup rings and juvenile jokes: for instance, 'why do cows lie down in the rain?' – the answer being, 'to keep each udder dry!'

I suppose I am stark staring mad, taking this on, three nights a week from seven to ten, plus the travelling time and the study? When people ask me why I am doing such a thing at this hour of my life, I have no convincing answer ready to reel off. I just say that I am doing this because I want to, or because it's a challenge, or just to keep the old brain ticking over. But basically, I think I am doing this, like so many other things in life, just because it seemed like a good idea at the time! I can't say that it is to improve my job prospects, or even to start a new career, because I have no notion of doing any such thing.

Lots of my fellow students, however, appear to have strong ideas along those lines, not that I have got to know that many of them yet. We are still at the stage of sizing each other up and wondering who is going to make the first move to strike up a conversation. And, as nobody seems particularly anxious to talk to me, one of the oldest students there, I find I have to make all the overtures. Then they appear glad enough to talk. But as I said, they are mostly disgustingly young. One young man just scraped in by the skin of his teeth, being twenty-one in December, or so he told me. There are no entrance qualifications, no points race for the night degree course, one must just be twenty-one by the first of January and be able to pay the fees. It is actually a great opportunity for anybody who missed out on University places first time round.

I am sitting in a different place each night, which helps me to meet people, although most of the others seem to stay in the one place. I, however, had a mighty good reason to change my seat after what happened to me there on my very first night. You see, I had treated myself to a present, the day before, of a really neat little tape-recorder, which I thought was quite bright of me. I then would not have to depend on my failing memory. I cannot but be very well aware of my loss of total recall with the doing off I get from the family from time to time, especially about forgetting or mixing up telephone messages, if I don't write them all down on the spot. I have to make shopping lists too, or I come away without the very thing that made me go shopping in the first place. But then again, as often as not, I forget to bring the list with me!

My brilliant master plan was to tape all my lectures with my unobtrusive little tape-recorder, and if anybody made any objection, I'd get awfully deaf and old on the spot! I thought it wiser not to look for permission, even on those grounds. If there is one thing I have learned in life it is never to look for permission for anything: just go ahead and do it! Asking permission only draws attention to what one is doing, and gives somebody in authority the chance to say no. My recording yoke is so small and silent that, if I was discreet, I thought that no one, not even my fellow students, would be any the wiser. Why should I give away any advantage too easily anyway? I am going to need every leverage going.

Now, I must admit that I am absolutely hopeless with any modern gadget. I have never succeeded in putting my digital watch forward, or back, the hour. I have never once used the timer on my electric cooker so as to have the meal cooked when I got home. The timer on the video recorder is even more of a mystery to me. Play, record, fast forward and re-wind are the only buttons I have ever used, and even then I manage to make mistakes. So, bearing all this in mind, I got my youngest to give me a lesson on using my new tape-recorder. Eoin Óg gave me a lesson all right, and a fair old teasing too, while he was at it, testing out the machine.

'Here comes Professor Kavanagh. Now what is Professor Liz Kavanagh going to lecture on tonight?... The wonderful works of a wheelbarrow? Or could it be...' He went on and on, ably assisted by Eoin, my dearly beloved! You know you'd badly need a good thick skin around here! I am left with no illusions whatsoever about my little weaknesses. But what matter. My little machine worked. It had picked up every word of the teasing, crystal clear, right the full length of the kitchen.

So now I need only write down anything written on the blackboard. My full attention could be given to the lecture. Time enough to make all the notes I might need, on replay, at home. Or I could even play the whole lecture over and over, while feeding the calves, working in the garden, or even doing my bit of housework. I'd surely get to understand, and retain, the lectures that way. I am absolutely determined I must never get left behind, or give it to say I took on too much at my age!

I was quite ridiculously nervous going in to the first lecture, not knowing what to expect. My subjects are English, Sociology and Applied Psychology. The first night was Applied Psychology, which is the subject I think I will like best. I went in early, but the lecture hall was practically full even then, but mostly at the back. That was no problem to me as I wanted a front seat, to be as near as possible for my recorder. Our lecturer came in shortly after, did his introducing bit, and then started into the lecture proper. Then

I switched on my tape recorder, or so I thought. But floating loud, and horribly clearly, came Eoin Óg's voice:

'...Here comes Professor Kavanagh... Now what is Professor Kavanagh going to lecture on tonight?.. The wonderful works of a wheelbarrow?... Or could it be the art of housekeeping, yes, the removal of spiders...'

It was worse than awful. Somehow I had pressed the wrong button. I had pressed play instead of record. And in the fuss I just couldn't seem to locate the stop button. I did everything, yet Eoin Óg's mocking voice boomed on... The lecturer stopped. A titter arose in the hall. Everybody, I presumed, was looking at me and I nearly died of embarrassment. I didn't know whether to sit on the infernal thing to muffle the sound or to run out of the hall and never again come back. Finally, fortunately, I found the stop button, and to his credit the lecturer carried on without comment and so the titter died away. But I am not over the shock of it yet. Not only did I get no recording made that night, I got precious few notes down either.

Then, when we finally got out, early, as it was our first night, I scooted away to my car as fast as I possibly could, looking neither to the left nor to the right of me as I went. I just couldn't face talking to anybody, that night anyway. Then, of all things, when I got to my car didn't I find that I had left the car lights full on, in my rush and fuss to be in early. Of course the battery was quite dead. There wasn't even a kick in it. Talk about the last straw! However, not having any choice in the matter, I gathered myself together and stopped a group of passing young men for assistance, explaining what I had done. They were great, even to the extent of taking the wheel from me, and push starting it in no time flat. I got back in my car, thanking them most effusively, and gratefully drove off. Then, through the still open window, came 'Safe home so, Professor Kavanagh...' the male voice full of laughter and his companions doubled up at his wit.

I died all over again. But thank God the car did not as I accelerated away. Trust me, out of the whole campus, to pick men from the psychology class I had just left, for help. What a fiasco of a first night in my attempt to become a 'Hiley Edukated Pursun'! (1991)

What a difference a wife makes

I discovered something this week. It is only in my own kitchen that my plate weighs a ton. I have always known that my plate must weigh at least that, because, in all the years they lived with me here, no son of mine has ever been able to lift my plate off the table and put it into the dishwasher. Then, this week, Eoin and I had two little parties given for us, for our anniversary, and on both occasions my sons managed to lift my plate, and all by themselves too, and got it safely into their dishwashers.

We were invited to dinner by the sons and their wives. Now this is not that unusual a thing. They do feed us from time to time, but not so formally, one night after the other. Both decided, separately I think, that we needed cheering up a bit, which was true enough, so they each put on a special meal for us. We had also gone out to a hotel to eat on the anniversary proper, and so this week I am suffering the consequences, as my waistband shows. But sure, I will never be thirty-six years married again. And what changes those years have brought, in us and our sons, especially this past year, with the last of them now married.

The biggest change in them I must say is in their own kitchens, in comparison to their behaviour as single men in mine. In their own kitchens they can lift just about anything, and do much else besides. They clear tables to the manner born. They serve food, and, indeed, take their turns at cooking it as well. In fact they are examples now to all of their sex, married or single.

And, God forgive me, I do take a wicked pleasure whenever they are feeding me at their tables, at becoming quite helpless myself in my turn. I don't lift a hand to help, only let them have at it. I just sit there and let them serve me. And my plate no longer weighs a ton, it seems, it gets whisked away so easily. What a difference a wife makes.

Now my sons were never the helpless kind about the house. They all learned to cook. As one of them succinctly put it during one fault-finding session, it was either that or starve! I also well remember one comment from my own mother to me. 'I've often noticed how bad mothers make good children!' she had observed one day out of the blue. I don't think she meant to make it sound as it did, a reflection on me. However, she had been commenting on how great her grandsons were, getting themselves off to school by themselves. Perhaps my conscience must have been a little bit on the tender side, because I was quick to defend the fact that my sons had to make their own lunches going off to school of a morning. I was, after all, outside with cows and calves. They were more than capable at this stage of buttering a bit of bread for themselves, anyway, and filling up their own milk bottles. Still, they did tell me, years later, that they used to be the only ones in school with doorsteps of bread, while all the others had beautifully and neatly made sandwiches, with the crusts off. Now there could be a little bit of exaggeration there, I hope, but the point they were making was valid enough.

Nevertheless, their wives now should thank me for husbands who are able to do every single thing for themselves, and for their wives too, if, and when, they have a mind to. Though I do hear from other parents about their sons who never had to do a hand's turn in the home, all their young lives, simply because they had such 'good' mothers. Nevertheless, once married, those sons, who once disdained any kind of housework, are now only too delighted to demonstrate their new skills in their own homes. Strange to relate, not all mothers really like this state of affairs. Some think, with rueful pity, of their poor darlings having, as they put it, to turn in and help in the kitchen, after their proper day's work!

The odd thing some of us mothers forget, and fathers too, is that doing things for yourself, and in your very own home, is a completely different matter from doing the same things in your parents' house. I, for instance, always swore growing up, when I had to do all kinds of hated farm work, from milking cows to thinning turnips, that I was never, ever, going to marry a farmer. And, even if I did, I would not be seen dead outside my own back door, at any kind of farm work, ever! I remember even telling Eoin as much, when he said that it was important to him too that his wife would not be required to do farm work.

And then look what happened! I got involved in everything: sheep and lambs, cows and calves, pigs and bonhams, tractor work and mucking-out work. It almost became the case that I was not to be seen dead inside my own back door when I grew to thoroughly dislike the endless monotony of housework. The house was always neglected in favour of the farm and garden.

Nevertheless, sitting there in my sons' kitchens, both nights, quite relaxed through being deliberately lazy, or maybe because it was the wine talking, I once again made the mistake of not having the zip for my lips fully fastened. I commented on the change in my sons.

And immediately I started hearing that echo once more in my head, as I so often do of late. This is when I have just said something, and then realise that I have heard those exact words, in just that same tone of voice, somewhere before, many years ago. Then I knew I was hearing them issuing from my mother's mouth. Her voice is the echo to mine. And this gives me something of a shock of recognition every single time I hear it.

Now that does not stop me in full flow, of course. I just carry on. But I am horribly aware of that echo there in the back of my head all the same. I wonder was my mother aware too of an echo in her head from her own mother, who echoed in turn her mother, back through the generations. It is like the reflections of reflections between two mirrors, going on and on for ever, back through those generations, always there, even though progressively smaller and fainter until no longer discernible to our senses.

Now, I can give all sorts of good advice, for all the good that will do, to stop that inevitable echo. Remember that no matter how often the phrase 'I told you so' comes to a mother's lips, it never does to utter it. Just recall how you felt yourself when it was said to you long and merry ago, probably by your own mother in similar circumstances. Of course, every young girl swears that when they get to their mother's age, no matter what, they are never, ever, going to say those sort of things to their children. But you can take it from me that, despite yourself, you will some day hear just that echo in the back of your head and there is not a damn thing you can do about it.

My poor 'neglected' sons, some day, will also hear the echo of my voice coming out of their mouths! I await that day with pleasure, which will be mine alone, as were my pleasures of wilful idleness, this week, in their kitchens, while I watched them clear up after me. (1993)

Liz presses the flesh

'You ease my pain for me,' said he to me. 'I lost a cow to tetany too that same week as you did, so I felt better knowing that I wasn't the only one!'

Suddenly it was all right. I wasn't all kinds of a fool to have gone to the Ploughing Match, which was how I had felt up to that very minute. It was my first ever public appearance, last Wednesday, and I was scared stiff of the whole affair. I thought I would be standing there, like a fool, and nobody would want to talk to me. So why did I do it?

Umpteen people asked me why I had chosen to break cover, after all these years, and the simple reason I gave was that Mairead McGuinness, our editor and my boss, was the first person ever to ask me to do more than send in my weekly copy. And I said yes because it seemed like a good idea at the time, the main reason why I seem to do most things. For those who probed further, however, I gave the reason that I thought, perhaps, nobody wanted me much, any longer, writing for the *Journal*, that I had run my course and my time was up. So this was one way I could find out, by actually meeting people from all over Ireland.

Immediately I said that, however, I was sorry that I had opened my big mouth, because it sounded as if I was fishing for compliments. Indeed, several times during the day I was sorry I opened my mouth, that I hadn't made the right answer to a person's problems, or that I had revealed too much of myself so that they wouldn't, couldn't, really like me. We all like to be liked, you know, however much we may pretend to be strong-minded enough to take no notice of what other people think.

I know now too, after my few days, that flattery can go to a person's head so easily. It was marvellous. I was on a decided high with everybody telling me how much they enjoyed reading my column. I wasn't just standing there like a fool: in fact I was surrounded by complimentary people a lot of the time. But a younger and wiser head told me that people only say the nice things to your face. However, there were complaints too. I was asked, please, never again to address God as 'the Man upstairs': I should always give due respect to God our creator. All I can say is point taken. I would hate to think I would offend people's religious sensibilities by being even slightly flippant. But sometimes country people have a lovely comfortable familiarity with their God, as part and parcel of their daily lives, which may sound disrespectful, even satirical, to others.

Another man told me that he didn't like my glasses, why didn't I change them and improve my image? So I tried on his glasses to see what difference those would make. I could not, however, see anything at all clearly out of his glasses. You know we all see the world through our own eyes, regardless of what glasses we don, and I have lived long enough to know that there is always more than one way of looking at things. I write as a dairy farmer principally, and this was a complaint too:

'Wouldn't you once in a while give the old cows a rest! The smell of milk rises up and sickens me once I sit down at my ease to open the *Journal* after my tea, each Friday night. Everything in it is for the dairyman. And you are just as bad at times, with your cows, your calves and the price of milk. Nobody takes the slightest notice of the man like myself growing potatoes and vegetables: 'tis only recently they started putting in market prices for potatoes, but vegetables still don't figure.'

What could I say to that, but tell him to write a letter to the editor stating his case. But at least he believed I was real when I wrote about cows and calves and those dreaded TB tests. That was more than the other man, who paid me the very dubious compliment of saying I didn't look the part of a farmer's wife at all, and who really wrote the weekly articles? I showed him my hands as proof that I really am a farming wife. Eoin is really there, as are all the boys and my daughters-in-law and my dearly loved Michaella. As to the two young and very pretty girls who wanted to know were all my sons taken, I had to say that I was afraid they are. They said they would love to have me as a mother-in-law, so what nicer compliment could any woman hope for?

More than one older woman, however, said that my daughters-in-law must really detest me, that it wasn't fair to make my poor relationship with them so public. That staggered me because I thought that the fact that I wrote about them showed the exact opposite. If they were a trouble to me, or I to them, I would say precisely nothing about them. My silence could be much more revealing than my speech, suffer and all as I may do for opening my big mouth occasionally: the intended meaning is not always the one taken. I think my daughters-in-law are great girls, not perfect by any means (only their husbands think that), but still I wouldn't swop them for any others that I know or hear about.

I also think I understand them far better than they do themselves, at times, because I too was once a daughter-in-law and I know from experience the difficulties of that, the most difficult of all relationships. My daughters-in-law won't and can't be expected to feel as I do until they have daughters-in-law themselves. And I will lay you any odds you like that they will, one day, consider me the best mother-in-law that ever drew breath, once I am safely under the ground!

Family relationships are a problem to such a lot of people it seems, from all I heard during my three-day stint at the Ploughing Match. But what is the magic answer? One thing that won't work, anyway, is everybody living too much on top of each other. As another man, a son-in-law this time, said to me, it is too much, after working all day with his father-in-law, to be expected to sit down and watch television all night with him as well. I couldn't agree more. Your own TV set, your own kitchen, car and front door are primary essentials for both generations.

By the way, people also told me they thought I was from Donegal, Kerry, somewhere in the Midlands, definitely from Wicklow way, and practically from every other county as well. 'Christ!' one man was overheard to say, leaving the tent. 'In all the years reading that woman I never knew she was such a close neighbour of my own!'

I had a great few days at the Ploughing Match. But when we got home, it was to discover we are to have a herd test next week. That quickly brought me back to earth with a bang. We escaped having it a long time, but our neighbours have just had second rounds and still more bad news everywhere. And me having just spent three days telling everybody how much I loved farming! I am already booked to go back to next year's Ploughing Match, so I am beginning to get nervous about that as well. It cannot possibly be as good the second time around. (1994)

No escape!

There was major commotion here this week. Michaella was sitting on my lap, as she is wont to do while I read to her, when, out of the corner of my eye, something moving caught my attention. No, it wasn't a mouse. It was something even smaller. Missy Michaella had head lice. I still feel my head getting itchy, even telling you about them. But Sara reacted much worse, almost as if I was blaming her for the lice on Michaella. God love her head. There hasn't been a child ever that did not get head lice at some stage or another in their career. And, as I hastened to reassure her, it is the children with the cleanest hair which the lice particularly target.

But an infestation of head lice is a hard thing for both parents to accept. I discovered head lice on Michaella's father in exactly the same circumstances many years ago, and all five of my sons were found to be badly infested that same afternoon. I went to the chemist on the spot, never mind the fact that I was due to go milking the cows that evening. Funny, isn't it, the things one remembers? As well as the lice-killing lotion I bought a fine comb, and for the rest of their childhoods I regularly used that fine comb on their heads.

The extraordinary thing is that head lice always seemed to develop in the autumn months. This somehow is the danger period, as I already knew to my cost. I was sent off to boarding school the September I was thirteen and to me it was a great adventure. However, a few days after I went there the whole class had to report to the Infirmary, immediately after lunch. There we all stood, in line, while this nun took out a fine comb and started to comb through our hair. I took not the slightest bit of notice since my mother had regularly done that with all my family. Each girl, as she was finished, was then allowed to leave and I assumed gathered outside for our walk, from lodge gate to lodge gate, which seemed to be the practice, immediately after lunch.

Then my turn came. The nun combed through my hair and told me to stand over there, in front of all the girls remaining. I did not take a lot of notice because the whys and wherefores of that school were a total mystery to me at the time, and, I presumed, to the rest of the newcomers as well. The only ones who were totally at ease were those who had come up through the prep school and knew the ropes. Those of us who had got our Primary Certs at our local national schools went straight into second year.

Standing apart, I soon noticed that those old hands at the game were sniggering and seemed to be looking pointedly at me. I was the only one standing on my own. And, as girl after girl was allowed go away, I finished up being the only one left in the room. Then I really got uncomfortable. But that was nothing to what I was soon feeling as the nun took me over to the sink and started in on washing my hair. And she started asking me pointed questions about did I have a mother, and finding out that I did, asking me if she washed my hair or had I to do it for myself, poor lamb.

Nobody had ever called me a lamb before, not to mind a poor lamb, so I laughed out loud, as much out of nerves as real amusement. Then, when asked why I was laughing I explained exactly why. This was a very big mistake. The poor nun decided I was mocking her, got very cross and told me what a dirty little girl I was with nits in my hair and how my mother was a disgrace to have let me come away to a decent school in that condition.

I can still feel the shock of that moment to this day. Nobody had ever, in all my life, criticised my mother in front of me. It was the most horrendous thing that could have happened, because up to then I really must have believed my mother was not alone invincible but quite incapable of doing anything wrong. Now here was a nun telling me that my mother was a disgrace and that I should therefore be ashamed both of her and for her.

But there was further shame waiting for me when I got out to join the rest of my class, who were impatiently waiting for me so that they could go for their walk. For the formal walks we had to proceed in little groups of three or four, in front of our accompanying class nun. I had quite enjoyed the walks up to this, making new friends and then being with the same two girls for every walk after the first day. We seemed to get on fine, with plenty in common to talk about.

But not this day. As I went to join them as usual, my hair still wet and plastered to my head with vile-smelling lotion, somebody hissed 'Crawly' at me and with a giggle those two girls turned their backs on me and joined up with another pair so that I could not tag along. We were strictly forbidden to walk either in twos or in anything more than fours.

I was left with no choice then but to try to tag onto the girls who were walking beside the nun. Favourites always got to walk beside the nun, and the misfits fitted themselves in as best they could on the sidelines. And so started my year of misery. The name 'Crawly' stuck for ages, as did the necessity to try to fit in with the misfits on the edges.

Yet I never told my mother of the real reason I was so unhappy my first year in that school. Somehow I couldn't. After what the nun had said it would have seemed like a direct criticism, even when I learned that, only a week after I was gone away to school, all the younger family members at home were found to have head lice as well. My mother was afraid of her life I might have them, she said to me, years later. 'But when you said nothing in your letters about that, I knew you had escaped.'

And, to this day, how I wish I had. (1994)

I only licked my lips

Michaella loves school with a passion which is absolutely lovely to see. She can't wait to go there each morning and rushes her mother out the door so as to be there ages before the time, for play. I even heard her mother, one night I was over visiting, threatening Michaella that if she wasn't good and didn't go to sleep fast she'd be kept at home from school next day! And you should have seen her scoot off to bed there and then. And there wasn't another word out of her that night. Sara told me that she often does that to get her to bed and it works a treat.

And I can't help thinking how lovely it is to be young now in comparison to when I was a child. I hated my national school, and one particular teacher with a passion, the bitterness of which has never died and is once again all stirred up inside me with the publicity on the Goldenbridge story. My old school is a ruin, but it still stands as a constant reminder to me of the very worst period of my life. How I, and many more, suffered there. The cold, the dirt, the stinking dry toilets, and the never-ending corporal punishment, gives me the horrors to this day. I really hated school with a passion.

When I was in the middle classes, so about ten years old, one day this woman teacher – I refuse to call her a lady teacher – told me straight out, as I was pulled to the front of the class, that she was going to slap me until I cried, for each missed spelling. One slap on the palm of the hand with her swinging stick, per missed spelling, was the usual thing anyway. And our spellings were examined every day of the week. I so well remember the dryness of the mouth that came with pure fear as one's turn, and the stick, approached along the line as we stood outside our desks. All the time I had spent the night before learning the page off, word by word, just went for naught as the dreaded moment arrived and it was a question of luck whether one got an easy or a hard word.

Anyway, this particular day when my turn came I licked my lips, nervously, so as to get some lubrication to speak. That was my downfall. I was grabbed by my hair, dragged out in front of the class and told that she would teach me to stick my tongue out at her. And so my ordeal began. Of course there was no way I would have dared to stick my tongue out at her. Children then were so cowed, so beaten into submission, that never, ever, did they dare give cheek in any form to a teacher.

Well, maybe total submission never comes about, even for a child, because the injustice of what was happening to me so affected me that I determined, no matter what she did, I was not going to cry. That was my only pitiful path of resistance. So the spellings started. And, believe it or not, I got the first six right. But she then selectively picked the hard words. So of course the inevitable happened. I missed one. Then she started in on me, right hand, left hand, right hand... as she went on to the pages we hadn't even covered as yet. She made the other children count out loud the number of slaps. At fifty-seven I still wasn't crying, so she used the stick on my legs, my head, my back, so totally out of control was she by then. I don't remember how it finished. But I did not cry. For the rest of my time with that teacher I remembered that fact whenever the stick came down on my tender flesh and it helped me to bear the pain. I had won, just that once, and that was vitally important to one helpless child.

Of course, with hindsight, I was just plain stupid. I should have cried, or even pretended to cry, and got my punishment over as quickly as possible. My older brother, and the brother next in line, were never punished by that teacher in quite the way I was. So something about me must have annoyed her greatly. When I went up to the top classes, to a male teacher, I was still slapped regularly, especially when the copybooks came back after corrections of our exercises, but I was never singled out. We all suffered equally, which, in a way, was not quite as bad.

Once we saw him coming into school in the morning with a bundle of copy books under his arm we knew we were for it. One by one he would go through them and it was a question then of how many slaps one got, since it was a slap per mistake. Never, no matter how hard one tried, could one escape a slap. Even if one's sums and spellings were all right, there was sure to be an ink blot, or crooked writing, or something else wrong. There was just no escape. That was the awful part of it. But his worst punishments were for any poor misfortunate who wasn't at Mass on a Sunday or Church holiday and he attended all Masses. And he also was severe on any girl who came to school with skirts above the knee or uncovered elbows.

So, personally, I think that truth in the Goldenbridge saga lies somewhere between the two opposing sets of memories. The spunky girls got badly treated. The nice, good girls who didn't buck the system got treated reasonably well. Those were tough times, make no mistake about that. Everybody had to conform. I, at least, escaped at three o'clock each day, which the poor children in Goldenbridge did not. But on escape, never once did I tell of my ill-treatment when I got home.

That to me is the really extraordinary part of my story because I am convinced that I would not have been beaten again at home. But the reign of terror worked so well that we kept our pain and misery hidden lest even worse befall us. I even remember explaining my cut and swollen hands, that awful day, by saying I fell in the school yard. Now it is too late to discover if that story was really believed at home or if parents too, in those days, were unable to make a difference once they had handed their children over to the 'tender care' of the schools, who were, after all, in *loco parentis*.

Those were not times of great communication between parents or teachers, or indeed between parents and children either. I remember being hugged and kissed by my mother only twice during my entire childhood. The second time was the awful night when she came home from the hospital, all dressed in black, and told us that Dadda was dead. The first time was one morning as I was standing on a chair, reaching up to get a piece of twine off the big ball of binder twine that was kept on top of the dresser. I was crying quietly to myself because I knew I did not know my Irish spellings for that day. Mamma came into the kitchen, saw me and put her arms around me and both hugged and kissed me. She must have been going to town, because, to this day, when I think of that little girl, reaching up both arms to the top of the high dresser, I can still smell the combination of Ponds vanishing cream and pinkish face powder which my mother always wore when she was going out anywhere. Strange that that comforting smell and the noxious smells of the old school house are inextricably linked in my memory. (1996)

Hallowe'en doings

What a beautiful October it has proved to be after all the rains of summer. I know the best of it is over, or so the weather men are telling us, but I am enjoying this Indian summer. I don't think that the garden was ever lovelier for the time of the year. It has a hectic flush on it as though it too knows that time is short: winter will soon bring all to naught. The autumn foliage was never better. Those fallen leaves and the dahlias, Michaelmas daisies, alstroemerias, kaffir lilies, etc. are all sprawled and intermingled all over the place, but it all does make a wonderful and glorious sight.

So why did I spend this past week cleaning and planting when I should just be enjoying the garden instead of worrying about what is not done, and still frantically trying to catch up? Thoughts cross my mind about how winter will bring all to naught for me too as well as for the flowers and leaves. No real point in dead-heading or tidying them up now. And is there really any point in my keeping up such a big garden either? Such are the wise thoughts of autumn, doubtless to be forgotten once more in the joys of spring.

And autumn is nearly over. Shopping this week, I noticed the place full of Hallowe'en displays and mothers being harassed by children to buy them some of those vampire masks and cloaks and things. Women were also stocking up with fruit and nuts and sweets for the children calling to the door on the night, or so one told me when we started to chat in the check-out queue. Now is that just a town custom? No child ever called here on Hallowe'en night!

There was nothing whatsoever like that when we were young. We had our customs all right but they were strictly in the house. Well, nearly in the house, because there was that excited going out in the dark to the field by the house, to pull up a cabbage stump to bring it in. The way that the earth fell on the floor then was supposed to tell us something, which we were told we were too young yet to understand. And there were other games played in the kitchen too, of which my mother disapproved, and lots of ghost stories told, and when they started late on Hallowe'en night we were always sent off to bed, and she and my father left the kitchen.

It was such a different time. Every farmer's house had men living in and a servant girl who milked cows, and did all other kinds of farm work as well as housework. The statistics of the time prove that only one in three women working on farms were the wives of the landowners. Life was so hard for these servant girls that it is no wonder they all preferred to take the boat to England than work for farmers. But that is another story. My big regret now is that I never questioned my mother on precisely what were those games going on, on Hallowe'en night in my home, when I was very young, and get the full details of why she disapproved and hushed us off to bed.

I remember, of course, the fun of ducking for apples in the great big tub that was normally used for washing the clothes on a Monday morning. Apples were also strung from the beams where the salted bacon hung, and those we tried to bite, with much laughing and jostling and our hands behind our backs. My father would stick pennies and the occasional silver sixpence in some of the apples in the tub and the thing was to bite that particular one and bring it out in your mouth, and get to keep the money. There were tears too, tears of frustration at the impossibility of being the one to get the apple with the silver sixpence. It took me years to learn that the only way was to take a deep breath and then take the apple down to the bottom of the tub and bone it there. And each time I did that there was war with my mother because I had long hair and getting your hair wet was considered the surest way to pneumonia. Hair was washed infrequently and with great care. Do you remember that jug of cold water always poured over, the very last thing, to prevent you somehow catching a cold? And now I see my daughters-in-law washing their hair at least once every day and just letting it dry naturally. Times sure do change.

We really half-believed that if we peeled an apple completely, without breaking the peel at all, and then threw it over our shoulders, on landing it would form the initial of the one we were destined to marry. But even worse was the routine, at precisely midnight, when with no other light on in the room, only the firelight, one looked into a mirror. Then one was sure to see the face of one's future mate looking in over one's shoulder. How I longed to do that, but of course we were never allowed up to midnight. But lights were turned down really low so that we could all try it before going to bed, and be scared half silly. One night I took a candle and went out into the hall to look in the mirror there, all by myself. And I nearly died with fright when I really did see a face looking over my shoulder! But it was only my brother who had spotted me leaving. There was a fight on the spot and we were both sent to bed.

My bedroom was over the kitchen and the fun used to go on below, it seemed, all night. Of course Hallowe'en is really a pagan festival, which the church took over and tamed down with its Feast of All Saints. And with hindsight I now know that some of the games played had decided sexual connotations. And I am not talking about the brack with its symbols for wife-beating and marriage and such. I never got fully straight in my head that Hallowe'en night I went out on my own to pull a cabbage stump for myself and saw more than I bargained for. (1994)

NOVEMBER

The bet that the sheds won't be ready on time

There is a bet down in this place at the moment. Well, actually it has been down since August, the day that none of them seemed to be too busy in themselves, so I suggested that maybe it might be a good idea to start in on the winter quarters for the animals!

'Time enough for that, Mom!' they choroused, almost in unison, and in quite annoyed tones as well. That needled me and once more the rot set in, with me trying to get them to accept my opinion, and they determined that whatever I said, right or wrong, had to be wrong.

I should have known better, of course. I've been long enough, God knows, at the game. Because it is a sort of a game that we play, wittingly or unwittingly. If I want anything done I can never come out baldly with it. I must somehow contrive that the idea comes from one of my menfolk in the first place – by planting the seed well in advance – or else taking an entirely different tack.

That was my mistake this week. I really should have said something like 'Will you all ever come and paint the windows upstairs for me, and the chutes on the house as well, while they are all nice and dry, and you have some little bit of time to spare? Next month I know you will be fully occupied in getting all the sheds ready for the winter – but sure there's plenty of time for that!'

Then I can guarantee you that the sheds would have become their number one priority, and the more I'd insist that there was plenty of time to tackle them, the more urgent that job would become. However, there is no point in talking like that now. I didn't and that's that. Instead, I compounded my mistake by reminding them of last year, and the year before, and probably the year before that as well, when the cows were badly cutting up the fields and just could not come in because of some building or repair work that wasn't quite finished.

And even if the weather stays fine, for every week we leave the animals out too late into November, we lose up to three weeks at the other end, when fresh spring grass is much more valuable to freshly calved cows. Grass is like ourselves. It needs an overcoat to protect it from the elements in the winter-time. So, if we eat off that protective coat in late November and December, we pay the price in the spring, when the cows respond so well to early grazing with increased milk in the bulk tank. The uptake of the nitrogen dressing is also much more effective if there is some length in the grass to utilise it, and the boys know that as well as we do.

'Wasn't it our idea getting that nitrogen out before Christmas last year, and look at the great early grass we had this year?' Eoin Óg retorted crossly, with some justification. That, they tell me anyway, is the most annoying of the many annoying things I do, pointing out the obvious.

Anyway one cross word led to another that August day, the culmination of which was one of my sons saying that he'd bet me anything I'd like that this would be the year that they'd just open the gates, with every wire hanging, and every gate in place in the yards... 'And the new cubicles finished, and all the holes in the concrete repaired?' I interjected, scenting an easy victory. 'Done,' said he. 'Twenty pounds says that everything will be ready by the second Monday in November.'

I told him I'd bet him a hundred pounds on that if he liked, but he backed off that figure. Another one of my more annoying habits, as they once also told me in a rare moment of mutual understanding, is of being right much too often for comfort. They still don't realise that I only bet on what I know are sure things, from either long experience or else insider knowledge. Experience has told me that never once, in well nigh thirty years of farming, has everything been ready in time for the winter, either here or on friends' or neighbouring farms. And, as well as that, I had just been talking to our builder, who told me that he is up the walls at the moment building for farmers.

'And they are all wanting everything as of yesterday...' he complained, explaining how he was concentrating on silage and slurry pits and things like that and leaving what wasn't immediately urgent to wait, as he classified our new cubicle house. Dan has put in the world and all of slurry pits and waste water systems, he explained, because the county council was now breathing down a lot more necks than ours!

And then Dan said something which was very true, but which you rarely hear anyone not in farming admit. He said that it is always the same: whenever the farmers have money everybody has money, because they always spread it around. He personally had never had such a good year. The building trade on the whole has been so good that he just can't get concrete lorries to deliver enough, or on time, as they do not seem to be able to manufacture it fast enough for the demand.

And it is the same in every line. Every dairy farmer around, like us, is doing some capital work and so everybody, like my builder friend, is benefiting to a greater or lesser extent, be it the young people getting jobs, or the local shops and pubs where they spend their money. Plus, of course, the substantial slice that goes back to the government through PAYE, PRSI, VAT or the good old excise duties. However, it would be even more painful for the farmer, who earned that money in the first place, to hand it over to the government through straightforward income tax.

It has been a very good year for us dairy farmers. There is no denying that, with milk freely making over £1 a gallon. Did we ever think we'd live to see the day? The only problem, of course, is that with the quota system we cannot take full advantage of this. We are only allowed to produce so much and nowhere near as much as we would like to, or indeed are capable of doing. Just think of the money that would go around and around then!

And around and around it would go. The apocryphal story is told of the two men, one of whom was a farmer, who shared the biggest lottery prize ever. The first man, when interviewed, said that he was going to buy a flash car, a new house, a long cruise holiday for all the family and then he'd put whatever was left over into the bank. The other winner, the farmer, on being interviewed, said quite simply that he was just going to put it into his farm. 'Are you going to buy more cattle, then?' questioned the interviewer. 'Aye,' said your man. 'Put up new sheds?' came the next question. 'Aye,' again came the answer. 'And what will you do then with the rest?' was the final question when the interviewer's knowledge of farming needs was exhausted. 'What rest?' came the question in reply. 'Don't you know quite well that I am going to put it into the farm 'till it's all gone, and I still won't have enough!'

And that is just about the way it is here. There is no amount of money that a farm can't soak up, no bother at all. So I did my calculations, and a new cubicle house is much better for us and our cows, not to mention our builder, than handing over most of it to the tax-man a few weeks ago. The building, although due to start last month, is still delayed according to my inside information. So it looks as if my twenty is quite safe. But come hail, rain or shine, I am not going to remind my sons of that until next Monday morning. Even under new management, it looks to me that Eoin's dream still won't come true of being able to merely open up the gates and let all the animals in when the weather turns bad in November. (1989)

Answering machines & accents

'What did the telephone ever do to you?' said Eoin to me this week, when he asked if I had returned those calls on the answering machine. I hadn't. I hate ringing up people for fear of bothering them at the wrong time; fearing they might not want to talk to me, even when I am returning their calls. So I know quite well that I do not have a logical relationship with that thing on the table. My sons, bless their cruel hearts, tell me that I also have what they call my 'telephone voice' a posher accent, when I am speaking on the phone!

Of course I denied categorically that I ever do any such thing, but the vote went against me. But then again, does anyone speak quite normally on the phone? Our speech is only fully normal when we have another person there in front of us to react with. Did you ever notice how much we all do react, with encouraging nods, eye contact, and inviting interjections, when being told a bit of news we want to hear? And the surest way to shut somebody up is not to react in any way to them, to keep a totally straight face and say nothing. Just try it and see what happens. We are trained to give the right reactions, the smiles, the nods, the eye contact, to people from babyhood. 'Look at me when I am talking to you' echoes through the generations, from parent to child and teacher to pupil.

That is the trouble with the phone. There is no one to look at, no signs to read. I avoid the phone like the plague when it is a silent lump just sitting there. But once let it ring and I am incapable of not answering it, regardless of how inconvenient it is at that precise moment. Eoin has a much more sensible attitude. He says that if they really want us they will phone back and he is able to go on with whatever it is he is doing, letting the answering machine pick up the message. The vast majority of the people who phone only want something anyway; there is nothing in it for us ever, only trouble. But I will get out of the bath, or leave my food, in order to get to that phone in time. I will tear into the house if I hear the shrill of that bell outside, and if the doorbell and the phone ring together the phone will always be answered first.

Which I know is all unutterably stupid, since the phone is connected to the answering machine and that will answer the thing for me. But I cannot break the habit of a lifetime, and anyway, often people will not leave a message on the answering machine. It kills me then not to know who phoned. I imagine all sorts of things. Could that be the deep breathing of someone with asthma, or a nastier form of deep breathing? Whose voice was it that said 'Blast it anyway!' before the phone on the other side was put down? And even worse are the half messages when somebody does not wait for the tone, when we know that they gave their phone number, but it is not on our machine. We rarely get answers to all these questions, even though sometimes we do get great amusement from overheard bits and scraps that people are not aware are being recorded.

Not long after we got the answering machine we got this message on the machine in a male voice, muttering away to himself, 'Cripes, they've got f...ing grand over there.' And it wasn't my voice he had heard inviting him to leave his message, either, but that of the son who later accused me of false grandeur on the phone. Why didn't I realise that until this very minute. Why do the best retorts always come too late?

Yesterday, I could have done without either the phone or the answering machine. I had gone out to calve a cow when I really should have been heading in to college for a lecture. And, with that job safely done and a message left for someone else to feed the calf since I was off, I found the light was winking on the answering machine. And on it Eoin was in full spate, damning and blasting, and hello-ing, before silence descended. He's in trouble somewhere, was my first thought, the jeep has broken down on his way back from the mart, and he thinks I am gone off to college and nobody inside. I gave out yards that he hadn't said where he was phoning from. Lisa wasn't yet back from her farming class. The milking was on. So there was no choice but for me to go and look for my dearly beloved. He became less and less my dearly beloved the further and further I went along the usual road he takes to the mart. And I finished up with some damning and blasting of my own when there was no trace of him all the way there. I prayed for every answering machine there ever was: without it he would just have kept phoning until he got a reply.

My prayers were even stronger when I got home to find the jeep safely in the yard and Eoin with his feet comfortably up before the fire. And he was cross with me!

'You never left a note to tell me what was happening...' he said accusingly. Whenever one of us is going away anywhere we always leave a note for the other, to tell where and report the latest. It keeps things running smoothly. So I waded into the attack about him not leaving a proper message on the machine.

'What message?' he interrupted. 'I left no message... I never phoned.'

So I took him and played back his message for him. But all he did was laugh. 'That must have been last night. Do you remember when the phone woke us up after midnight and I dropped it and finally when I got the thing right there was nobody there after all... I said a few choice words... The bloody machine must have been clicked in by then...'

So all was plain. The message was old. I had wasted so much time and energy. I had missed most of my first lecture. Eoin thought it all fierce funny. I didn't. But I'll tell you this much, whatever about me, nobody could accuse Eoin of putting on an accent when he recorded that message on the machine. Nobody could doubt his opinion on all the phones there ever were, either, or the people who use them. (1994)

A real family occasion

Do you know, it is a very dangerous thing to pontificate on any subject at all. Because the longer I live, the more and more I find I can change my mind on practically every subject under the sun. When circumstances change, my opinions change. It is as simple as that really, however strong-minded I may think I am. And the longer I live the more circumstances do change on me.

For years now I've said that I'd pay good money not to have to go to a wedding, any wedding, they being far more a penance than a pleasure to me. I had better not say that I find them totally boring. But I can only take so much of all that hanging about in freezing churchyards, with me in my finery, making inane chatter, while the photographer lines people up for yet another photograph of the happy couple and their close relations. It seems to be the photographers who totally dictate the pace of weddings these days, in that long-drawn-out period before the meal. If we had any sense we'd just skedaddle off to the bar and warmth.

When we finally get to eat, it can be very hard work making conversation sometimes, if you find yourself at a table where all the others appear to know each other, making you the odd one out. And then the music, if you can call it such, once the dancing starts, stops any further attempts at conversation, should one find congenial companionship.

Why must the volume be so high that it hurts? That, to me, is one of the great mysteries of modern-day living. I tell my lot here that they will be stone-deaf, long before they get to our age, if they don't cop themselves on. The first thing Eoin and I automatically do, when we get into a car after them, is to turn the volume of the car radio down before we ever dream of switching on the engine. Too long we have been literally blasted out of it once we touched the ignition key. And I don't know for the life of me how the cows can stand the radio in the milking parlour. It can be heard a full half a mile away.

Last month, at the Station Mass, a neighbour told me that the radio going on in our milking parlour is always the signal for herself and her husband to get up in the mornings, better than any alarm clock. I don't think she was being nasty about it, although of course you never can be sure. But this remark came after her commenting how regular the boys are to start the cows in the mornings, and she wished her son John would do the same.

I did not tell either of my sons that last part, the good part. I just had a vague hope that the thought of disturbing the neighbours might prove a more effective volume control than all my warnings of future deafness. They will remember my words, of course, but only when it is too late. That whole generation is going to be deaf, and/or suffer dreadful tinnitus, from not only night after night, during their road fever days, but now also day after day of endless noise, and all in the name of enjoyment.

But before I get back to my subject matter, from being side-tracked on the noise question, the radio left on continually works wonders in one place and that is the calf house. There the radio is never turned off, night or day. The result is that anybody can walk in there, at any time, and the calves take not the slightest bit of notice, so used are they to continual noise. You know yourself how calves normally behave, if they associate voices or footsteps with somebody coming to feed them; the noise of them bawling for milk would deafen you worse than any radio.

Now back to the subject of weddings. The wedding this week was a totally new experience for us, because we went there as a family: sons, daughters-in-law and special girlfriends. This is the first time that has ever happened. And not only did we all stay together in the church and eat together at the one long table, but all my sons actually danced with me, and we shared the same corner table by the bar, in between dances.

That was the furthest we could get from the band, in fact, a gesture on their part towards us. We were proud of our family, if truth be told. And for the very first time I began to see why so many people talk about the pleasure they get in having their families around them on special occasions. Indeed, I could see quite a few other fathers, besides Eoin, swelling with pride as they surveyed their extended families. We were by no means the only family table around that dance floor.

It was that kind of wedding, a real family occasion, with whole families invited and not the usual token one or two. There was plenty of mixing and chat at the bar, of course, and in the passing up and down. But each lot seemed to find great security in returning to their own particular corner after each sortie away. I never noticed that at weddings before. But then again I never had all my own about me at a wedding before. Doubtless the usual mating game would start with the afters. But my lot are settled, thank God.

This had a lot to do with the fact that we were all enjoying ourselves so well. I was happy because they all seemed so happy. As for Eoin, he had a ball. And why wouldn't he, with pretty young girls to dance with, and no shortage of lubrication to give him confidence. One young man, a neighbour, even asked Eoin Óg if his father had had a face-lift or something. He had never seen Eoin smiling so much before, only always worried about something and rushing madly about the place. He was describing Eoin's normal working face in fact. When people see only one side of us I suppose it is normal enough to conclude that that is all there is to a person. Eoin Óg thought it hilariously funny, his father having a perpetual smile deliberately grafted onto his face. But Eoin Óg, basking in his girlfriend's smiles, would have thought anything perfect right then, as his father waltzed her onto the floor, saying he hadn't had the pleasure of dancing with her yet.

Eoin Óg thought his father was being quite the ladies' man, dancing with everyone all evening. I knew better. Eoin was, in fact, exhausted from all his duty dances. Yet, because of my training, that concept of duty dances did not go over that son's head entirely when I pointed out, as gently as possible, that he had not given his old mother her duty dance yet. I was whirled onto the floor on the spot. Although I noticed that we never danced far away from his father and girlfriend. I wonder which was he keeping an eye on?

Actually all my sons danced the legs off me. Which was great because Eoin always gives more duty dances than I ever get in return : the husbands in question are usually only to be found bellying up to the bar. How often, at dinner dances and elsewhere, I have been left the wallflower at the table while my man is on the floor! I have longed in vain for the courage to tell various men that they more than owe me a dance, even if they don't fancy me personally. Yet while the present system prevails, of women having to wait to be asked, I, with a perfectly good husband of my own, will be left sitting much too often on my own, because the other men in the party lack the same code of manners.

Like all brides, the bride on this occasion was beautiful, the bridegroom as proud as punch, and no calamities at all befell as far as the guests could see. I laughed heartily at the meal when a newly-married young man regaled us with the true tale of how his best man had actually forgotten the rings until they were sitting down in the church together, waiting for the bride. So another brother was dispatched the fifteen miles home to get them, and a friend was sent off in an equal rush to stop the bridal car from getting to the church on time.

'And you can imagine how I felt in the back of that car when I saw John swerve in, in front of us, blowing his horn madly and shouting out his open window,' chimed in his young wife.

'Were you afraid I had thought better of it, while I still had the chance?' teased her young husband, obviously still deeply in love. Anyway, she and her father had to suffer being driven round and round in circles, until the brother got back with the rings and they got the all-clear to finally stop. They both think it highly amusing now, as we all did. But I bet it was no joking matter at the time. We all get so het up about having everything right on the day. And does it really matter one whit in the long run?

By the way, I did hear one new joke during the wedding speeches, and new jokes in that context are few and far between. This priest, a family relation, got up to speak. When he had silence, he said: 'Now I have only one serious matter to cover. Remember, dear children, that what was a sin last night is a duty tonight.' And he sat down on that note to tumultuous applause. Would that all the speeches were that short. (1994)

Poor as students

Eoin was very cross with me one night this week. I knew that I was in trouble when I drove up to the house, in the wee small hours of the morning, and I saw him looking out the window. And as I came in the door his face warned me that was not the time to remind him that many was the night, over the years, I had waited and watched for him to come home safely from some farming meeting or other.

You see, there was a bit of a Christmas party on in college. All the class were going to it, with our last seminar of the term over, and right or wrong they insisted on my going along too. I was loth to go, feeling that I'd be sticking out like a sore thumb among all the youngsters. Still and all I was flattered that they felt I'd fit in.

When I discovered the first port of call was the pub I very nearly balked. And I would have too, except that I had a full car-load who were depending on me to take them on the next step. The thought did cross my mind that my car was the reason they were so insistent I should come along too, but I quickly banished that because they are a great bunch of youngsters. Not once has one of them made me age-conscious all this first term.

They are all broke of course, living from hand to mouth, or so it seems. The paying of their grants was the really big occasion this term. That was the one weekend that all were not heading for home, a good feed and hopefully a few pounds from the mother. Since I did my degree by night, where no grants are applicable, I was not aware that so many students survive on their grants alone. They are all student poor, but still that does not prevent them smoking heavily and ordering pints nightly. Those two things seem to be part of the student culture, for the girls as well as fellows, and, since I never had family at college, the whole scene is new to me and I have to work hard at being understanding.

I did enjoy the party, when we eventually got to it, mainly because of the novelty of the thing. It was a bottle party, which is the usual thing in college. Somebody provides the venue and the guests bring all the necessary. Actually, although I brought a bottle, when we finally got there it was more of a can party; they all came well supplied with six-packs. Not that the bottle I brought lasted that long either.

But during the night, what really brought it home to me how poor some of them must be was when I saw a group in the corner sharing the one cigarette between them, back and forth, boys and girls. Being full of the Christmas spirit, except that I think they are stupid to be smoking at all, I would have gone out on the spot and bought cigarettes for them all. But I disciplined myself by thinking of the pints I saw them having at the pub earlier!

All the talk was college talk at this party. Because we have just finished correcting the end of term assessments, our first real taste of power over our students, we, the tutors were full of that. And each had a tale to tell of the things the first year students had said. One of my fellow MA students, who is quite an ardent feminist, was spitting fire about a girl student who had written of secretaries always 'wearing short skirts, black tights and high heels', the subject being sexual discrimination in the work-place.

The funniest note was the answer one of us got to the question that 'Debt is the biggest problem faced by Third World countries today'. This student, who must have heard the question only verbally, wrote quite a good paper that *death* is indeed the biggest problem faced by Third World countries today.

One of my students had chosen to answer a question on power in Ireland. And I was somewhat amused to read that:

'every farmer's child in Ireland, regardless of size and income, is entitled to every grant going for third level education, as well as paying no tax unless the farmer, or his wife, has employment outside farming. Now is that justice?'

I can't resist quoting her in full here, and I was really tough marking her as well, because she trotted out every cliché you ever heard, as if the mere saying a thing was so was proof enough.

But my personal story fell flat enough that night. Even though all there could see the stupidity of stereotyping all secretaries as bimbos, only one other person there would agree with me that farmers are subject to precisely the same tax code as everybody else. And so the argument ran fast and furious about the actual power of the farming lobby, etc. I do so love a good argument when each side is prepared to listen and accept what they hear even if it goes against their deepest held beliefs.

I was highly amused when, during another argument, having once more valiantly fought for my minority position on divorce, something arose about how long I personally was married. Immediately my opponent, who is a lecturer in a different department at college, said that if he had known I was as old as his mother he would never have been so hard on me. I was delighted when some of my companions rowed in then on my behalf, with the accusation that he was being completely ageist in his comment, since what on earth had my age got to do with anything?

And all this time poor Eoin was at home all on his own. And once he knew I was safe he calmed down and wanted to know all about my night. But it was my sons, next day, who put me straight about the poor students who were so poor they all had to share the one cigarette. (1996)

An E-Mail affair

Did I ever think at my age that I'd have a young man sending me demented messages of undying love almost daily? And I, the coy young maiden, have allowed him to teach me all I know about the latest modern technology. The whole saga started on the first day of term too, to make things even better. But it's all right. I have told Eoin all about it.

Dear, dear, the double entendre is catching. I am mixing too much with the young, who think that they are the first to discover the doubtful delights of double-meaning jokes. So I had better just give you the facts straight up. Now that I have started in on my Master's degree, I decided to have yet another go at coming to grips with modern technology in the shape of E-Mail and the Internet. Every University student, now, because of some EU directive, is entitled to an E-Mail number and access to the Internet.

Which is fine if you know how to work the damn things. With help from a fellow female student, I managed to get logged on some months ago, when I got my user name and password, which was my birth date backwards. This password had then to be changed to one of my choice, which never appears on the screen and so nobody else can accidentally access my messages. But with me, it has been a case of what messages? I mean, after all, who do I know with E-Mail who would be likely to be sending me messages?

Then, that first day, not having a lot to do for an hour or so since nothing much seemed organised, I decided to give this thing another go, having discovered that, as a postgraduate student, I didn't have to queue up with all the undergraduates; I could work away, in total privacy, in the research room of my faculty building. I do hate making a total and utter fool of myself in front of knowledgeable youngsters.

But anonymity is truly wonderful, I have now discovered. It was a real pleasure to have nobody near as I struggled with the terminal and my leaflet of instructions which I got when I originally logged on. You know there is a whole new language in this game. I personally am what is known as a 'lurker'. I get onto programs and discussion groups in which others interact, but they do not know I am there because I keep as quiet as a mouse, and I don't mean my computer mouse either.

But I am quite sure you do not want to know so much about computer data as about my computer date. As I said it all began first day back when I tried once more to come to grips with this Internet and E-Mail thing. E-Mail means electronic mail. Then I discovered that the computer screen was flashing at me that I had E-Mail, four new messages awaiting my attention. That was real exciting, and I eventually got to make out how to display messages on screen.

Three of the messages turned out to be weeks old. They were from my fellow MA student, Eithne, who had helped me to get logged on in the first place last year. In the first one she was welcoming me to E-Mail, and then twice she asked me why I wasn't answering her messages. But the fourth message was dated that very day and said:

'Hi there whoever you are! Will you talk to me please? My name is David. I am doing my Masters degree and I am so lonesome out here with just my research work and me. I am learning how to work this damn thing, which of course I shall conquer since I am dynamite at everything thing I touch, except girls. Nobody even sent me a Valentine card last year, boo-hoo. Please mail me if you are there and make contact with this poor defenceless soul who is completely lost in the E-Mail morass.' And he gave his E-Mail code for a return call.

Now who could resist something like that? I couldn't anyway, so I wrote back on my computer, addressing it to Dynamite Dave and signing it Lonesome Liz. I E-Mailed it, using, I hoped, the right instructions, and went back to my lurking on the Internet. Then, before I knew what was happening, my screen was flashing at me. A new message was in.

'Thanks a million for leaving a message for me. When I logged on today, for the first time ever, somebody listened to me, so now it is great to have someone to write to. At the very least it spares me from the ordeal of having to stare at an empty screen, wondering what the hell to do next! Now I am no longer an electronic virgin, and Liz, I will always remember you as my first electronic experience!'

I went off chuckling at the fellow and thought I would leave it at that. But the next time I logged on there were two new messages from Dynamite Dave calling on Lonesome Liz, which I couldn't resist. So it has continued ever since, with puerile jokes on both sides as I try to remember what is was like to be young again and quite silly. Anonymity does allow you to be that, you know.

But there has also been a very useful side to it as I too confessed my total inexperience, my virgin state on the electronic front, my history as a lurker and my total timidity in exalted company, which I feel this electronic world is, and the whole Masters experience in college. Dave rushed back a message asking me to allow him to be my mentor in all things. He said that my full education would be his pleasure. Every time he found out something new, about anything, he would pass on the knowledge and the technique to me, he wrote.

And so far it is all working out very well. He didn't even balk at my main research topic being farming. But I have never asked him how he originally got my E-Mail number. I don't want to embarrass him, or indeed myself, by finding out that he is being unfaithful to me regularly on the Internet and has a girl on every terminal. If he has I just do not want to know. Anyway, how much more embarrassed would Dynamite Dave be to find out I am a grandmother seven times over?

So far, therefore, when he suggests we meet, I invent one excuse after another. Just to keep him keen, I tease. But what happens when I run out of excuses? (1996)

DECEMBER

I'm the real Granny now

My mother died on Wednesday, so I really am a Granny now. She was always the Granny, you know, the one who counted, who kept all the family together. I was only her daughter, a young one really, despite all evidence to the contrary. Now all is changed utterly. She is gone and we are now the older generation, the next in the firing line. We have not had time to miss her yet, the pain is too much, but I know we will miss her, in ways that we have yet to realise.

She was eighty-seven, eighty-eight next June, so we should be grateful for having had her so long. We should also celebrate her life, not mourn her death. You see, she was quite ready to go. It was just that we were not really listening to her. We were the ones delaying her.

Last March she was found unconscious in her room, rushed to hospital in an ambulance, and the next day recovered practically completely from that seizure. But when she woke up, that fine sunny day in March, she was bitterly disappointed to do so. 'Why didn't you just let me go?' she said sadly to me at her bedside, where I had kept vigil. So, of course, I made all the right noises about how she would be fine again, that the good Lord still had work for her to do here below, that her children and grandchildren, not to mind her great-grandchildren would miss her too much. I hushed her gently with easy words.

But I was not actually listening. She really meant what she was saying. Time and again, over the following months, in different ways to different people, she repeated her words. With hindsight, I now know that she had prepared each one of us for this time of her going. Late autumn, when my son Padraig and Michaella called in one fine evening and went up to her room, she was sitting in her rocking chair by the window. Her knitting had fallen to her lap, and she was looking out the window. Then, when the pleasantries had all been said and Michaella was ensconced in her favourite place of all, being rocked gently on Great-Gran's lap, my mother turned to Padraig and remarked that all the leaves were almost off the tree now, outside her window. She, however, had just been looking at the buds on the twigs. She pointed out how fat they were already, how they were even then getting ready to burst open in the spring, ready to repeat the cycle all over again. She then gave her great-granddaughter a quick hug and said that it was the same way, now, with herself and Michaella. She was ready to fall off the tree and, again hugging Michaella, she said that this little lady needed room to grow, that the old cannot live for ever and nobody should ask them to.

'Nonsense,' said Padraig, just as his mother would do. 'You'll dance at Michaella's wedding yet. Do you remember that waltz we had together at my wedding, when I was hard set to keep up with you?' Yes indeed, my mother dearly loved a proper old-time waltz. She must have been quite a lively lass in her day.

She also told Eoin Óg and Lisa, when they went up with their Christmas presents, that she had her bags packed and she was only waiting for the off. Lisa wanted to know where. But my mother laughed and said her bags were packed for a very different reason, and then changed the conversation to something else entirely. The penny having dropped, my young pair came home quite upset. But those words have been a great comfort to us all since, in a strange sort of way.

I would say that in recent times our own mother-daughter relationship, with all the stresses and strains that that implies, turned into a friendship between two grown women. She then told me things about her past that never before had she even hinted at, in all the years and circumstances. I too was able to talk to her about my present. She was a great woman for holding her own counsel and never, ever, told one of her children what any of the rest of us had said or even done.

And she advised me too, with great good sense, about my own family and how to adjust to daughters-in-law. One day when I had some little complaint or other about one of them, so little that I cannot now even recall what it was, important and all as it seemed at the time, she said to me, 'Always remember, Liz, that there is no winning with young people. Even if you try to oppose them and do win, that is when you lose. So sidestep every time and you'll do fine.'

Then my mother got a massive stroke, last Saturday, and never regained consciousness. We all loved her enough not to wish her to recover from that. Her right side was paralysed. Nevertheless, we really thought she would go on forever, or for another ten years at least. Her health was excellent. She had never had a serious setback: she had recovered fully from each little seizure before this. She had a better appetite than any of us and really enjoyed her food too. She was at Eoin Óg's wedding last summer, in all her finery, and enjoyed meeting everybody, it didn't matter in the least to her whether they were strangers or not.

And she was a very keen follower of the Irish soccer team. None of us would dare ring her up or go near her when there was a soccer match on. She would not want to see us, and would flatly refuse to come to the phone. With the grandchildren she was more than able to hold her own, discussing *Top of the Pops*, which is more than Eoin and I could. I swear too she knew all about AIDS and the like, long before any of us, she kept up so much with the times, and, for a woman born in 1906, had extraordinarily liberal views when she and her grandchildren got into deep discussions.

The day after the funeral, in the course of conversation, someone asked me what precise relationship there was between him and us, and without thinking I said that I'd ask my mother that, the next time I saw her, because she was the only one who kept great track of that sort of thing. And then the stupidity and uselessness of what I had just said hit me. I can never ask my mother anything again.

And that is how it has been all week. I don't know how many times I have said to myself that I must tell Mamma that, when I heard a bit of local gossip. I always, for years past, store up in my mind bits and pieces to tell her, of what was going on locally, because she dearly loved to know everything about everybody. She would genuinely enjoy even my talk about what I was doing in college and read again quite a few of the novels on my English course because she had read them herself, for pleasure, long ago, and was interested in what was being said about them now.

I often used a point or two she had come up with, in my essays, because her viewpoint was so valid. And I never ceased to be amazed at just how widely read and well educated was her generation, the last to be educated under the British system. Much of the body of work that came to be frowned upon under the new regime of nationalistic Catholicism was quite widely read in her youth. Reading was the sole entertainment after all, on long winter nights by the fire, when one family member would read aloud while the others did fine needlework. Hands were never allowed to be idle and my mother still knitted to the end, although this autumn she said she would take on no more big jumpers for any of us, that small things would be enough. A cap for Michaella she had just finished, except for the sewing up, the Saturday she got the stroke. I must sew that up for her and finish it.

Every night my dreams are full of my mother in a most extraordinarily normal manner. They are not nightmares by any means. And she is never dead or even sick in them. She is just doing things or going places with us. And, as usual, all my dreams are set in my old home. Never once do I ever dream of here, where I have lived all my married life. In dreams, I still return to the place of my formative years.

My mother went back in time too because her last intelligible words, on the first of the four nights I spent up with her, was when she opened her eyes and looked straight at me. But she did not see me. However, she did see somebody else, because she then squeezed my hand and said quite clearly 'Are you awake, James? You know, I don't think I'll get up quite yet.' Then she sighed and became more deeply unconscious, still and peaceful, and never spoke again.

Before this she was trying, although unconscious, to get out of the bed to go somewhere. It appeared she wanted to go out into the farmyard. She was obviously back in the time before my father died, when the morning drill was that he got up first to bring in the cows and she snuggled down for a little while longer, before she had to get out as well. Her final years may have been very comfortable but she had things hard when my father died suddenly, a young man.

Quite a few people at that time advised her to sell up and go back to her own people, that a woman could never make it on her own in farming. But fortunately for her family, she would not accept that, and with the considerable help of her only brother she held on to the farm and educated all of us in those days before free education, when boarding schools were the only choice for people in remote areas.

Going through her things this week, I came across a letter from her sister-in-law, wife of that uncle who did so much for us, and in it she said for him not to be in any hurry back, that two calves were born, and ten lambs, and they were all perfect, that things were going fine, every bit as good as if he was there himself. My father's anniversary is in early January, so it must have been tough going for that woman with a houseful of really young children, in the depths of winter, to have encouraged her husband to stay away longer – for as long as he was needed, she wrote. That was true generosity of spirit. She did more than enough.

All I can say this week is for those who have parents still living to look after them, because how you'll wish you too had done more than enough, when they are gone. Now I know that guilt is part of bereavement, just as is the pain, and it also has to be worked through. And we did have a few days before my mother died to get accustomed to the idea of not having her any more.

Yet when we found a diary of hers with, among many other things, an entry for the pitifully few times I did anything special for her, I felt truly terrible. She was not a diary keeper, but I think she tried this for a little while when she found her memory not quite as reliable as it used to be. Those were the sorts of entries she made, when she had written to my brother out foreign, when some of the rest of us had phoned her and things that happened at home, odd things like them selling some fodder beet and taking animals to the mart. How I wish now that there were more entries made of good things I had done for her. It would have cost me so little at the time. And now it is all too late. (1993)

The keepers of Christmas: the weavers of dreams

Christmas came to this house twice yesterday. The young pair were in town and they came in with a glow on their cheeks and a Christmas tree sticking out the boot of the car. 'Did you buy it or swipe it?' I asked and Lisa looked at me in horror and said that of course they bought it. To her, a town girl, there was no other way to acquire a Christmas tree. Little did she know that her darling husband was not quite so guiltless in Christmases past. But then he has grown up since, and so has that particular plantation. Therefore, this year the saw stayed at home when they went Christmas tree hunting, and I myself went out quickly to be the one to cut the red-berried variegated holly in the garden for them. There is still a hole in that bush where it was attacked with more enthusiasm than skill last year. But I do hope that they also go to the wood for the more humble green holly and ivy. That, the smell of the green mossy dampness, was always an integral part of the magic of Christmas for me and mine.

Christmas is after all about the making of magic. Christmas is about dreaming, wishing and hoping. What difference if the reality of those hopes, wishes and dreams is finally less? It is the anticipation, the time before, that is really the best of anything in life. And Christmas is no exception. Take that from one who knows.

And that is why I love to see my daughters-in-law weaving their own Christmas magic about the place when they each put so much time and energy into transforming their homes so totally for Christmas. It really shouldn't matter to me that most of the decorations, even the greenery, in the house is artificial now and came originally from Taiwan, Hong Kong or God knows where. Their Christmas tree laden with glitter and glamour, and the good spicy smells from the kitchen prove that those girls too have a soft romantic core and the future of Christmas for the generations of Kavanaghs to come is safe in their hands.

Women are the keepers of Christmas. Women are the weavers of dreams. And the men then go along willingly enough. Left to themselves, however, they'd do nothing only wish things were as they used to be, once upon a time, when they were young and innocent. And then feel both vaguely guilty and hard done by, if they are not. But I find it is up to their wives to make their Christmas dreams come true, even if in a slightly different form, and to weave the magic spells for their children, born and unborn. The magic they weave now will be transmitted through the generations in one form or another, because it will live on forever in somebody's memory.

Once, long ago, I too was very good indeed at making magic, or so my sons tell me. They talk wistfully at times of their Christmases past and how great it all was. But that is not wise talk. It is continuity that counts, not necessarily repetition. They now have the chance to be part of the magic-making themselves, to join in the making of the crib, the going to town to see Santa, or whatever else their wives best remember.

Sometimes, however, it is the husband's memories that prevail. This year, Eoin and I are going to the pantomime in town with Michaella and her parents, just as my mother always and ever came to the pantomime with us and our sons. Sara said that she'd get the tickets since Padraig never is done talking about the pantomimes when he was young and how marvellous they used to be. He recalls, especially, that famous night his Dad, on his outside seat, tripped up the Dame coming down the aisle in the dark, and how she/he said all those really naughty words out loud!

Funny the things small children remember. That night Eoin had the outside seat in the central aisle downstairs, which he always gets for his long legs. At one point, the Dame was offstage but his voice could be heard in an occasional commentary of the action on stage, where snow was falling on a winter wonderland scene. Every child in the place, including mine, craned his neck to see where the voice was coming from, rich with wonderful threats to pelt them with snowballs and lollipops and more snowballs and still more lollipops. Down the central aisle came the Dame, to hoots of surprised and delighted childish laughter with each cotton wool snowball and multi-coloured lollipop thrown at random into the audience. But the f...ing and blinding when the Dame was totally taken by surprise and went flat on his face over Eoin's outstretched legs, and he said more than his prayers, live on the mike, really brought the house down. This is what has stuck in Padraig's memory as the highlight of all his wonderful pantomimes. No other pantomime was ever as good again.

Sara said that she never had that big thing about going to the pantomime when she was young. In the city, once Christmas was over, it was over, she said. There were none of our extras, before and after. So she wants Michaella to have all the happy Christmas memories that Padraig had of a country Christmas. So that is why they would love us to come with them to make the night perfect for them all. A lump came to my throat, and I wouldn't be at all surprised if a tear came to my eye as well. But it was partially a tear of thankfulness for Eoin.

You see, last year I was very tempted to take Michaella myself to the pantomime. But Eoin's wiser counsel prevailed. Firstly, he said Michaella was too young at three, and secondly, he said that it was up to her parents to invite us along with their family, if and when they were ready, and not having us make all the running. So I did nothing, and said nothing, and yesterday I had my reward. It would have been lovely if my mother had lasted just a few more weeks, to have come along too, to see the magic she had made for me, when we were taken in a pony and trap fifteen miles to see the lights of the city and the same pantomimes, now all being repeated in a modern form for her great-granddaughter. But perhaps I shall go with my great-grandchildren some day, in whatever mode of transport is then in vogue!

I really must go to the trouble of telling my granddaughters all about my Christmases of long ago. They too are the ones who will grow up, some day, to be the keepers of Christmas, the weavers of dreams, just as I once was, and my daughters-in-law are now, and my mother was before us all. (1994)

Of corsets & pigs & Christmases past

How many are left, I wonder, of those who remember Christmas times without electricity? Whenever I personally think of the Christmases long ago I think of darkness suddenly pierced with glowing light. By this I mean both the lighting of Christmas candles in every house window, and the coming of Christmas in the dark dead depths of winter, when, except for the moon and stars, not a stem of light showed in the countryside once night descended. At Christmas everything changed. And the very first signal for this was the killing of the Christmas pig.

With the awful power of all our yesterdays, the Christmases I still regret, and want to recreate, are those I had before I was made grow up, which, coincidentally, were also those before the rural electrification scheme robbed the countryside here of its magic. The very last Christmas of my childhood was when I was twelve. And my memories of the beginning of the end of mysterious wonder are punctuated by the piercing shrieks of the Christmas pig being killed, and the discomfort of whalebone corsets and suspenders.

Christmas was magic when I was a child, growing up safe and secure on a reasonably big farm, where we never seemed to have spare money but we were never hungry, not even during the war years. We milked cows and made our own butter for sale in the town. We kept pigs and had bacon for dinner five days a week. The hens provided eggs, chickens for sale, and the odd one for dinner if we, or they, were sick. My mother was a great believer in the efficacy of well salted chicken broth when we were too sick to eat anything solid.

Geese were also reared for sale, as well as for our own Christmas dinners and as gifts to the parish priest, the curate and the various relations in town. There were also guinea fowl, whose eggs, little hard bullets of sweetness, we loved if we could find them in time: they were really wild birds but quite beautiful with their painted heads. And do you remember their call? We were told that they kept saying 'Two o'clock, two o'clock', over and over, to remind us to give them their dinner on time. They were thrown some of the scraps after our dinner, with fistfuls of grain from the loft, so it was always about two o'clock all right before they got fed, and they knew the time for food as well as ourselves. After dinner someone was also free to track them back to their nests for the eggs. Which was fine until one of the workmen told us children that the guinea fowl were really saying 'You f... off, you f... off!' to us all! So, after this nugget of knowledge was stored away in our delighted memories, every time the guinea fowl called when the parents were around, or 'two o'clock' was ever said, in any context whatsoever, we would burst out laughing and never, ever, explain our private joke. Our mouths would literally have been washed out with soap if such a word crossed our lips, even in explanation.

Children inhabited a world of their own in those times, with their own jokes and knowledge, quite different to the grown up serious world of work. Keeping out of the way was an art we developed to the full, since neither our father nor our mother could ever see us idle, especially wasting time reading a book, without giving us a job to do instead. After school we collected the eggs at four o'clock, we helped with the milking at five, we fed the calves and the pigs, and there was endless pulping of mangolds and turnips in between. But we made our own fun as well, our own play, apart from the adults altogether.

The adults in our world were the farm-workers, our parents and our teachers in school. All we learned came from those three sources: we knew no other world. The class distinctions were very marked, in those far-off times, between farmers and farm-workers. But the children floated quite happily between the two worlds. My ambition was always to be allowed eat at the same table as the men and especially to be allowed grow a fingernail long enough to peel my potatoes with it, as Mick could do. At that table I grew expert at spearing a piece of potato with my knife, balancing a piece of butter on top of that, and then putting the lot in my mouth!

But the day came when it was decided I was growing up too wild by far for a girl. A corset was put on me literally and figuratively. And thus a pink corset came, all wrapped up in tissue paper, among my presents that last Christmas of my childhood when I was all of twelve. I delighted in that present of a corset when told how grown-up it would make me, often fingering it in its box, only being allowed to wear it at Mass. Off it had to come, together with my good clothes, immediately on our return. I was secretly delighted to be rid of the discomfort, but was assured by my mother once I got used to wearing it full time I would find that I would not be able to do without its support.

But be that as it may, come January, it was the most hideous torture imaginable to be sent off to school tied up in this thing, from armpits to thighs, and long black stockings attached to that, and then my normal strong boots with their iron tips for good wear. I stuck it until first playtime, when the impossibility of fluid movement drove me into that terrible noisome hole that was our dry-closet toilet. I took the lot off, boots and all, and was free. And, as a child, not the young lady my parents were demanding, I went back to playing football, barefoot once more with the boys, winter time or not. I stuffed the long stockings in my pockets and wore the boots home. But I left the corset stuck for good between two stones, in the stench!

Was it any wonder that the following September I was sent off to my mother's convent school, but with three suspender belts, all marked with Cash's name tapes, and not the statutory three corsets on the list. Those six pairs of brown lisle stockings, part of the school uniform, had to be kept up somehow, since there was an appendix onto the list about garters not being suitable. But I had prevailed on the question of corsets.

Then, in October, while I was away at school, the rural electrification scheme reached our area. With no half-term breaks, all was changed on my return for the Christmas holidays. They were no longer dependent on paraffin and candles and Aladdin lamps in the house, or the Tilly lantern going out to check the cows at night. The house had been re-papered after the wiring of each room. The smells seemed somehow different to what I remembered. Paddy the workman was gone. So was my pony Joey. Everything and everybody was changed.

I too had been changed, both subtly and forcefully. I also saw things now in a different light. I had been laughed at when, in reply to the questioning nun about the meaning of Christmas in all our homes, I said that the first thing about Christmas in our house was the killing of the pig. The laughter of my class of young ladies in the making effectively killed the magic of Christmas for me. In my country-bred innocence I had continued on, for far too long, about how I, out of all my family, was the one who got to hold the bucket for the blood for the black puddings. And that nun led the laughter, for which I hated her with a venomous hatred for years, long after I had left that school. On her, to boot, I had already blamed my perceived unpopularity with my peers.

Poor woman, she ill-deserved that. I fully understand her now. Tact was just not her forte. She laughed, not from derision, but, I would think, from honest amusement at my open earnestness. But the laughter of my peers was quite different, and effectively stopped my mouth from telling them other things. I was going to tell them how the killing of the pig was best because it was first, and signalled all the magic to come. The other girls, who had spoken before me, were practically all daughters of teachers, doctors and business people, and had nothing much to tell beyond repetitive mundane chatter of Christmas dinners, presents and visiting relations.

But I knew that Christmas was much more to me; Christmas was a truly magical time. Those girls' parents bought their Christmas; we made ours. Our going for holly and ivy was an outing and special, as was the decorating of the house from top to bottom with home-made decorations. I was starting in on my long list, prepared while I awaited my turn, and was only telling the direct truth when I said that Christmas, in my old home, always started with the killing of a pig. My sons are horrified at this now, that I was the one who willingly stood with the bucket to catch the blood which came out of the wound made by the long pig-killing knife, straight into the heart. But I do not remember those occasions for the cruelty to the poor pig, but for the warm glow I got from pleasing my father greatly. And I did not mind in the least the odd little splash of warm blood on my face or on my neck. That, instead, was a form of benediction since these were the days my father made the greatest fuss of me all year long.

I had an older brother who wouldn't do this job, which rightfully should have been his. My mother backed her first-born: she would not do this job either. A workman couldn't be ordered to hold the container, and anyway they weren't wanted for the job since a workman once got in my father's way and spilt the entire contents of the bucket. The blood-catcher had to get in under his butchering arm and neatly hold the freshly-scalded, galvanised, two-gallon bucket pressed hard against the pig; a child was the perfect size. And I would have walked on hot coals all day for a word of approval from my much-loved Dad.

Pig-killing was just a normal event in the farming calendar anyway for most farmhouses. Our Christmas pig-killing always took place the first day of our holidays from school, when we were home to help. So the fell deed was done after the usual morning milking and the separating of the cream was finished and all the separator parts put to soak. Then buckets of hot water, heated in the big black pot on the crane over the open fire in the kitchen, were used to scald and shave the carcass. We all would like to have had a go at this, but the cut-throat razors were deadly sharp, and it was very important for the curing process that the skin not be cut.

After our dinner came the trip to the small river, three long fields away, with those buckets now sloppingly full of pig intestines, which needed the flow of water to turn them inside out. This was my mother's part of the proceedings and I know I was slower to learn the knack of turning the end enough so that the strength of flow of water then turned the intestine fully inside out, with no further human intervention.

I can still feel the desperate cold of that river water, in December, on my hands, and my bare legs freezing since my skirts had to be tucked into my knickers to keep the edges out of the water. (Girls did not wear trousers, ever, in those days.) The intestines had then to be completely cleansed of any extraneous matter, with handfuls of river gravel, before the river flow was used to turn them right way around again. Finally and thankfully once that horrible part of the job was over we trudged back through the fields with our buckets, our spirits lifting with the thought of the big night ahead, in the warmth, making the sausages and puddings.

And nothing ever tasted as good as those sausages and puddings made that same night, when, immediately after the usual supper of bread and tea, the table would be cleared and brought out a little from the wall. The biggest pot of all would be filled with water and swung on its crane over the open fire, to boil up all in readiness for the first batch of sausages. We children were given the job of turning the fire machine or fanners. In between our turn at that, there were dozens of loaves to turn into bread-crumbs in the great big timber container that usually held the cream before the butter-making. This was on the floor so that we could all sit around it in comfort and crumb the bread, when it wasn't our turn for blowing the fire. Another big bin held all that was going to go into the sausages, which was every single bit of the poor pig that couldn't be turned into bacon: the liver and lights, the trimmings and the fat. While my mother had all of us down at the river and out of the way, my father had cut up the carcass so that it now looked nothing whatever like a pig. The bits that hadn't been given their first salting, or set aside for immediate use, or to give away, were in that bin for sausages. These were all boiled up now in that big pot on the open fire, and how we exulted as the sparks flew up that wide chimney Santa Claus was to come down a few days later. The chimney was never cleaned with its furze bush until the day after this big night, so there was plenty of burning soot to ignite and excite.

And it was a really big night because the workmen, who usually made themselves scarce after supper for a few hours (I thought they went to bed for a stretch, but I now know they were gone to the pub) stayed on. Paddy, who was with us forever, always took the seat by the mincer, which was screwed onto the table-top, and he twisted that handle all night long, and, even as he weakened, would give way to no one, while my mother and the maidservant, known only as 'the girl', took turns in taking bits of cooked meat out of the pot on the fire, and feeding them into the mincer.

It really must have been like a picture from the Old Masters; the great big roaring turf fire, with the steam rising out of the huge black pot, the pools of light only at each work station, the wall lamp illuminating the table with its mincer and Paddy's determined face, and that one paraffin lamp swinging off its centre hook on the ceiling shining down on all the children (the girls with wide red ribbons in their hair, the boys in short pants) getting into everything, and all of us up to our elbows in breadcrumbs. Hollowed-out half-loaves of baker's bread we had done with lay scattered about the floor. My mother, wearing the snow-white apron kept specially for major cooking jobs, directed operations, and my father, at the edge of the picture now that his work was done, opened the bottles of stout which were to refresh the working men, and for use in the black puddings. The girl was never offered any sustenance. She wore only her usual wrap-around pinny, and was never allowed do the actual mixing up of minced meats, breadcrumbs, allspice, salt and pepper, herbs and the rest. That rested firmly in my mother's control.

By the way, I found the handwritten recipes my mother used for making the sausages and puddings those nights among her things when she died, so in theory I could repeat that wonderful taste and smell. But nothing will ever bring back the feeling of being up to my elbows, on my knees on the bare concrete floor, in the glow of the turf fire, and mixing together all this glorious concoction. Then occasionally being allowed to feed fistfuls of it into the mincer, which now had the sausage attachment on the end and our carefully cleaned sausage casing (that sounds a heck of a lot better than pig's intestine) slid all the way up over that. The trick was to hold the end of the casing while it filled up with sausage meat and to let it slide off all the way, very slowly, just as it filled, without any air-pockets at all, yet not so full that it burst under pressure. Then, when finally full, it would be laid on the scrubbed table, doubled and deftly twisted into sausages by my mother's quick hands. A bit of twine to tie the ends tight and together, a long loop left for catching it, and into the pot it would go, the pot that had already boiled up all the bits and pieces and so was really a soup.

Quite some time had, of course, passed by now and hunger was overtaking us. But the only sausages we could have would be any which, unfortunately, because of possible air-bubbles or overfilling, burst in the boiling. And, extraordinary to relate, the first sets of sausages had always a lot of them well burst when they came out of the pot. Small fingers, and not such small ones either, always made sure to break through the skin, in the putting of them into the pot.

When all the tummies, both big and small, were full, we just could not be bothered any more, so perfect specimens then emerged each and every time! And it was important that the skins were unbroken because, shrunken when boiled, they preserved what was inside, when all were hung from the hooks in the kitchen ceiling for later consumption.

They never lasted that long anyway. Both supper and breakfast were now special with sausages. I cannot recall any ever going off. But my mouth waters to this day with the memory of them and sitting, eating so late, and everyone in harmony. We were just too tired, man, woman and child, to be anything else. This, the first day of Christmas for us, had always been a mighty busy one. And we slept soundly that night. But visions of sausages for breakfast, and not sugar-plums, danced in our heads that night.

It was the done thing then in my home to give all the poorer neighbours some fresh meat, and some bacon, butter, eggs and fuel, each Christmas, the day after we killed the pig. 'You can't be mean! And anyway it was done this way before I came here,' my mother would say firmly, that day, when there might be some discussion about what to give. She was a great believer in never making or breaking a custom, even though she wasn't always thanked for her generosity. A remark once found its way back from one of the relations in town, on my father's side, that really she should have kept her butter for 'greasing the axles of the butts.' And this in the war years when food was so scarce everywhere! But then, trust close relations always for the bitter word!

Some people really were hungry then, you know, and the poorer neighbours were welcome, God knows, as far as I was concerned, to the bacon and the rest. But I did begrudge anyone sausages. The bacon usually was what was unused from the last kill anyway, which was taken down from the hooks, to make way for the new: the rusty marks of the hooks in the fat were a dead giveaway. But these families didn't see much meat then, so that and the fresh bit of pork, which was included as well, probably was their Christmas dinner; the bacon, having held six months, probably held a little longer. Now the quality of the cuts, as well as the quantity, was carefully judged for the recipient households. Two old dears, who had once had land but had fallen on hard times, always got one of the pork steaks and a string of sausages, with my father telling them that after killing the pig we had more than we could safely use in time. We, however, were strictly warned to stay outside if we came along for the spin when my father went delivering: seeing a child, the recipients would feel compelled to give us a stand they could ill afford.

Not everyone got a goose. Those only went to specific people since they were really a cash crop. The plucking of the geese was fun, if a chore, because we coloured the wing feathers to make Red Indian headdresses and made whistles of a sort from their windpipes. We also made a football from the slaughtered pig's bladder, once it was dried up the chimney.

There was the excitement of making our own Christmas cards and watching the post for envelopes, or even parcels for us, with enclosures. The postman coming drunk, and late, was in itself a sight to behold, and to await, for children who never saw drunkenness. There was interest in everything come Christmas. Even going to confession on Christmas Eve, and watching out ourselves for 'the hardy annuals', was an outing.

Everyone, even the most obdurate, had to go to confession on Christmas Eve. I well remember my father telling my mother, who would have stayed at home to mind the younger ones, of 'the hardy annuals' who had turned up on the night, naming all of them out. The community then was so close knit, with only the one church within easy distance, that these hardy annuals were conspicuous by their absence from confession for the rest of the year. They always stuck out a mile anyway from the awkward way they would throw down their caps on the ground and then go down on one knee only. They also were loth to move along in an orderly fashion like the rest of us, sliding on our bottoms from seat to seat in the queue. They were liable at any moment to suddenly take a mad dash for the confessional door, out of turn, especially if a child was going in next; I suppose this was lest their courage fail them. Children had no rights then anyway. This we accepted without rancour.

Neither did we mind being taken from our beds before dawn, to be taken to the double Mass of Christmas morning, and us just gone back to sleep after exploring our stockings at the foot of the bed. Three Masses were said in a row that morning, a special privilege for each priest, and the people were expected to stay for at least two. Only a very brave soul got up to leave after the first. Just as only the saintly maiden ladies of the parish and the schoolmaster pointedly stayed on for the third.

The unreal feeling of travelling to Mass in the pony and trap, in the dark, was a large part of that special Christmas morning feeling. With not a stem of light anywhere, the stars seemed bright and near, and the faint luminosity of the dawn sky made me wish to reach out and grab great fists of it to keep for ever.

My father would point out the Star of Bethlehem to us, and tell of the three wise kings even then making their way, and we believed him utterly. The tiredness and excitement combined to form a tight knot in my stomach. I can still feel it and smell the candles and the hot-house chrysanthemums on the altar. I can see the altar boys, like me all glassy-eyed with exhaustion, gently swaying the thurible for the incense. Then the exultant *Adeste Fidelis* breaking the stillness. How the Latin added to the magic and the mystery. As did the queueing up of the children to see the crib, with the baby Jesus now in place, and everyone taking a straw home to their own cribs for luck, and talking to each other, out loud, there in the church itself, each wishing friend and foe alike a Happy Christmas. All those things made my Christmas and I was a happy child.

Before I went to boarding school my parents' way of life and this, their kind of Christmas, was all I knew. But the laughter of my peers, and of the nun in charge, taught me that those were the things to keep quiet about. I was learning my lesson well, that there are things girls do not do, like farming. Girls only talk about dresses and parties and helping their mothers with the cooking.

Before that I assumed every option in life was available to me. Hadn't I thinned beet faster than any, even the workmen? I could milk cows, drive the tractor, tackle the horse, in fact do absolutely everything on the farm better than my older brother. But I had never boasted of those accomplishments in my convent school, precisely because my father had quietly told me, the day I first left home, not to mention these facts, that the rest of the girls might not understand and it would sound as if I was boasting. He was sparing my feelings, and of course retaining his excellent little worker as well. But it obviously never occurred to him that I might stand up in class when asked and boast how Christmas always started for us, at home, with the killing of the pig and me holding the bucket for the blood. The laughter of my peers ended my childhood innocence and turned me fastidiously feminine and a total pain in the neck for a period. I had deliberately escaped that corset a year earlier: laughter and contempt took a lot longer.

Happy Christmas everybody! (1995)

The end of an era &
the beginning of another

Everywhere we go, friends, neighbours and relations are wishing us a very Happy New Year and the best of continuing health, wealth and happiness. I am afraid that each time that salutation comes, Eoin and I look a little wryly at each other as we both wonder the same thing. How will 1997 work out for us all, with the big changes that started here last summer twelve months, which are to be finally completed and rubber-stamped by the first of January?

Over the years I have been accused by my readers of starting to tell a story and never, in the weeks that follow, giving the full details of its conclusion. So now, looking back at the end of the year, I can see that I did precisely that once again in 1996. But as always, there were perfectly good reasons for so doing at the time. I must watch my back occasionally.

I especially had to watch my back, in 1996, when it came to telling about problems with planning permission which, thanks to conditions imposed and neighbourly objections, took us well over twelve months and led us all the way to an Bord Pleanála appeal, and a mountain of paperwork, before we finally got permission to build a new milking set-up, way inside in the middle of the farm the sons bought some years ago. And, at the same time, I also had to watch my back in dread of rocking the family boat in what could have been potentially stormy waters.

I know that there are a frighteningly large number of farmers around the country who would dearly love to have our problems. Our problems are those which arise from having two fine sons, and their wives, committed to farming, while so many others now find that their heirs want nothing at all to do with the land. Those young people, for one reason or another, have found their ways into all sorts of other easier and possibly more lucrative careers. But I bet, were the land to be sold, or when it eventually comes to will-reading time, they'd all be back with their expectations.

Our expectations were that our set-up here would continue on indefinitely since we were making quite a nice living for us all with our cows, our beef enterprise and, of course, family labour. Therefore it doesn't help our pride in the slightest that many people will now be saying 'I told you so', to our faces or behind our backs, when they hear that the herd is now being divided and each son and respective daughter-in-law will be more or less on their own from January the first. By then the new milking unit should be finally up and running and all the buildings, changes and divisions completed.

Actually, what bothers me more than the opportunity people have of saying 'I told you so' is that this really is the first non-productive piece of investment we have made here since we started farming. Building a new milking parlour, and all that goes with it, does not give us one more gallon of quota or put one more pound into our collective pockets. There is no denying that.

The really sensible way to run this farm was in partnership, sharing the same milking facilities and machinery, benefiting from buying in bulk and each partner allowing the others plenty of time off. Those sons of ours and their wives had no bother at all in heading off for their full annual holidays, and being sure of every second weekend off as well, purely and simply because the other one was always there to take over the work and the usual emergencies.

We never had it so good in our day, as we were never done telling them, lest they think that this was a normal thing in farming. The cows and the calves were always there, waiting for us, when we got home from any outings we took at their age – as they will be for them from now on, unless they organise relief milkers or the like.

Yet there is no denying the fact that we have been told, time and time again, for much longer than the fourteen years our sons have been working together, that partnerships between brothers do not work, whatever about those between fathers and sons. One very good friend, who works in the advisory service, so has had a lot of experience, didn't put a tooth in it, years ago, when he told us, 'You'll do fine until the second woman comes into the partnership. Then your troubles will start. I don't care how good and nice she is. It will be small things at first. But the finish is always the same. Each will want to go out on their own and there will be no peace for anybody until they do.'

Now, we met that man again over the Christmas. And when we were telling him how the family was going, the usual start to conversation these days when old friends meet, he had the grace not to remind us of what he had said to us, all those years ago, when our two sons first decided to go farming in partnership with us. He possibly had forgotten all about it. But his words had stuck in our memories because, at the time, they seemed so unfair, unlikely, and sexist as well.

As it turned out, however, he was only the first of many to express the same sentiment. You have no idea of the yarns we heard from time to time when the talk turned to how our farming partnership was doing. Parents would tell us how, if one family household got a new anything, be it a car, carpet or even a new hat, there'd be no peace until the other had as good if not better. We laughed at the sheer ridiculousness of some of the tales we were told. But the stories had the habit of sticking in our memories nevertheless.

One farmer, a widower, told us how, years ago, he had got a beast of his killed before Christmas, for the deep freeze, for his two married sons who were farming with him. He picked the best beast out of his fattening shed and got his butcher to pack each side separately and mark the boxes of frozen meat A and B so as there would be no confusion. The father himself collected and delivered the sides to each house, thinking no more about it, beyond perhaps the value of the present he was giving them.

But a month or two afterwards, when it was his birthday, the whole family were invited to dinner at the house of one of the sons, where the *pièce de résistance* of the meal was a grand roast of beef, tender and perfect as only a large roast can be. All were enjoying it, and remarking on how good it was, when – and he didn't know how it started – the visiting sister-in-law got into full spate about how the side of beef she and her husband got was obviously not the same quality as what his brother had got. He had been given the A side while they were expected to be happy with the B side, which was tougher. And how it was always the same, that that son was favoured above her husband in absolutely everything. And out she stormed from the table, taking her reluctant husband with her.

That storm in a teacup took a long time to subside, as do many family rows, especially those which erupt around Christmas time. We never had anything even remotely like that here. But I'll tell you this much for nothing: after hearing that story, we never did get an animal killed here for division, even though it might have made great sense from time to time. We always said to let each lot go and buy their own meat, and everything else personal to each separate household as well. How family members spend their personal money is an entirely private matter. That is one rule which should never be broken, no matter how tightly one has to guard the zip on the lip.

And, to finish the other part of the unfinished happenings of the past year, I'll tell you about another 'rule' which we never knew about. That is, if you are thinking of building anything at all, you had better go about it a good year, at least, before you absolutely have to have it. I have yet to meet anybody who got permission to build after the two-month compulsory waiting period, when planning must be granted by default if nothing is heard to the contrary. Precisely on the day before, a registered letter arrives, with all the ifs, ands and buts, which mean starting another two-month period, all over again.

We had intended to put up a new shed in 1995, a beef unit actually, because we had too much stock on our hands, being tied up with TB and all the rules and regulations which follow that. But we knew nothing about how bad, and binding, and long-drawn-out regulations can be, until we started down the planning permission road. Never again do we want to face the endless hassle of that.

But what am I talking about? All such hassle, in theory anyway, will never again be our affair but our sons'. And the delay forced on us proved a blessing in disguise since the sons in the meantime decided that they would rather work two separate units, each being responsible for his own, so it was rather an elaborate milking shed, with everything under the one roof, that went up instead of the beef unit.

Now that it is all done, I can see something very clearly which is more important than the fact that I am to give up being financial controller and pacifier of families and bank managers. They now have the excitement of making their own way, mistakes and all. We may have fallen into the trap, which many parents do, of stealing their problems from them, and so preventing them growing by coping for themselves. A week or so ago I saw Sara, who never really had got involved in farming, out there driving staples straight and true, securing the fencing wire her husband was stringing along, to the posts. It did my heart good so see them so united and happy even in the desperate cold.

Each family is a unit in itself, after all. And yes, they did work out a marvellous system to keep the children safe while they are milking. They built a room over the dairy, with deep windows which overlook the milking parlour, the calving boxes and the paddocks east and south. The parents can see into this room from outside and the girls, warmly heated by the bulk tank compressors which are installed up here, can see their parents as they milk the cows. And Michaella tells me, now that she is six, she will soon be tall enough to milk the cows herself.

Personally I don't care who milks the cows just so long as it isn't me, and the milk cheques keep rolling in each month, because they are managing their quota properly. Because, while the sons are now responsible, pro-rata, for all existing debts, most importantly, for every pound they take in personal money we must get the same sum, again pro-rata, as a right and not a handout. So the money must keep coming in or we are all in trouble. This way if they do well, so shall we. Thus, in addition to having the tax-man, each October, as a perpetual curb on their personal spending, they will also have us, every month of the year, with our hand out for our fair share to live on, which is no harm at all.

During the quiet days after Christmas, when it was too miserable to go out and I was fed up to the back teeth with television and food, I did a very interesting calculation. I took the present day value of our share of the land, buildings, milk quota, cows, cattle, machinery etc. and added them all together. Then I divided the result by the income we expect to get each year from the farming enterprises of our sons. The answer, of course, should be the number of years which would be break-even point for the sons. If we live less than that number they are on a winner. And if we should live longer? Well, tough!

I'll let you know how things progress as the year goes on. But I am telling nobody, not even the sons, the result of my calculations on the break-even number of years I have to live to make a real profit out of the changes we are making in 1997. Stay tuned and perhaps I'll finally finish the telling of that story too, sometime in the third millennium.

Happy New Year, everybody. (1996)

Out of Sight

by Joe Bollard

The remarkable and compelling story of musician and broadcaster Joe Bollard. Fascinating, moving and often witty, it is the life story of a man who has triumphed over adversity, prejudice and the fact that his eyes 'don't work'.

Joe Bollard was born in the 1930s in Dublin's inner city. One of 13 children, he was pronounced blind at the age of two. Through the senses of a four-year-old blind boy, we share in Joe's experience of starting in a Dublin blind school. Shortly afterwards, his family moved to Liverpool, where Joe grew up. In his early twenties he returned to Ireland as a pianist with the Ballina-based Jack Ruane Band. The reader is treated to witty descriptions of touring with the band in Ireland and England (and smuggling home condoms to sell on the black market in Ballina).

In 1964 Joe moved with his wife and children to Dublin where he worked as resident pianist at the Silver Tassie in Loughlinstown and later at the Dalkey Island Hotel. He also became organist at his parish church in Bray, where he continues to play thirty years on. Having worked for some years on local radio in Bray, he went on to work with RTE's *Listen and See* and, latterly, *Audioscope*.

Joe has been involved in several fund-raising cycles in aid of the National Council for the Blind of Ireland, whose audio magazine he edits. The cycles on the back of a tandem have taken him to the US, Europe and Africa.

ISBN 0-86327-623-7

Available from:
WOLFHOUND PRESS
68 Mountjoy Square
Dublin 1
Tel: +353 1 874 0354
Fax: + 353 1 872 0207